中英对照

澳大利亚联邦证据法

Australia

Evidence Act 1995

王进喜◎译

中国法制出版社
CHINA LEGAL PUBLISHING HOUSE

译者导言

　　澳大利亚的正式名称为澳大利亚联邦（the Commonwealth of Australia），是大洋洲最大的国家，也是全球土地面积第六大的国家，其首都位于堪培拉。澳大利亚是 1901 年由当时 6 个独立的英国殖民地所组成的联邦制国家。澳大利亚现在由 6 个州和 10 个领地组成。这 6 个州分别是：新南威尔士州（New South Wales (NSW)）、昆士兰州（Queensland (Qld)）、南澳大利亚州（South Australia (SA)）、塔斯马尼亚州（Tasmania (Tas.)）、维多利亚州（Victoria (Vic.)）和西澳大利亚州（Western Australia (WA)）。每个州都有其自己的州宪法，像联邦政府一样，各州政府也分为立法、司法和行政三个部分。此外，在州边界之外，尚有 10 个领地（territories），即州边界之外的地域。澳大利亚首都领地（The Australian Capital Territory (ACT)）和北领地（The Northern Territory (NT)）这两个大陆领地和诺福克岛（Norfolk Island）这个离岸领地，已经被联邦政府授予了有限的自治权，由地方选举的议会处理一系列政府事务。另外 7 个领地，则仅受联邦法律所辖，通常通过联邦政府任命的行政长官来治理，这些领地是：亚什摩及卡地尔群岛（Ashmore and Cartier Islands）、澳大利亚南极领地（Australian Antarctic Territory）、圣诞岛（Christmas Island）、科科斯群岛（Cocos (Keeling) Islands）、珊瑚海群岛（Coral Sea Islands）、杰维斯湾领地（Jervis Bay Territory）、贺得岛及麦唐纳群岛领地（Territory of Heard Island and McDonald Islands）。澳大利亚首都领地、北领地和杰维斯湾领地被称为内部领地。其他领地则被称为外部领地。

　　澳大利亚证据法（the law of evidence）的当前样态，是由制定法、普通法和法院规则所组成的混合体。1995 年之前,澳大利亚的证据法主要表现为普通法,即法院在长期的历史中发展出的证据规则。它们反映了各种原则和价值,因而缺乏连贯性和体系性,也因为复杂而难以查找。"人们对重大改革期待已久。然而法院并不准备从事这一工作,法院认为这最好是交给立法机关来做。多年以来,立法机关并没有准备着手这一庞杂的任务"。[1]

1979 年 7 月,澳大利亚联邦司法部长 Peter Durack 提出,要对联邦法院和领地法院适用的证据法进行审查,以形成一个综合性的证据法。澳大利亚法律改革委员会(the Australian Law Reform Commission)就此提议,分别在 1985 年提出了中期报告(ALRC 26),在 1987 年提出了最终报告(ALRC 38)和证据法案草案。1995 年澳大利亚联邦和新南威尔士州通过的《1995 年证据法》(以下 1995 年澳大利亚联邦《1995 年证据法》简称《1995 年证据法》),是澳大利亚法律改革委员会近十年工作的成果。这些法律在绝大多数方面是一样的,常常被称为《统一证据法》(Uniform Evidence Acts)。[2] 这些法律在澳大利亚产生了重大影响。塔斯马尼亚州和诺福克岛分别于 2001 年和 2004 年通过了与此类 似的立法。北领地、西澳大利亚洲、南澳大利亚州、昆士兰州也有类似的动向。[3]

1　S Odgers, *Uniform Evidence Law* (8th edition, Thomson Reuters (Professional) Australia Limited, 2009), [1.1.20].

2　也有观点认为应当把统一证据法更为准确地描述为"镜像"(mirror)立法而不是统一立法。镜像立法是指不同司法辖区的立法机关依据同一立法草案制定的立法。1995 年澳大利亚联邦和新南威尔士州通过的《1995 年证据法》就是这样制定的。这种机制在开始的时候能够形成统一性,但是随着各立法机关不断地行使其权力,这种统一性就不断地遭到了侵蚀。See Australia Law Reform Commission, *Uniform Evidence Law*, *ALRC Report 102* (2005), 55.

3　See Australia Law Reform Commission, *Uniform Evidence Law*, *ALRC Report 102* (2005), 38-9.

2004年7月，澳大利亚联邦司法部长要求澳大利亚法律改革委员会对《1995年证据法》的运作进行审查。此后，新南威尔士州司法部长也对本州法律改革委员会提出了类似要求。2004年11月，维多利亚州司法部长则要求本州法律改革委员会审酌《统一证据法》的现行规定在引入维多利亚州之前是否需要进行修改。这三个委员会就统一证据法进行了联合研究，并于2005年公布了名为《统一证据法》的联合报告（ALRC 102）。该报告建议对《1995年证据法》进行重大修改，并在附录提供了修正草案。

2007年7月澳大利亚联邦司法部长常设委员会批准了《统一证据示范法案》（Model Uniform Evidence Bill）。2007年11月新南威尔士州议会制定的《2007年证据修正法》，反映了ALRC 102的建议。2008年11月，澳大利亚国会通过了《2008年证据修正法》，该法在主要方面与新南威尔士州议会制定的《2007年证据修正法》是相同的，从而使得联邦和该州的证据立法近乎统一。2008年9月，维多利亚州也以《统一证据法》为据制定了《2008年证据法》。因此，在澳大利亚，出现了以《统一证据法》为基础的证据法一体化趋势。

本导言将以澳大利亚联邦《1995年证据法》及其相应的修正为核心，对《统一证据法》的运作框架、政策背景、特点等事项进行说明，并据此略论我国相关立法的得失。

一、运作的政策框架

审判程序在很大程度上是由证据法所决定的。而审判程序是诉讼程序中最为核心、最为公开的部分，公众将通过对审判的观察，评估法律是否得以施行，正义是否得以实现。因此，证据法是程序正义的重要组成部分。

澳大利亚法律改革委员会经过审慎的研究，将以下政策作为证据法的政策框架：

第一，事实认定。法院的事实认定在政策中被赋予了首要地位。澳大利亚法律改革委员会认为，审判制度的可信性最终取决于其在事实认定方面的表现。因此，证据法要使当事人能够提出他们可得到的证据，从而促进准确的事实认定。

第二，区分民事和刑事审判。《1995 年证据法》的一个重要特点，是没有就陪审团审判和非陪审团审判进行区分，而是在刑事程序和民事程序进行了区分。尽管该法的某些规定与陪审团直接相关，例如法院对陪审团作出的指示（如第 116 条、第 4.5 节），以及法院在就预备性问题作出决定时陪审团是否在场（如第 17 条、第 18 条），但是关注的重点并不是陪审团审判与非陪审团审判的区别。人们经常提起的观点是，制定证据法是出于对陪审团适当评估证据能力的不信任，证据法要使陪审团与他们可能误用或者误解的证据隔离开来。美国证据法学家 Thayer 的证据法是"陪审团制度之子"的观点最常被引用。[4] 但是澳大利亚法律改革委员会认为，法官以及治安法官尽管受过训练，并具有经验，但是在误用传闻证据、品性证据等方面并不比陪审员技高一筹。[5] 就证据法目的而言，区分民事审判和刑事审判更有意义。

澳大利亚法律改革委员会认为，刑事审判在以下几个方面不同于民事审判：（1）采用弹劾式（刑事审判不是解决双方之间的争端；刑事被告在被证明有罪之前被推定无罪，没有帮助检控方的义务）；（2）要将错误定罪的风险最小化（刑事审判要符合社会利益，即宁可错放而不可错判）；（3）核心问题鲜明（刑事审判的核心问题是检控方是否将被告有罪证明到了排除合理怀疑的程度）；（4）认可个人权利（不能不计代价地达成有罪判决，要认可刑事被告的个人尊严和权利）；

4　JB Thayer, *A Preliminary Treatise on Evidence at the Common Law* (Little, Brown & Co, Boston, 1898, reprinted 1969 by Rothman Reprints, New Jersey), 266.

5　See Australia Law Reform Commission, *Evidence*, ALRC 38 (1987), [28].

（5）要帮助对造进行对抗（刑事被告有权获得某些保护，以保证对抗制的公平性）。[6] 因此，在刑事审判中，在采纳反对刑事被告的证据时，应当采取更为严格的方法。在刑事被告被强制作证、交叉询问等方面，也应当反映这种特点。

第三，可预测性。澳大利亚继承了英美对抗制审判的衣钵。在诉讼程序中，由当事人决定何为争议问题。"在我们的对抗制中，当事人有权利并有责任选择推进其案件的方式，以及他们提出用以支持其案件的证据。他们也有责任就对方当事人提出的证据提出异议并对之加以检验。他们——包括刑事被告——必须接受其选择的结果。"[7] 因此，需要通过具有可预测性的证据规则对当事人进行引导和控制，以有效地进行审判。为此，立法应当将司法自由裁量权最小化，特别是在关于证据可采性的规则上。在可能的情况下，都应当以规则的形式体现这一点。只有在虑及相关政策因素不能这么做的情况下，才能采用自由裁量权的形式。换言之，明确的规则优于自由裁量权。

第四，成本、时间和其他关切。澳大利亚法律改革委员会认为，在任何时候都应当虑及诉讼时间和成本的影响，以及对庭外活动的时间和成本的影响。在任何时候，清晰性和简洁性都是目标。[8]

二、立法技术

《1995 年证据法》采用了娴熟的立法技术，使得该法清晰、可读，成为一部使用者友好型的立法。这体现在以下几个方面。

第一，条文结构依次采用了章、节、目、条、款、项等层次，并在每一条列明条题，排列清晰，便于援引。在历年根据立法和判例的

6 See Australian Law Reform Commission, *Evidence*, ALRC 38 (1987), [35].

7 Australian Law Reform Commission, *Evidence*, ALRC 38 (1987), [28].

8 See Australia Law Reform Commission, *Evidence*, ALRC 38 (1987), [34].

发展进行修正时，增加的条文序号仅在需插入处原相应条文序号后，缀加 A、B、C 等插入（如第 8A 条，第 78A 条，第 108A 条，第 108B 条），删除的条文则直接删除而不改变其他条文顺序（如直接删除第 105 条）。此外，立法后附有《修正表》，分别就增添或者插入、修正、取消、取消并取代四种立法修正模式的发生情况予以明确说明，便于读者对立法史的了解。

第二，包含引言性注释和法内注释。《1995 年证据法》在每章开始，有引言性注释，对各章的主要内容进行概述，便于使用者对该章内容进行整体把握。

《1995 年证据法》与新南威尔士州《1995 年证据法》同属基于同一立法草案而形成的镜像立法，二者大同小异。这些差异主要是因为二者在联邦司法管辖权和州司法管辖权方面的差别而形成的。为便于对照，立法在文内增加了注释，对这些差异进行了必要说明。

第三，附有详尽的术语定义。术语含义的清晰性和前后一致性，是一部立法质量优劣与否的最重要表征之一。《1995 年证据法》在法典正文后附有术语，对立法所使用的术语进行了详尽界定。这避免了在正文中进行术语定义所带来的繁琐、冗赘，最大限度地维护了正文的清晰与简洁。

三、范围与结构

任何一个学科，首先应当明确的就是自己的研究范围。证据法所涵盖的范围有多大？阅读一下各国的相关法律或者教科书，就会发现这是个很棘手的问题。以英美若干典型证据法为例，在其所涵盖的内容上，可以说是千姿百态，千差万别。美国《加利福尼亚州证据法典》对证明负担、推定与推论等事项作了详细规定。美国《联邦证据规则》并没有包括争议点禁止反言、判决既判力、补强、证明负担等内容，推定问题也没有在《联邦证据规则》中得到实质规定。[9]英国证据法没有美国这样的系统性法律，而是散见于制定法与判例法中。但是，英国学者的证据法著作中往往涵盖证明负担、争议点禁止反言、推定等事项。[10]此外。英国证据法学家 Stephen 制定的《印度证据法》（Indian Evidence Act）也规定了补强、推定、争议点禁止反言等事项，尽管这些规定很有限。

澳大利亚法律改革委员会认为，"证据法应当被归类为裁判法（adjectival law）的一部分"。据此，澳大利亚法律改革委员会在证据法的范围问题上，采用了二分法，即就哪些应当包括在证据法内，哪些不应当包括在证据法内，进行了区分。澳大利亚法律委员会认为，应当从证据法中排除的事项包括：（1）应当被分类为实体法的内容，或者与实体法有着密切联系，只有在该背景下审酌方为适当的内容。这些内容包括法律和证据负担、推定、争议点禁止反言、判决既判力、口头证据规则（parol evidence rule）等。（2）应当被分类为程序法而不是证据法的裁判法事项。这包括与证据收集、证言固定、就不在犯罪现场的证据进行通知等事项。（3）诸如检控方传召证据的职责、法官传唤证人的权力、法证科学服务的组织与运作等事项。《1995 年证据法》很大程度上反映了这种方法。它并没有就争议事实的证明负担、推定、争议点禁止反言、判决既判力、口头证据规则等事项作出规定。

《1995 年证据法》除去附录（宣誓与郑重声明）和术语部分外的主体，分为五个部分，其结构如下：

9　美国《联邦证据规则》仅在规则 301 中就民事推定作了一般性规定（"在民事案件中，除联邦制定法或者本证据规则另有规定者外，推定所反对的当事人负有提出证据反驳该推定的负担。但是，本条规则并未转移说服负担，该证明负担仍由原先承担它的当事人承担"）。

10　例如，可参见［英］克里斯托弗·艾伦：《英国证据法实务指南》，王进喜译，中国法制出版社 2012 年版。

可以看出，《1995 年证据法》是按照审判活动中通常出现的证据事项的顺序组织的。其核心部分是关于证据可采性问题的第 3 章。这一部分开始于基本规则，即所有具有相关性的证据都具有可采性，该法另有规定者除外；不具有相关性的证据不具有可采性。[11] 此后，是关于不同类型的证据的可采性规定，各个具体规定遵循了这样的模式：规定了排除该类型证据的基本规则后，又规定了该基本规则的例外。最后，该章还规定了法官排除证据的自由裁量权和有限使用证据的自由裁量权。[12]

四、《1995年证据法》是法典吗？

法典有两个含义，广义而言，是指详细而全面记述一个法律体系的所有法律的成文法；狭义而言，是指某个法律体系内关于某一方面的所有法律的成文法。证据法的法典化当然是指后者。证据法的法典化要实现何等目标？新西兰法律委员会在思忖新西兰的证据法法典化问题时认为："真正的法典可以被定义为具有综合性、结构系统性、先发性（pre-emptive），并阐明了所适用之原则的立法规定。其先发性在于其取代了该领域的所有其他法律，仅在法典另有规定时除外。其系统性在于其所有部分构成了一个连贯的、完整的一体。其综合性在于其具有足够的包含性与独立性，使其能够以相对自足的方式适用。然而，最后一个因素特别突出，使法典与其他立法规定区别开来：与更为有限的立法规定相比，法典的目的就是在原则的基础上建立法律秩序。"[13]

从技术角度看，《1995年证据法》这种统一证据法并不是无所不包的证据法典，并不是要完全取代普通法，而是试图对证据法的某些

11　澳大利亚《1995年证据法》第56条。

12　澳大利亚《1995年证据法》第135条和第136条。

13　New Zealand Law Commission, *Evidence Law: Codification-A Discussion Paper*, PP14 (1991),3.

方面进行改革。例如,《1995年证据法》第8条规定,该法并不影响诸多其他法律的运作,尽管该法没有就普通法和衡平法中的证据法原则和规则的运作作出明确规定。[14] 新南威尔士州《1995年证据法》第9条则明确规定,该法并不影响普通法或者衡平法证据规则在该法所适用的程序中的效力,除非该法另有明确规定或者这些法律及此后产生的判例法,构成了新的证据法体系。这些法律及此后产生的判例法,构成了新的证据法体系。如一些学者所指出的那样,这些法律在解释和适用上存在着特定的困难。这些法律在某些方面的规定是原则性的,在其他一些方面的规定则具有高度的规定性;在某些方面,它们完全是为了取代普通法,在其他方面则对普通法纹丝未予触动;在某些方面它们规定得非常清晰,在其他方面则需要法院运用解释工具和法庭规则来进行界定。[15] 还有的学者指出了该法中存在的许多缺隙(例如谁来承担证明负担),认为该法并不是对现行的法律进行完全重述意义上的法典,也不是穷尽性的法典,因此不能简单地回答要在多大程度上诉诸该法之前存在的判例法的问题。这些法律既有法典化的因素,也有改革的因素。[16] 因此,普通法在这些立法框架下的证据法运作中仍然发挥着重要作用。

14　澳大利亚《1903年司法法》第80条规定,如果联邦法律并不适用,或者它们的规定不足以实施,或者不足以提供救济或者处罚,在适用并且不与宪法或者联邦法律不一致的情况下,为宪法或者行使管辖权的法院所在的州或者领地的有效法律所限定的普通法,规制所有行使联邦管辖权的法院所管辖的民事和刑事事项。根据《1995年证据法》第8条的规定,《1995年证据法》的适用优于《1903年司法法》第68条、第79条、第80条和第80A条之规定,但是在这些普通法与《1995年证据法》不一致的情况下,这些普通法继续有效。

15　See J Anderson, J Hunter and N Willliams SC, *The New Evidence Law* (LexisNexis Butterworths, Australia, 2002), xix.

16　J D Heydon, *A Guide to the Evidence Acts 1995 (NSW) and (Cth)* (2nd Edition, Butterworths, 1997), 9.

　　《1995年证据法》第3章的规定，就被视为是一种法典化的做法。[17]该法第3章规定了证据的可采性问题。该法56(1)规定，"除本法另有规定者外，程序中具有相关性的证据在该程序中具有可采性。"因此，这一规定排除了关于证据可采性的其他法律，任何规定证据不可采的普通法可采性规则，将与该法不一致。Branson 法官在 *Quick v Stoland Pty Ltd* 案件中曾指出，"第3章旨在在这个问题上具有穷尽性，从实践意义上看，这在该法所涉的程序中，构成了关于证据可采性的法律"。[18]

　　即使是一些没有被视为法典化的规定，也对现行法律中的证据规则进行了相当程度的删减。例如在司法认知问题上，144(1)规定，不能合理质疑并且属于下列情况的知识无需证明：(a) 程序进行地的常识或者一般性常识；或者 (b) 能够为其权威性不受合理质疑的文件所核实。144(2)规定，法官可以采取其认为适当的任何方式获得上述知识。在 *Gattellaro v westpac Corp* (2004) 204 ALR 258; [2004] HCA 6 案件中，法官认为，在制定第144条后，看上去没有为关于司法认知的普通法原则的运作留下空间。

五、对普通法的变革

　　《1995年证据法》是对澳大利亚证据法的重大改革，而不仅仅是就普通法和早期的制定法所进行的重述(restatement)。《1995年证据法》虑及科学性、简明性、公平性、可操作性等因素，对许多普通法证据规则进行了重大改革，但需要注意的是，《1995年证据法》并没有完全取代普通法，而仅仅是改革了某些方面。以下是部分变革的例子。

　　1. 证人刷新记忆与敌意证人问题。《1995年证据法》第32条规

17　See S Odgers, *Uniform Evidence Law* (6th ed, 2004), [1.1.40].

18　*Quick v Stoland Pty Ltd* (1998) 87 FCR 371,373.

定，经法院许可，证人在作证过程中，可以使用文件来试图唤醒其关于某事实或者意见的记忆。但是证人在庭上刷新记忆时，不是必须要使用其记忆清新时所制作的文件。根据32(2)，证人对有关事件是否"记忆清新"，仅仅是法院要虑及的一个因素。而在普通法上，则要求所制作的文件具有同时性，即必须是证人在记忆清新时制作的。此外，普通法上要求该用于刷新记忆的文件应当是证人制作或者采认的文件。而这在《1995年证据法》中也不再是一个绝对的法律要求，而仅仅是法院在决定是否准许时所要考虑的因素。在 *R v Cassar; R v Sleiman*[19] 案件中，法官允许警察使用了一个并没有为 32(2)(b) 所规定的文件来刷新记忆，因为该文件所包含的信息及其制作环境使得其具有可靠性，并且它所包含的信息与证人在记忆清新时记录的文件所包含的信息基本上是一致的，只不过后者丢失了。从这一案例可窥第32条与普通法的差异之一斑。

《1995年证据法》第38条规定，在当事人自己的证人作出了不利证言的情况下，允许当事人对该证人进行交叉询问，而不需要首先认定该证人是敌意证人。而在普通法上，当事人在对自己的证人进行交叉询问之前，该证人必须首先被法院宣布为敌意证人。《1995年证据法》对"不利（unfavourable）"一词并没有进行界定，但显而易见的是，与普通法上的"敌意（hostile）"相比，这一术语设定了更低的要求。澳大利亚法律改革委员会建议废止与"敌意"证人有关的法律，因为在证人仅仅作出不利证言的情况下，无法认定其敌意，因而无法对其证言进行检验。[20] 因此，《1995年证据法》第38条之规定降低了对不利证人进行交叉询问的门槛，更有利于导出事实真相。

2. 法院对交叉询问中的诱导性问题进行控制的权力问题。《1995

---

19 （No 28）[1999] NSWSC 651.

20 See Australia Law Reform Commission, ALRC 26, vol 1, paras 294, 295, 625.

年证据法》第 42 条规定，在适当情况下，法官可以不允许当事人在
交叉询问中向证人提出诱导性问题。一般而言，对证人的交叉询问，
是指由传唤证人作证的当事人之外的当事人对该证人的询问。诱导性
问题是交叉询问的重要标志。尽管依据普通法，当事人在交叉询问中
并没有适用诱导性问题的绝对权利，[21] 但是《1995 年证据法》第 42 条
大大扩大了法院不允许当事人在交叉询问中提出诱导性问题的权力。
42(2) 规定，在决定是否不允许诱导性问题时，法院应当虑及的事项包
括但是不限于：(a) 证人在主询问中所作证言是否不利于传唤该证人的
当事人；(b) 证人与交叉询问者是否具有一致的利益；(c) 证人在整体上
或者就具体事项是否同情进行交叉询问的当事人；(d) 证人的年龄、证
人患有的任何精神、智力或者身体上的残障，是否可能影响证人的回答。
42(3) 规定，如果法院确信，如果不使用诱导性问题将能更好地查明有
关事实，则法院应当不允许该提问或者指示证人对此不予回答。这些
规定反映了法院对诱导性问题对准确事实认定和诉讼公平性之影响的
关切。

　　3. 原件规则问题。《1995 年证据法》第 2.2 节规定，废除普通法
证明书证内容的"原件"规则，[22] 而代之以更为灵活的做法，即可以使
用 48(1) 规定的"某种或者多种方法来就有关书证的内容提出证据"。
这一修改的目的是简化证明书证内容的规则，并虑及现代信息存储媒
介和复制技术的特点。澳大利亚法律改革委员会认为，普通法上的原
件或者最佳证据规则"复杂、缺乏灵活性，并且会带来高成本"。尽
管要求提出原件会减少争论，但是该规则缺乏灵活性，会"大大增加
诉讼成本"。"这些评论特别适用于现代书证和复制技术。对（这些）

21　See *Mooney v James* [1949] VLR 22 at 27–8.

22　参见《1995 年证据法》第 51 条。

法律的批评支持进行改革"。[23]

4. 观察作为证据问题。《1995 年证据法》第 54 条规定，观察可以作为证据，即法院（如果有陪审团的话，还包括陪审团）可以根据其在演示、试验或者勘验过程中的所看、所听或者以其他方式进行的察觉，作出任何合理的推论。事实认定者可能会对地点或者物品进行勘验、检查或者是观察演示和试验。这样的行为叫做观察（view）。澳大利亚法律改革委员会指出，"尽管就现行法律（特别是英国的法律）而言并不确定，但是 [这些法律] 在观察和演示之间要进行区分——只有后者才被归为证据。前者是帮助事实裁判庭理解在法庭上提出的证据的材料。"[24] 澳大利亚法律改革委员会认为，上述观点应当被废弃，观察应当被视为事实裁判庭作出认定的合法的事实信息来源。第 54 条贯彻了这一建议。[25]

5. 传闻规则问题。《1995 年证据法》第 3.2 节就传闻规则作出了重大修改。60(1) 规定："如果先前表述证据之所以被采纳，是因为其就证明主张的事实之外之目的具有相关性，则该先前表述证据不适用传闻规则。"换言之，如果传闻可以为非传闻目的所采纳，则该证据也可以作为所主张事项的证据而采纳。而根据普通法，如果先前表述证据因非传闻目的而被采纳，则该证据仅能用于该目的，而不能用于证明所主张事项的真实性，除非其属于某个传闻例外。澳大利亚法律改革委员会认为，"根据现行法律，为非传闻目的而可采的传闻证据不被排除，但是法院不得将其用作证明所陈述事实的证据。这是在进行不现实的区分。这个问题可以这样解决，即将传闻规则界定为防止采纳这样的传闻证据，即其在理性上仅仅是影响法院对所意图

23　See Australia Law Reform Commission, ALRC 26, vol 1, para 648.

24　Australia Law Reform Commission, ALRC 26, vol 1, para 1027.

25　See Australia Law Reform Commission, ALRC 26, vol 1, para 1028.

主张的事实的评估时才具有相关性。这将产生这样的效果，即为非传闻目的而具有相关性的证据（例如证明先前一致陈述或者不一致陈述，或者证明专家意见的基础的证据），也将作为关于所陈述事实的证据而可采。"[26]

6. 最终争点与常识规则问题。《1995年证据法》第80条规定，废除最终争点与常识规则。以常识规则为例，普通法上的传统做法是，如果意见证据所及的仅仅是"常识"事项，则该意见证据不可采。澳大利亚法律改革委员会认为，"仅仅因为'普通人'就有关领域有某些知识而排除证据，是完全错误的，这不应当是证据法的一部分。显而易见，如果专家试图作证的事项浅显，为众所周知，则提出这样的证言会浪费法院的时间。在相关性上的自由裁量权足以排除这样的裁判。然而，即使在大多数人都知晓的领域，专家仍能够对法院有帮助。因此，我们建议删除常识要求，依赖于相关性规定、自由裁量权来保证不采纳不必要的证据。"[27]

7. 品性证据问题。在普通法上，品性证据因为证明价值难以评估、可靠性难以确定而被排除。这种排除主要是为了保护刑事被告不被错误定罪。因此，该排除仅适用于不利于刑事被告的品性证据。在《1995年证据法》中，该排除更为广泛，不再局限于刑事案件，但是也顾及了刑事案件的特殊性。第3.6节规定，倾向与巧合证据不可采，除非进行了预先通知，并且证据具有重大证明价值。但是第101条对检控方提出的倾向证据和巧合证据进行了进一步的限定，即检控方提出的关于被告的倾向证据或者巧合证据，不能用于反对被告，除非上述证据的证明价值严重超过了（substantially outweigh）其可能给被告造成的任何损害后果。

26　Australia Law Reform Commission, ALRC 26, vol 1, para 685.

27　Australia Law Reform Commission, ALRC 26, vol 1, para 743.

8. 委托人法律建议特免权问题。就律师为委托人提供法律建议的特免权，澳大利亚最高法院在 *Grant v Downs* (1976) 135 CLR 案件中曾确立了唯一目的标准。澳大利亚法律改革委员会认为，这一标准破坏了"正确的平衡"，而主要目的标准则更为有效。[28] 因此，《1995 年证据法》第 118 条规定，用委托人法律建议特免权的主要目的标准取代了唯一目的标准。该条规定，如果根据委托人的异议，法院判定提出证据将会导致披露下列因为一个或者多个律师向委托人提供法律建议之主要目的而进行的交流或者制作的文件的内容，则不得提出该证据：(a) 委托人与律师之间的秘密交流；或者 (b) 为委托人而行动的 2 个或者 2 个以上律师之间的秘密交流；或者 (c) 委托人、律师或者他人所制作的秘密文件的内容（无论是否已经交发）。这一规定实际扩大了委托人法律建议特免权的保护范围。

9. 证人反对被迫自我归罪的特免权问题。Griswold 曾说"反对被迫自我归罪的特免权是人类在自身文明化的斗争过程中最伟大的里程碑之一"，[29] 曾被称为"自由的基本堡垒"。[30] 赋予证人反对被迫自我归罪的特免权，有利于维护证人尊严，有利于鼓励证人作证，从证人这里获得证言，有利于避免伪证。证人反对被迫自我归罪的特免权一度被认为仅仅适用于司法程序，即允许证人或者当事人在审判或者具有中间性质的审前程序中拒绝回答问题或者披露文件。但是澳大利亚最高法院在 *Pyneboard Pty Ltd v TPC*, (1983) 152 CLR 328 案件中明确反对这一限制，使得这一特免权适用于任何强制取得信息的情形。在司法程序中，这一特免权被判定适用于可能披露"任何惩罚、刑罚、

28　See Australia Law Reform Commission, ALRC 26, vol 1, para 881.

29　E Griswold, *The Fifth Amendment Today*, Harvard Uni Press, Cambridge, 1955, 7.

30　*Pyneboard v Trade Practices Commission* (1983) 45 ALJR 609, 621 (Murphy J); *Baker v Campbell* (1983) 49 ALR 385.

没收或者开除教籍"的情况。[31]《1995年证据法》第128条则将其限定在司法程序中。128(1)和(3)规定，在证人反对作出具体证言或者关于具体事项的证言，是因为该证言可能倾向于证明该证人存在实施了违反或者起因于澳大利亚法律或者外国法律的犯罪；或者应当对民事处罚承担责任，则法院应当确定该异议是否存在合理根据，以决定是否使用该特免权。128(4)规定，如果法院确信有关证据并不倾向于证明该证人实施了违反或者起因于外国法律的犯罪，或者根据外国法律应当对民事处罚承担责任，并且正义利益要求证人作证，则法院可以要求证人作证。在法院据此要求证人作证的情况下，要为证人提供证人豁免。因此，该规定改变了普通法的规定，使得该特免权仅仅适用于审判，且不适用于证言可能使证人牵涉没收或者开除教籍的情形。

10. 排除证据的一般自由裁量权问题。《1995年证据法》第135条规定，如果证据的证明价值将会为下列危险所严重超过，则法院可以拒绝采纳该证据：(a) 该证据可能给一方当事人造成不公平的损害；或者 (b) 该证据可能具有误导性或者迷惑性；或者 (c) 该证据可能导致或者造成不合理的时间耗费。这一规定既适用于刑事程序，也适用于民事程序，与普通法主要存在以下不同：（1）135(a)既适用于民事案件也适用于刑事案件，而在普通法上则不适用于民事案件。换言之，在普通法上，在民事案件中，在证据的损害效果超过其证明价值时，不存在拒绝采纳该证据的自由裁量权。（2）135(b)和(c)对应的是普通法上的法律相关性概念。根据普通法的法律相关性概念，在存在损害、混淆、时间耗费等情况时，要由提出证据的当事人使法官确信证据具有足够的证明价值。第135条则改变了普通法的做法，由反对该证据的当事人说明证据应当被排除。

---

31 *Redfern v Readfern* [1891] P139.

11. 非法证据排除问题。《1995 年证据法》第 138 条规定，不当或者非法取得的证据不得被采纳，除非采纳这些证据的可取性大于其不可取性。这一规定既适用于民事程序也适用于刑事程序。在普通法上，自由裁量权也要求进行政策权衡。然而进行权衡的天平一侧是证据表明被告有罪的程度，另一侧则没有得到清晰的界定。[32]澳大利亚法律改革委员会认为，"在处理非法和不当取得的证据问题上，自由裁量方法似乎是最适当的方法。……这个领域相互冲突的关切，以及情况的复杂多变，使得这样的方法成为必需。"[33] 为了减少法官行使自由裁量权的困难，避免判决的过大差异，138(3) 规定了法院在进行这种权衡时所要考虑的因素，包括但是不限于该证据的证明价值；该证据在程序中的重要性；相关犯罪、诉因或者抗辩的性质以及程序标的的性质；不当行为或者违法的严重性；该不当行为或者违法行为是故意的还是过失造成的；该不当行为或者违法行为是否违反了《公民和政治权利国际公约》所认可的人的权利或者与此不一致；是否就不当行为或者违法行为已经提起或者可能提起任何其他程序(无论是否为法院程序)；在不从事不当行为或者违反澳大利亚法律行为的情况下获得证据的难度（如果有的话）。这一规定大大提高了就非法证据排除进行抗辩的可操作性和可预测性。

12. 计算机证据问题。《1995 年证据法》第 146 和第 147 条以推定为工具，就采纳计算机生成的证据进行了程序简化。第 146 条适用于下列书证或者物证：(a) 全部或者部分是由设备或者工序生成的；并且 (b) 是由主张在该书证或者物证生成过程中，该设备或者工序生成了某具体结果的当事人提交的。146(2) 规定："如果可以合理地认定，该设备或者工序经适当使用通常会生成该结果，则应当推定在相关场

32　See Australia Law Reform Commission, ALRC 26, vol 1, para 468.

33　Australia Law Reform Commission, ALRC 26, vol 1, para 964.

合生成该书证或者物证时，该设备或者工序产生了该结果，除非就该推定提出了足够的质疑证据。"第 147 条就业务过程中由工序、机器和其他设备生成的书证作了类似规定。这些规定适用于计算机生成的证据。澳大利亚法律改革委员会认为，要求就计算机记录的可靠性的各个环节进行证明，将给提交该证据的当事人带来沉重、昂贵的负担，给对方当事人带来策略上的优势，并增加法院的工作负荷。因此，由对方当事人提出质疑更具效率。[34]

尽管《1995 年证据法》对普通法进行了修正和补充，普通法在澳大利亚证据法的运作中仍然发挥着重要作用。这是因为《1995 年证据法》对普通法的诸多方面并没有触及。在这些领域，普通法仍然是主要的法律渊源，例如证明负担问题。此外，对《1995 年证据法》进行解释的法官所受的训练，也是普通法的训练。从实践层面来看，他们对于该法的解释必然会受到普通法的影响。

2008 年，根据澳大利亚法律改革委员会 2005 年公布的名为"统一证据法"的联合报告（ALRC 102），《1995 年证据法》进行了较大幅度的修正。这些修正一定程度上吸收了英国、美国近年来在证据立法上的成功经验，[35] 吸收了普通法发展所取得的成果，[36] 进一步促进了《1995 年证据法》的科学性和可操作性，但是没有从根本上否定《1995 年证据法》的政策框架和立法模式。

---

34 See Australia Law Reform Commission, ALRC 26, vol 1, para 705.

35 例如在证人作证能力问题上，对《1995 年证据法》第 13 条的修正，就借鉴了英国《1999 年少年司法与刑事证据法》第 53 条的规定。例如 13(1) 原先规定，证人能力的一般标准是能够作出宣誓证言，这一标准被认为过于严苛而会排除有证明价值的证据。该条的修改借鉴了英国上述立法，该标准经修正后表达为：证人无能力理解就该事实提出的问题；或者证人无能力就关于该事实的提问作出可被理解的回答，且该无能力不能克服。

36 例如，根据澳大利亚最高法院在 *TKWJ v The Queen* (2002) 212 CLR 124 案件的判决，《1995 年证据法》增加了第 192A 条，允许法院在证据提出之前，就证据作出预先裁决和认定。

六、争鸣、经验与借鉴

对以《1995年证据法》为代表的统一证据法趋势，并不乏批评的声音。这些批评主要是：采用制定法形式，将使得证据法变得越来越僵化，失去了普通法的澎湃发展动力；面对新型证据，法院在制定新的证据规则时可能会面临困难；制定法会需要更多的判例法来澄清制定法所制造的不确定性因素；对制定法修正常常是一个困难的、复杂的过程。[37]

确实，《1995年证据法》不是解决所有问题的万灵丹。作为规制对象的复杂证明过程的诸多方面，例如证据的相关性问题，并不是一个适合法律来加以规制的问题；法官在证明活动中的自由裁量权，也必然带来不确定性。可以说，规制证明过程的证据法，必然会在某些问题上具有不确定性。但是，制定法形式所表达的证据法，能最大限度地简化证据规则，带来明晰性、便捷性等正价值。与普通法相比，《1995年证据法》更容易查阅，更易于理解；它适应了科技的进步，促进了对计算机等新技术生成的信息存贮证据的采纳；以《1995年证据法》为代表的统一证据法趋势，使得澳大利亚全国的诉讼程序在追求正义方面，有了更加实质的均衡性和可比较性。澳大利亚法律改革委员会就统一证据法的运作，经过18个月的调查，于2005年在ALRC 102中也认为，统一证据法运行良好，立法本身及其背后的政策没有大的结构性问题。[38]

澳大利亚《1995年证据法》的立法技术和立法内容对于我们均具有重要的借鉴意义。暂不论各立法内容上的比较借鉴意义，以立法技术为例，《澳大利亚1995年证据法》在立法体例上层次分明，引用方便，

---

37 S Odgers, *Uniform Evidence Law* (8th edition, Thomson Reuters (Professional) Australia Limited, 2009), [1.1.100].

38 See Australia Law Reform Commission, *Uniform Evidence Law*, ALRC Report 102 (2005), Executive Summary.

各项之间的关系清晰。我国立法技术则在这种层次上没有明确的标准。以 2012 年修改的《刑事诉讼法》关于证据的规定为例，第 48 条在证据的种类上，采取了分独立项列示的方式；而第 187 条对于证人作证的条件，则没有进行明确的独立性列示。第 187 条第 1 款规定："公诉人、当事人或者辩护人、诉讼代理人对证人证言有异议，且该证人证言对案件定罪量刑有重大影响，人民法院认为证人有必要出庭作证的，证人应当出庭作证。"因此，"公诉人、当事人或者辩护人、诉讼代理人对证人证言有异议"、"该证人证言对案件定罪量刑有重大影响"和"人民法院认为证人有必要出庭作证"三者之间是什么关系，在该立法中并不清晰。对此可以有三种解释：第一，这三个条件同时具备，则证人应当出庭作证；第二，为"公诉人、当事人或者辩护人、诉讼代理人对证人证言有异议"且"该证人证言对案件定罪量刑有重大影响"为条件之一，"人民法院认为证人有必要出庭作证"为条件之二，二者具备其一则证人应当出庭作证；第三，"公诉人、当事人或者辩护人、诉讼代理人对证人证言有异议"且"该证人证言对案件定罪量刑有重大影响"即为证人应当出庭作证之"必要性"，"人民法院认为证人有必要出庭作证"乃人民法院对该必要性进行审查之要求，因此，只要具备了前两个要件，则人民法院就应当通知证人出庭作证。毫无疑问，对同一法条的多种解释可能性，极有可能妨害人们对 2012 年《刑事诉讼法》的理解和执行，严重削弱了程序法本身应当具有的中立性。因此，在立法中采用科学的条件列示方式，是促进法律规则明晰性的重要手段和形式。

2012 年《刑事诉讼法》在术语使用上的不一致，也会影响该法的实践效能。例如该法第 54 条规定，"采用刑讯逼供等非法方法收集的犯罪嫌疑人、被告人供述和采用暴力、威胁等非法方法收集的证人证言、被害人陈述，应当予以排除。收集物证、书证不符合法定程序，可能严重影响司法公正的，应当予以补正或者作出合理解释；不能补正或者作出合理解释的，对该证据应当予以排除。"对照该法第 48 条规定的 8 个证据种类，该第 54 条仅及"犯罪嫌疑人、被告人供述"、"证人证言"、"被害人陈述"、"物证"和"书证"，而未及其他证据种类。因此，有观点认为，鉴于该规定在措辞上明确规定的是"物证、书证"，因而该规定并不适用于视听资料、电子数据等实物证据。[39] 而该法第 190 条、第 192 条等所称"物证"，[40] 显然又是广义的"物证"。而该法侦查一章第 6 节所称"查封、扣押物证、书证"所称"物证"，显然又是指书证之外的其他广义的"物证"。同一部法律由于没有就术语进行必要的界定，造成同一术语的使用上存在三种外延，这种术语的不一致，必然造成解释上的困难和困惑。事实上该法第 106 条对"侦查"、"当事人"、"法定代理人"等术语的含义是有界定的。这种界定技术适用的范围应当更为广泛。

2012 年《刑事诉讼法》在司法自由裁量权方面的规定，也大大减少了法律的可预测性。例如第 54 条规定："采用刑讯逼供等非法方法收集的犯罪嫌疑人、被告人供述和采用暴力、威胁等非法方法收集的证人证言、被害人陈述，应当予以排除。收集物证、书证不符合法定程序，可能严重影响司法公正的，应当予以补正或者作出合理解释；不能补正或者作出合理解释的，对该证据应当予以排除。"立法对"等

39　参见陈光中主编：《〈中华人民共和国刑事诉讼法〉修改条文释义与点评》，人民法院出版社 2012 年版，第 71 页。事实上该条之规定源于 2010 年两院三部联合颁布的《关于办理刑事案件排除非法证据若干问题的规定》。

40　2012 年《刑事诉讼法》第 190 条规定："公诉人、辩护人应当向法庭出示物证，让当事人辨认，对未到庭的证人的证言笔录、鉴定人的鉴定意见、勘验笔录和其他作为证据的文书，应当当庭宣读。审判人员应当听取公诉人、当事人和辩护人、诉讼代理人的意见。"第 192 条规定："法庭审理过程中，当事人和辩护人、诉讼代理人有权申请通知新的证人到庭，调取新的物证，申请重新鉴定或者勘验。"

非法方法"并没有作出任何界定；对何为"严重影响司法公正"，相关机关在判断"可能严重影响司法公正"时应当考虑何等因素并没有作出规定。这种模糊性使得对非法证据排除的操作最终为何结果皆有可能，大大降低了法律的严肃性和可预测性。同样，2012年《刑事诉讼法》第52条第2款规定："行政机关在行政执法和查办案件过程中收集的物证、书证、视听资料、电子数据等证据材料，在刑事诉讼中可以作为证据使用。"该款规定也出现了令人生疑的"等"字。而为填补2012年《刑事诉讼法》本身存在的罅隙，解决其中的模糊问题，最高人民法院、最高人民检察院、公安部等机关又以各种庞杂的解释来应对实践操作问题，[41]这反过来必然造成实践中《刑事诉讼法》的实然参考资料地位。这种以解释代替《刑事诉讼法》的做法，为公权力的扩展与私权利的限制留下了空间，使得即使是法定司法解释机关之外的下级机关也萌生了制定各类解释的非常冲动。[42]

自1979年《刑事诉讼法》制定，《刑事诉讼法》已经经过了1996年和2012年两次大的修正。这种修正在内容上涉及面广泛，但是在立法形式上几乎没有变革。法律执行效能的最大实现，要求《刑事诉讼法》做到形式与内容相统一。而当前修正的结果显然使得立法形式不能服务于立法的内容。因此，借鉴包括澳大利亚《1995年证据法》在内的各国成功立法例，确立可操作的重塑技术指标，对《刑事诉讼法》

41　2012年《刑事诉讼法》本身有条文290条；2012年12月最高人民法院公布的《关于适用〈中华人民共和国刑事诉讼法〉的解释》则有条文548条；2012年11月最高人民检察院公布的《人民检察院刑事诉讼规则（试行）》则有条文708条；公安部2012年12月公布的《公安机关办理刑事案件程序规定》则有条文376条。此外，最高人民法院、最高人民检察院、公安部、国家安全部、司法部、全国人大常委会法制工作委员会2012年12月公布的《关于实施刑事诉讼法若干问题的规定》也有条文40条。

42　参见最高人民法院、最高人民检察院2012年《关于地方人民法院、人民检察院不得制定司法解释性质文件的通知》。

进行重塑是非常有必要的。

澳大利亚《1995年证据法》是证据法比较研究的一个重要文本，目前国内对于该法的研究还不是很充分。我希望这个译本能够为证据法的深入研究提供相对准确的参考资料，并在此基础上看到更多的比较证据法研究成果。

本译本是教育部长江学者与创新团队发展计划"证据科学研究与应用"（IRT0956）项目的成果。本译本也是2011年度国家社科基金重大项目"诉讼证据规定研究"的阶段性成果。

王进喜

2013年7月

Evidence Act 1995

Act No. 2 of 1995 as amended

This compilation was prepared on 21 March 2012
taking into account amendments up to Act No. 132 of 2011

The text of any of those amendments not in force
on that date is appended in the Notes section

The operation of amendments that have been incorporated may be
affected by application provisions that are set out in the Notes section

Prepared by the Office of Legislative Drafting and Publishing,
Attorney–General's Department, Canberra

1995 年证据法

1995 年第 2 号法律，已经修正

本汇编制作于 2012 年 3 月 21 日，
已结合截至 2011 年第 132 号法律的修正。

截至该日未生效的修正条文，
见附录的注释部分。

已经纳入的修正的运作，
可能会受到注释部分所列规定之适用的影响。

司法部立法起草与公布办公室 制作
堪培拉

Contents

目　录

Contents

Contents

Contents

Contents

Contents

Contents

Contents

Contents

Contents

An Act about the law of evidence, and for related purposes

Chapter 1   Preliminary

INTRODUCTORY NOTE

Outline of this Act

This Act sets out the federal rules of evidence. Generally speaking, the Act applies to proceedings in federal courts and ACT courts (see section 4), but some provisions extend beyond such proceedings (see Note 2 to subsection 4(1)).

Chapter 2 is about how evidence is adduced in proceedings.

Chapter 3 is about admissibility of evidence in proceedings.

Chapter 4 is about proof of matters in proceedings.

Chapter 5 deals with miscellaneous matters.

The Dictionary at the end of this Act defines terms and expressions used in this Act.

Related legislation

This Act is in most respects uniform with the Evidence Act 1995 of New South Wales. The 2 Acts are drafted in identical terms except so far as differences are identified in the Acts by appropriate annotations to the texts, and except so far as minor drafting variations are required because one Act is a Commonwealth Act and one Act is a New South Wales Act.

If one Act contains a provision that is not included in the other Act, the numbering of the other Act has a gap in the

关于证据法和相关目的的法律

第 1 章—初步事项

引言性注释

本法概要

本法规定了联邦证据规则。一般而言，本法适用于联邦法院和澳大利亚首都领地法院（参见第 4 条）进行的程序，但是某些规定扩展超出了这些程序（参见对 4（1）的注释 2）。

第 2 章规定了如何在程序中提出证据。

第 3 章规定了程序中证据的可采性。

第 4 章规定了程序中的事项证明。

第 5 章规定了其他事项。

本法最后部分的《术语》界定了本法使用的术语和措辞。

相关立法

本法在大多数方面与《新南威尔士州 1995 年证据法》是统一的。除了对这两部法律的正文的适当注释所说明的差别，以及因为一部是联邦法律而另一部是新南威尔士州法律而需要在起草中作出的些微变化外，两部法律的起草工作使用了相同的术语。

如果一部法律中包含有另一部法律所未包含的规定，则

numbering in order to maintain consistent numbering for the other provisions.

Part 1.1   Formal matters

1 Short title [*see* Note 1]

This Act may be cited as the *Evidence Act 1995*.

2 Commencement [*see* Note 1]

(1) This Part and the Dictionary at the end of this Act commence on the day on which this Act receives the Royal Assent.

(2) Subject to subsection (3), the remaining provisions of this Act commence on a day or days to be fixed by Proclamation.

(3) If a provision referred to in subsection (2) does not commence under that subsection before 18 April 1995, it commences on that day.

3 Definitions

(1) Expressions used in this Act (or in a particular provision of this Act) that are defined in the Dictionary at the end of this Act have the meanings given to them in the Dictionary.

Note: Some expressions used in this Act are defined in the *Acts Interpretation Act 1901*, and have the meanings given to them in that Act.

(1A) The Dictionary at the end of this Act is part of this Act.

(2) Notes included in this Act are explanatory notes and do not form part of this Act.

(3) Definitions in this Act of expressions used in this Act apply to its construction except insofar as the context or subject matter otherwise indicates or requires.

Note: Subsection (3) does not appear in section 3 of the NSW Act,

另一部法律的条文编号就会间断，以保持其他规定在编号上的一致性。

第 1.1 节—形式事项

1 简称 [参见注释 1]

本法可被引为《1995 年证据法》。

2 施行 [参见注释 1]

（1）本节和本法最后的《术语》自本法取得御准[1]之日起施行[2]。

（2）在遵守（3）的情况下，本法的其他规定自《公告》[3]所确定的日期起施行。

（3）如果（2）所称之规定在 1995 年 4 月 18 日之前没有根据该款得以施行，则该规定自该日起施行。

3 定义

（1）本法（或者本法的具体规定）所使用的在本法最后的《术语》中界定的措辞之含义，见《术语》之界定。

注释：本法所使用的某些措辞已为《1901 年法律解释法》所界定，其含义见该法之界定。

（1A）本法最后部分的《术语》，为本法的组成部分。

（2）本法所含注释均为解释性注释，不为本法的组成部分。

（3）本法使用的关于本法中的措辞的定义，适用于对本法的解释，语境或者主旨另有表示或者要求者除外。

注释：（3）并没有出现在《新南威尔士州证据法》第 3 条中，

because it is covered by section 6 of the Interpretation Act 1987 of New South Wales.

Part 1.2   Application of this Act

4 Courts and proceedings to which Act applies

(1) This Act applies to all proceedings in a federal court or an ACT court, including proceedings that:

(a) relate to bail; or

(b) are interlocutory proceedings or proceedings of a similar kind; or

(c) are heard in chambers; or

(d) subject to subsection (2), relate to sentencing.

Note 1:   Section 4 of the NSW Act differs from this section. It applies that Act to proceedings in NSW courts.

Note 2:   *ACT court* and *federal court* are defined in the Dictionary. The definitions include persons or bodies required to apply the laws of evidence.

Note 3:   Some provisions of this Act extend beyond proceedings in federal courts or ACT courts. These provisions deal with:

• extension of specified provisions to cover proceedings in all Australian courts (section 5);

• faith and credit to be given to documents properly authenticated (section 185);

• swearing of affidavits for use in Australian courts exercising federal jurisdiction or similar jurisdiction (section 186);

• abolition of the privilege against self–incrimination for bodies corporate

因为《新南威尔士州 1987 年法律解释法》第 6 条涵盖了该问题。

第 1.2 节—本法的适用

4 本法适用的法院和程序

（1）本法适用于联邦法院或者澳大利亚首都领地法院的所有程序，包括：

（a）与保释有关的程序；或者

（b）中间程序或者类似程序；[4] 或者

（c）在法官办公室听审的程序；或者

（d）在遵守（2）的情况下，与量刑有关的程序。

注释 1：《新南威尔士州证据法》第 4 条与本条不同。它将该法适用于新南威尔士州法院的程序。

注释 2：**澳大利亚首都领地法院**和**联邦法院**的定义见《术语》。这些定义包括需要适用证据法的人员或者机构。

注释 3：本法的某些规定超出了在联邦法院或者澳大利亚首都领地法院进行的程序的范围。这些规定解决的问题是：

· 特定规定的扩展适用，以涵盖在澳大利亚所有法院进行的程序（第 5 条）；

· 对经适当验真的文件所赋予的信赖（第 185 条）；

· 用于行使联邦司法管辖权或者类似司法管辖权的澳大利亚法院的宣誓陈述书的宣誓（第 186 条）；

(section 187).

Note 4:   See section 79 of the *Judiciary Act 1903* for the application of this Act to proceedings in a State court exercising federal jurisdiction.

(2) If such a proceeding relates to sentencing:

(a) this Act applies only if the court directs that the law of evidence applies in the proceeding; and

(b) if the court specifies in the direction that the law of evidence applies only in relation to specified matters— the direction has effect accordingly.

(3) The court must make a direction if:

(a) a party to the proceeding applies for such a direction in relation to the proof of a fact; and

(b) in the court's opinion, the proceeding involves proof of that fact, and that fact is or will be significant in determining a sentence to be imposed in the proceeding.

(4) The court must make a direction if the court considers it appropriate to make such a direction in the interests of justice.

(5) Subject to subsection (5A), the provisions of this Act (other than sections 185, 186 and 187) do not apply to:

(a) an appeal from a court of a State, including an appeal from a court of a State exercising federal jurisdiction; or

(b) an appeal from a court of the Northern Territory or an external Territory; or

(c) on or after the day fixed by Proclamation under subsection (6)—an appeal from an ACT court; or

第 4 条

·法人反对被迫自我归罪特免权的废除（第 187 条）。

注释 4：就本法适用于行使联邦司法管辖权的州法院的程序问题，参见《1903 年司法法》第 79 条。

（2）如果上述程序与量刑有关：

    （a）只有在法院指示在程序中适用证据法的情况下，才适用本法；并且

    （b）如果法院在指示中明确规定，证据法仅仅适用于特定事项，则该指示具有相应的效力。[5]

（3）在下列情况下，法院必须作出指示：

    （a）程序的一方当事人就对某事实的证明，申请法院作出上述指示；并且

    （b）在法院看来，程序涉及对该事实的证明，并且该事实对于确定该程序所要科处的刑罚至关重要或者将会至关重要。

（4）如果法院认为出于正义利益作出指示是适当的，则法院必须作出指令。

（5）除适用于所有澳大利亚法院的程序的规定外，在遵守（5A）的情况下，本法的规定（第 185 条、第 186 条和第 187 条除外）并不适用于下列事项：

    （a）对州法院（包括行使联邦司法管辖权的州法院）裁判的上诉；或者

    （b）对北领地或者外部领地法院裁判的上诉；或者

    （c）根据（6）在《公告》确定的期日当日或者之后，对澳大利亚首都领地法院裁判的上诉；或者

    （d）在根据（6）在《公告》确定的期日之前，

(d) until the day fixed by Proclamation under subsection (6)—
a review of a decision or order of a magistrate (other than a
review of a decision or order of a magistrate of the Australian
Capital Territory) and any appeal from such a review; or

(e) on or after that day—a review of a decision or order of
a magistrate and any appeal from such a review;

except so far as the provisions apply to proceedings in
all Australian courts.

(5A) Despite subsection (5), this Act applies to an appeal
to the Family Court of Australia from a court of
summary jurisdiction of a State or Territory exercising
jurisdiction under the *Family Law Act 1975*.

(6) On a day fixed by Proclamation, the provisions of this
Act (other than sections 185, 186 and 187) cease to apply
to proceedings in an ACT court, except so far as the
provisions apply to proceedings in all Australian courts.

Note: Subsections (5), (5A) and (6) are not included in section 4 of
the NSW Act.

5 Extended application of certain provisions

The provisions of this Act referred to in the Table apply
to all proceedings in an Australian court, including
proceedings that:

(a) relate to bail; or

(b) are interlocutory proceedings or proceedings of a
similar kind; or

(c) are heard in chambers; or

(d) relate to sentencing.

对治安法官的裁决或者命令的复审（对澳
大利亚首都领地治安法官的裁决或者命令
的复审除外），以及对该复审的任何上诉；
或者

（e）在该期日当日或者之后，对治安法官的裁决
或者命令的复审，以及对该复审的任何上
诉。

（5A）尽管有（5），本法适用于根据《1975年家庭法律法》
行使司法管辖权的州或者领地简易司法管辖权法
院向澳大利亚家庭法院提起的上诉。

（6）截至《公告》确定之日，本法规定（第185条、第
186条和第187条除外）不再适用于在澳大利亚首
都领地法院进行的程序，适用于所有澳大利亚法院
的程序的规定除外。

注释：《新南威尔士州证据法》第4条并不包括（5）、（5A）
和（6）。

5 某些规定的扩展适用

下表所列的本法规定适用于澳大利亚法院的所有程序，
包括：

（a）与保释有关的程序；或者

（b）中间程序或者类似程序；或者

（c）在法官办公室听审的程序；或者

（d）与量刑有关的程序。

TABLE

Provisions of this Act	Subject matter
Subsection 70(2)	Evidence of tags and labels in Customs prosecutions and Excise prosecutions
Section 143	Matters of law
Section 150	Seals and signatures
Section 153	Gazettes and other official documents
Section 154	Documents published by authority of Parliaments etc.
Section 155	Official records
Section 155A	Commonwealth documents
Section 157	Public documents relating to court processes
Section 158	Evidence of certain public documents
Section 159	Official statistics
Section 163	Proof of letters having been sent by Commonwealth agencies
Section 182	Commonwealth records, postal articles sent by Commonwealth agencies and certain Commonwealth documents

Note 1:   *Australian court* is defined in the Dictionary to cover all courts in Australia. The definition extends to persons and bodies that take evidence or that are required to apply the laws of evidence.

Note 2:   The NSW Act has no equivalent provision for section 5.

6 Territories

This Act extends to each external Territory.

Note: The NSW Act has no equivalent provision for section 6.

表

本法之规定	主题
70（2）	关税检控和税务检控中关于标牌和标签的证据
第 143 条	法律事项
第 150 条	印章和签名
第 153 条	公报和其他公文
第 154 条	议会等机构公布的文件
第 155 条	官方记录
第 155A 条	联邦文件
第 157 条	与法院文书有关的公共文件
第 158 条	关于特定公共文件的证据
第 159 条	官方统计
第 163 条	联邦机构寄发的信件之证明
第 182 条	联邦记录、联邦机构寄发的邮品和某些联邦文件

注释 1：**澳大利亚法院**的定义见《术语》，该定义涵盖了澳大利亚的所有法院。该定义扩展到了取证或者需要适用证据法的人员和机构。

注释 2：《新南威尔士州证据法》没有第 5 条的相应规定。

6 领地

本法扩展适用于每个外部领地。

注释：《新南威尔士州证据法》没有第 6 条的相应规定。

7 Act binds Crown

This Act binds the Crown in all its capacities.

Note: This section differs from section 7 of the NSW Act.

8 Operation of other Acts etc.

(1) This Act does not affect the operation of the provisions of any other Act, other than sections 68, 79, 80 and 80A of the *Judiciary Act 1903*.

(2) This Act does not affect the operation of regulations that:

(a) are made under an Act other than this Act; and

(b) are in force on the commencement of this section.

However, this subsection ceases to apply to a regulation once it is amended after that commencement.

(3) This Act has effect subject to the *Corporations Act 2001* and the *Australian Securities and Investments Commission Act 2001*.

(4) Until the day fixed by Proclamation under subsection 4(6), this Act does not affect the operation of the following:

(a) provisions of the Evidence Act 1971 of the Australian Capital Territory that are specified in the regulations;

(b) any other Act of the Australian Capital Territory;

(c) an Ordinance of the Australian Capital Territory;

(d) an Imperial Act or State Act in force in the Australian Capital Territory;

(e) regulations that:

(i) are made under an Act or Ordinance of the Australian Capital Territory or under an Imperial Act or State

7 本法约束政府

本法对政府有约束力。

注释：本条不同于《新南威尔士州证据法》第 7 条。

8 其他法律等的适用

（1）除《1903 年司法法》第 68 条、第 79 条、第 80 条
和第 80A 条外，本法并不影响任何其他法律规定
的适用。[6]

（2）本法并不影响下列条例的适用：

（a）根据本法之外的法律制定的条例；以及

（b）在本条施行之日有效的条例。

然而，本款不再适用于在本条施行后修正的条例。

（3）本法应当遵守《2001 年公司法》和《2001 年澳大
利亚证券和投资委员会法》的规定。[7]

（4）在 4（6）规定的《公告》确定的期日之前，本法
并不影响下列法律、法令和条例的运作：

（a）条例中列明的澳大利亚首都领地《1971 年证
据法》的规定；

（b）澳大利亚首都领地的任何其他法律；

（c）澳大利亚首都领地的法令；

（d）在澳大利亚首都领地有效的王室训令或者州
法律；

（e）下列条例：

（i）根据澳大利亚首都领地法律、法令或者
根据在澳大利亚首都领地有效的王室训

Act in force in the Australian Capital Territory; and

(ii) are in force on the commencement of this section.

(5) Paragraph (4)(e) ceases to apply to a regulation once it is amended after the commencement of this section.

(6) Subsection (4) does not apply:

(a) in relation to provisions of this Act that apply to proceedings in all Australian courts; or

(b) so far as the regulations provide otherwise.

Note: Subsection (1) differs from section 8 of the NSW Act. Subsections (2), (3), (4), (5) and (6) are not included in section 8 of the NSW Act.

8A   Application of the *Criminal Code*

Chapter 2 of the *Criminal Code* applies to all offences against this Act.

Note 1:   Chapter 2 of the *Criminal Code* sets out the general principles of criminal responsibility.

Note 2:   Section 8A does not appear in the NSW Act, because Chapter 2 of the *Criminal Code* applies only to this Act.

9   Effect of Act on other laws

(1) For the avoidance of doubt, this Act does not affect an Australian law so far as the law relates to a court's power to dispense with the operation of a rule of evidence or procedure in an interlocutory proceeding.

(2) For the avoidance of doubt, this Act does not affect a law of a State or Territory so far as the law relates to:

(a) admission or use of evidence of reasons for a decision of a member of a jury, or of the deliberations of a member of a jury in relation to such a decision, in a

令、州法律制定的条例；以及

(ii)在本条施行当日有效的条例。

(6)(4)(e)不再适用于本条施行后修正的条例。

(6)(4)并不适用于：

(a)本法中适用于所有澳大利亚法院的程序的规定；或者

(b)条例另有规定者。

注释：（1）不同于《新南威尔士州证据法》第8条。《新南威尔士州证据法》第8条并不包括（2）、（3）、（4）、（5）和（6）。

8A 《刑法典》的适用

《刑法典》第2章适用于违反本法的所有犯罪。

注释1：《刑法典》第2章规定了刑事责任的一般原则。

注释2：《新南威尔士州证据法》并没有第8A条，因为《刑法典》第2章仅适用于本法。

9 本法对其他法律的效力

（1）为避免疑义，本法并不影响与法院在中间程序中免除适用证据规则或者程序规则的权力有关的澳大利亚法律。

（2）为避免疑义，本法并不影响与下列事项有关的州或者领地法律：

（a）在对有关法院的判决、裁定、命令或者量刑的上诉程序中，采纳或者使用关于陪审团成员裁决理由的证据，或者关于与该裁决有关

proceeding by way of appeal from a judgment, decree, order or sentence of the relevant court; or

(b) bail; or

(c) any requirement for admission of evidence in support of an alibi.

(3) For the avoidance of doubt, this Act does not affect a law of a State or Territory so far as the law provides for:

(a) the operation of a legal or evidential presumption (except so far as this Act is, expressly or by necessary intendment, inconsistent with the presumption); or

(b) the admissibility of a document to depend on whether stamp duty has been paid; or

(c) a requirement that notice must be given before evidence may be adduced; or

(d) evidentiary effect to be given to a certificate or other document issued under that or any other law of the State or Territory; or

(e) proof of title to property (other than by a means provided for by this Act that is applicable to proof of title to property).

Note: This section differs from section 9 of the NSW Act.

10   Parliamentary privilege preserved

(1) This Act does not affect the law relating to the privileges of any Australian Parliament or any House of any Australian Parliament.

(2) In particular, subsection 15(2) does not affect, and is in addition to, the law relating to such privileges.

的陪审团成员评议活动的证据；或者

（b）保释；或者

（c）关于采纳支持不在犯罪现场证据的要求。

（3）为避免疑义，本法并不影响规定下列事项的州或者
领地法律：

（a）法律或者证据推定的运作（本法的明文规定
或者必要的意图与推定不一致者除外）；或
者

（b）书证的可采性取决于是否已经缴纳印花税；
或者

（c）在提出证据之前必须发出通知的要求；或者

（d）根据该法或者州或者领地的任何其他法律，
赋予证明书或者其他文件的证据效力；或
者

（e）财产所有权证明（本法规定的适用于证明财
产所有权的方式之外的方式）。

注释：本条不同于《新南威尔士州证据法》第 9 条。

10 保留议会特免权

（1）本法并不影响与任何澳大利亚议会或者任何澳大利
亚议会的任何一院的特免权有关的法律。

（2）特别是，15（2）并不是影响，而是补充了上述关
于特免权的法律。[8]

11 General powers of a court

(1) The power of a court to control the conduct of a proceeding is not affected by this Act, except so far as this Act provides otherwise expressly or by necessary intendment.

(2) In particular, the powers of a court with respect to abuse of process in a proceeding are not affected.

11 法院的一般权力

（1）法院控制程序运行的权力不受本法影响，本法另有明文规定或者必要的意图者除外。

（2）特别是，法院针对程序中的滥用程序行为的权力不受影响。[9]

Chapter 2—Adducing evidence

INTRODUCTORY NOTE

Outline of this Chapter

This Chapter is about ways in which evidence is adduced.
Part 2.1 is about adducing evidence from witnesses.
Part 2.2 is about adducing documentary evidence.
Part 2.3 is about adducing other forms of evidence.

Part 2.1—Witnesses

Division 1—Competence and compellability of witnesses

12 Competence and compellability

Except as otherwise provided by this Act:

(a) every person is competent to give evidence; and

(b) a person who is competent to give evidence about a fact is compellable to give that evidence.

13 Competence: lack of capacity

(1) A person is not competent to give evidence about a fact if, for any reason (including a mental, intellectual or physical disability):

(a) the person does not have the capacity to understand a question about the fact; or

(b) the person does not have the capacity to give an answer that can be understood to a question about the fact;

第 2 章—提出证据

引言性注释

本章概要

本章是关于提出证据方式的规定。

第 2.1 节是关于由证人提出证据的规定。

第 2.2 节是关于提出书证的规定。

第 2.3 节是关于提出其他形式的证据的规定。

第 2.1 节—证人

第 1 目—证人能力与强制作证

12 证人能力与强制作证

除本法另有规定者外：

　　（a）任何人都有作证之能力；并且

　　（b）可以强制有能力就某事实作证的人就此作证。

13 证人能力：缺乏能力

（1）如果出于任何原因（包括精神、智力或者身体残障），导致某人存在下列无能力情形，且该无能力情形不能克服，则该某人就某事实无作证能力：

　　（a）该某人无能力理解就该事实提出的问题；或者

　　（b）该某人无能力就关于该事实的提问作出可被

Section 13

and that incapacity cannot be overcome.

Note: See sections 30 and 31 for examples of assistance that may be provided to enable witnesses to overcome disabilities.

(2) A person who, because of subsection (1), is not competent to give evidence about a fact may be competent to give evidence about other facts.

(3) A person who is competent to give evidence about a fact is not competent to give sworn evidence about the fact if the person does not have the capacity to understand that, in giving evidence, he or she is under an obligation to give truthful evidence.

(4) A person who is not competent to give sworn evidence about a fact may, subject to subsection (5), be competent to give unsworn evidence about the fact.

(5) A person who, because of subsection (3), is not competent to give sworn evidence is competent to give unsworn evidence if the court has told the person:

(a) that it is important to tell the truth; and

(b) that he or she may be asked questions that he or she does not know, or cannot remember, the answer to, and that he or she should tell the court if this occurs; and

(c) that he or she may be asked questions that suggest certain statements are true or untrue and that he or she should agree with the statements that he or she believes are true and should feel no pressure to agree with statements that he or she believes are untrue.

(6) It is presumed, unless the contrary is proved, that a person is not incompetent because of this section.

(7) Evidence that has been given by a witness does not become inadmissible merely because, before the witness finishes giving evidence, he or she dies or ceases to be competent to give evidence.

第 13 条

理解的回答。[1]

> 注释：就为帮助证人克服无能力问题而提供的帮助，可参
> 见第 30 条和第 31 条之示例。

（2）因（1）而无能力就某事实作证的人，可能就其他
事实有作证能力。

（3）就某事实有能力作证的人，如果并无能力理解其在
作证时有作出真实证言之义务，则无能力就该事实
作出宣誓证言。

（4）就某事实无能力作出宣誓证言之人，在遵守（5）
的情况下，有能力就该事实作出非宣誓证言。[2]

（5）在下列情况下，因（3）而无能力作出宣誓证言
之人，有能力作出非宣誓证言：

（a）法院就如实陈述的重要性对该某人进行了告知；
并且

（b）法院已经告知该某人，该某人可能被问及其不
知道如何回答或者不能记起答案的问题，如果
发生了这种情况，该某人应当告知法院；并且

（c）法院已经告知该某人，该某人可能被问及暗示
某些陈述为真或者为假的问题，如果该某人认
为该陈述为真，则应当对该陈述表示同意，并
且在其认为该陈述为假的情况下，则应当感到
没有对该陈述表示同意的压力。

（6）应当推定一个人并不因为本条而无作证能力，有相
反证明者除外。[3]

（7）已经由证人作出的证言，并不仅仅因为证人在作证
完成之前死亡或者不再具有作证能力而不具有可采
性。[4]

(8) For the purpose of determining a question arising under this section, the court may inform itself as it thinks fit, including by obtaining information from a person who has relevant specialised knowledge based on the person's training, study or experience.

14 Compellability: reduced capacity

A person is not compellable to give evidence on a particular matter if the court is satisfied that:

(a) substantial cost or delay would be incurred in ensuring that the person would have the capacity to understand a question about the matter or to give an answer that can be understood to a question about the matter; and

(b) adequate evidence on that matter has been given, or will be able to be given, from one or more other persons or sources.

15 Compellability: Sovereign and others

(1) None of the following is compellable to give evidence:

(a) the Sovereign;

(b) the Governor–General;

(c) the Governor of a State;

(d) the Administrator of a Territory;

(e) a foreign sovereign or the Head of State of a foreign country.

(2) A member of a House of an Australian Parliament is not compellable to give evidence if the member would, if compelled to give evidence, be prevented from attending:

(a) a sitting of that House or a joint sitting of that Parliament; or

(b) a meeting of a committee of that House or that Parliament, being a committee of which he or she is a member.

（8）为了确定起因于本条的问题，法院可以以其认为
适当的方式了解有关情况，包括从基于训练、学
习或者经验而具有专门知识的人那里获得信息。

14 强制作证：能力减损

如果法院确信存在下列情形，则不得强制某人就某具体
事项作证：

（a）为保证该某人有能力理解就该事项的提问，
或者能够就该事项的提问作出可被理解的回
答，将导致重大的耗费或者延误；并且

（b）关于该事项已经有，或者能够从他人或者其
他来源获得足够的证据。

15 强制作证：元首与其他人员

（1）不得强制下列人员作证：

（a）元首；

（b）总督；

（c）州长；

（d）领地行政长官；

（e）外国元首或者外国首脑。

（2）如果强制澳大利亚议会某院成员作证将妨碍其出席
下列会议，则不得强制其作证：

（a）该院的会议或者议会的联席会议；或者

（b）其担任成员的该院或者议会的某委员会的会
议。

16 Competence and compellability: judges and jurors

(1) A person who is a judge or juror in a proceeding is not competent to give evidence in that proceeding. However, a juror is competent to give evidence in the proceeding about matters affecting conduct of the proceeding.

(2) A person who is or was a judge in an Australian or overseas proceeding is not compellable to give evidence about that proceeding unless the court gives leave.

17 Competence and compellability: defendants in criminal proceedings

(1) This section applies only in a criminal proceeding.

(2) A defendant is not competent to give evidence as a witness for the prosecution.

(3) An associated defendant is not compellable to give evidence for or against a defendant in a criminal proceeding, unless the associated defendant is being tried separately from the defendant.

(4) If a witness is an associated defendant who is being tried jointly with the defendant in the proceeding, the court is to satisfy itself (if there is a jury, in the jury's absence) that the witness is aware of the effect of subsection (3).

Note: *Associated defendant* is defined in the Dictionary.

18 Compellability of spouses and others in criminal proceedings generally

(1) This section applies only in a criminal proceeding.

(2) A person who, when required to give evidence, is the spouse, de facto partner, parent or child of a defendant may object to being required:

(a) to give evidence; or

(b) to give evidence of a communication between the person and the defendant;

as a witness for the prosecution.

16 证人能力与强制作证：法官与陪审员

（1）担任某程序法官或者陪审员的人，无能力在该程序中作证。但是，陪审员有能力就影响程序运行的事项在该程序中作证。

（2）不得强制担任或者曾经担任澳大利亚程序或者海外程序的法官的人就该程序作证，除非法院许可。

17 证人能力与强制作证：刑事程序中的被告

（1）本条仅适用于刑事程序。

（2）被告没有作为检控方的证人作证之能力。

（3）不得强制关联被告作证来支持或者反对刑事程序中的被告，除非该关联被告正在与被告分开审理。[5]

（4）如果证人是正在与程序的被告共同受审的关联被告，法院应当自己确信（如果有陪审团，则陪审团不在场）证人意识到了（3）的效力。

注释：**关联被告**的定义见《术语》。

18 在刑事程序中强制配偶和其他人员作证的一般规定

（1）本条仅适用于刑事程序。

（2）如果某人在被要求作证的时候是被告的配偶、事实配偶、父母或者子女，可以反对被要求作为检控方的证人从事下列活动：

（a）作证；或者

（b）就该某人与被告之间的交流作证。

(3) The objection is to be made before the person gives the evidence or as soon as practicable after the person becomes aware of the right so to object, whichever is the later.

(4) If it appears to the court that a person may have a right to make an objection under this section, the court is to satisfy itself that the person is aware of the effect of this section as it may apply to the person.

(5) If there is a jury, the court is to hear and determine any objection under this section in the absence of the jury.

(6) A person who makes an objection under this section to giving evidence or giving evidence of a communication must not be required to give the evidence if the court finds that:

  (a) there is a likelihood that harm would or might be caused (whether directly or indirectly) to the person, or to the relationship between the person and the defendant, if the person gives the evidence; and

  (b) the nature and extent of that harm outweighs the desirability of having the evidence given.

(7) Without limiting the matters that may be taken into account by the court for the purposes of subsection (6), it must take into account the following:

  (a) the nature and gravity of the offence for which the defendant is being prosecuted;

  (b) the substance and importance of any evidence that the person might give and the weight that is likely to be attached to it;

  (c) whether any other evidence concerning the matters to which the evidence of the person would relate is reasonably available to the prosecutor;

  (d) the nature of the relationship between the defendant and the person;

（3）该异议应当在该某人作证之前提出，或者在该某人
    意识到该异议权利后尽可能早地提出，以上述两种
    情况较迟者为准。

（4）如果在法院看来，某人可能有权根据本条提出异议，
    法院应当自己确信该某人意识到了本条适用于该
    某人时的效力。

（5）如果有陪审团，法院应当在陪审团不在场的情况下
    听取根据本条提出的异议并作出决定。

（6）在某人根据本条反对作证或者反对就有关交流作证
    的情况下，如果法院认定存在下列情况，则不得要
    求该某人作证。

    （a）如果该某人作证，将导致或者可能导致对该
        某人，或者该某人与被告的关系产生损害，
        无论直接或者间接；并且

    （b）该损害的性质和范围超过了让其作证的希求
        性。

（7）就（6）之目的而言，法院必须考虑的事项包括但
    是不限于：

    （a）被告正在被检控的犯罪的性质和严重程度；

    （b）该某人可能提供的证言的要旨、重要性，以
        及该证据可能被赋予的证明力；

    （c）就该某人所要陈述之证据之相关事项，是否
        有其他能为检控方所合理获得的证据；

    （d）被告与该某人之间关系的性质；

      (e) whether, in giving the evidence, the person would have to disclose matter that was received by the person in confidence from the defendant.

(8) If an objection under this section has been determined, the prosecutor may not comment on:

      (a) the objection; or

      (b) the decision of the court in relation to the objection; or

      (c) the failure of the person to give evidence.

19 Compellability of spouses and others in certain criminal proceedings

Section 18 does not apply in proceedings for an offence against or referred to in the following provisions:

      (a) an offence against a provision of Part 2, 2A, 3, 4 or 5 of the Crimes Act 1900 of the Australian Capital Territory, being an offence against a person under the age of 16 years;

      (b) an offence against section 374, 375, 376 or 389 of the *Children and Young People Act 1999* of the Australian Capital Territory;

      (c) an offence that is a domestic violence offence within the meaning of the *Domestic Violence and Protection Orders Act 2001* of the Australian Capital Territory.

Note: This section differs from section 19 of the NSW Act.

20 Comment on failure to give evidence

(1) This section applies only in a criminal proceeding for an indictable offence.

(2) The judge or any party (other than the prosecutor) may comment on a failure of the defendant to give evidence. However, unless the comment is made by another defendant

第 20 条

（e）在作证的过程中，该某人是否将不得不披露其从被告那里秘密获悉的事项。

（8）如果根据本条提出的异议已经被确定，公诉人不得就下列事项进行评论：

（a）该异议；或者

（b）法院就该异议作出的决定；或者

（c）该某人未能作证。

19 在某些刑事程序中强制配偶和其他人员作证

第 18 条并不适用于有关违反下列规定的犯罪或者下列规定所称犯罪的程序：

（a）违反澳大利亚首都领地《1900 年犯罪法》第 2 章、第 2A 章、第 3 章、第 4 章或者第 5 章之规定，针对不满 16 岁之人所实施的犯罪；

（b）违反澳大利亚首都领地《1999 年儿童和少年法》第 374 条、第 375 条、第 376 条或者第 389 条的犯罪；

（c）澳大利亚首都领地《2001 年家庭暴力和保护令法》规定的家庭暴力犯罪。

注释：本条规定不同于《新南威尔士州证据法》第 19 条。

20 对未能作证的评论

（1）本条仅适用于可诉罪之刑事程序。[6]

（2）法官或者任何当事人（公诉人除外）可以就被告未能作证进行评论。然而，该评论不得暗示被告之所以未能作证是因为被告犯有有关罪行或者被告相

in the proceeding, the comment must not suggest that the defendant failed to give evidence because the defendant was, or believed that he or she was, guilty of the offence concerned.

(3) The judge or any party (other than the prosecutor) may comment on a failure to give evidence by a person who, at the time of the failure, was:

    (a) the defendant's spouse or de facto partner; or

    (b) a parent or child of the defendant.

(4) However, unless the comment is made by another defendant in the proceeding, a comment of a kind referred to in subsection (3) must not suggest that the spouse, de facto partner, parent or child failed to give evidence because:

    (a) the defendant was guilty of the offence concerned; or

    (b) the spouse, de facto partner, parent or child believed that the defendant was guilty of the offence concerned.

(5) If:

    (a) 2 or more persons are being tried together for an indictable offence; and

    (b) comment is made by any of those persons on the failure of any of those persons or of the spouse or de facto partner, or a parent or child, of any of those persons to give evidence;

the judge may, in addition to commenting on the failure to give evidence, comment on any comment of a kind referred to in paragraph (b).

Division 2—Oaths and affirmations

21 Sworn evidence of witnesses to be on oath or affirmation

(1) A witness in a proceeding must either take an oath, or

信其有罪，除非该评论是程序中的其他被告作出的。[7]

（3）法官或者任何当事人（公诉人除外）可以就下列人员未能作证作出评论：

（a）在未能作证时，是被告的配偶或者事实配偶；或者

（b）在未能作证时，是被告的父母或者子女。

（4）然而，（3）所称评论不得暗示，配偶、事实配偶、父母或者子女未能作证是出于下列原因，除非该评论是程序中的其他被告作出的：

（a）被告犯有有关罪行；或者

（b）配偶、事实配偶、父母或者子女认为被告犯有有关罪行。

（5）在下列情况下，法官除了可以就未能作证进行评论外，还可以就（b）所称任何评论进行评论：

（a）2 个或者 2 个以上的人因某可诉罪正在一起受审；并且

（b）任何一名上述人员对任何其他上述人员或者其配偶、事实配偶、父母、子女未能作证进行了评论。[8]

第 2 目—宣誓与郑重声明

21 证人经宣誓或者郑重声明所作的宣誓证言

（1）程序中的证人在作证之前，必须进行宣誓或者郑重

make an affirmation, before giving evidence.

(2) Subsection (1) does not apply to a person who gives unsworn evidence under section 13.

(3) A person who is called merely to produce a document or thing to the court need not take an oath or make an affirmation before doing so.

(4) The witness is to take the oath, or make the affirmation, in accordance with the appropriate form in the Schedule or in a similar form.

(5) Such an affirmation has the same effect for all purposes as an oath.

22 Interpreters to act on oath or affirmation

(1) A person must either take an oath, or make an affirmation, before acting as an interpreter in a proceeding.

(2) The person is to take the oath, or make the affirmation, in accordance with the appropriate form in the Schedule or in a similar form.

(3) Such an affirmation has the same effect for all purposes as an oath.

23 Choice of oath or affirmation

(1) A person who is to be a witness or act as an interpreter in a proceeding may choose whether to take an oath or make an affirmation.

(2) The court is to inform the person that he or she has this choice.

(3) The court may direct a person who is to be a witness to make an affirmation if:

　(a) the person refuses to choose whether to take an oath or make an affirmation; or

　(b) it is not reasonably practicable for the person to take an appropriate oath.

声明。

（2）（1）不适用于根据第 13 条作出非宣誓证言的
人员。

（3）经传唤仅为向法院出示书证或者物证的人，在向法
院提交上述书证或者物证前，无需宣誓或者进行郑
重声明。

（4）证人应当遵照《附录》规定的适当形式或者类似形
式进行宣誓或者郑重声明。

（5）上述郑重声明与宣誓具有完全同等之效力。

22 传译人员须经宣誓或者郑重声明而行为

（1）一个人在程序中充任传译人员之前，必须进行宣誓
或者郑重声明。

（2）该某人应当遵照《附录》规定的适当形式或者类似
形式进行宣誓或者郑重声明。

（3）上述郑重声明与宣誓具有完全同等之效力。

23 宣誓或者郑重声明的选择

（1）在程序中充任证人或者传译人员的人员，可以选择
宣誓或者郑重声明。

（2）法院应当告知该某人其可进行该选择。

（3）在下列情形下，法院可以指示充任证人之人进行郑
重声明：

（a）该某人拒绝就宣誓或者郑重声明作出选择；
或者

（b）该某人没有进行适当宣誓的合理可行性。

24 Requirements for oaths

(1) It is not necessary that a religious text be used in taking an oath.

(2) An oath is effective for the purposes of this Division even if the person who took it:

   (a) did not have a religious belief or did not have a religious belief of a particular kind; or

   (b) did not understand the nature and consequences of the oath.

Division 3—General rules about giving evidence

26 Court's control over questioning of witnesses

The court may make such orders as it considers just in relation to:

   (a) the way in which witnesses are to be questioned; and

   (b) the production and use of documents and things in connection with the questioning of witnesses; and

   (c) the order in which parties may question a witness; and

   (d) the presence and behaviour of any person in connection with the questioning of witnesses.

27 Parties may question witnesses

A party may question any witness, except as provided by this Act.

28 Order of examination in chief, cross–examination and re–examination

Unless the court otherwise directs:

   (a) cross–examination of a witness is not to take place before the examination in chief of the witness; and

   (b) re–examination of a witness is not to take place before all other parties who wish to do so have cross–examined the witness.

24 宣誓的要求

（1）宗教经卷并非为进行宣誓所必需。

（2）就本目之目的而言，即使在下列情况下，宣誓依然有效：

（a）宣誓之人没有宗教信仰，或者没有某具体种类的宗教信仰；或者

（b）宣誓之人并不理解宣誓的性质和后果。

第 3 目—作证的一般规则

26 法院对询问证人的控制

法院可以就下列事项作出其认为正当的命令：

（a）对证人进行询问的方式；以及

（b）出示和使用与询问证人有关的文件和物品；以及

（c）当事人询问证人的顺序；以及

（d）与询问证人有关的任何人员的在场和行为。[9]

27 当事人可以询问证人

当事人可以询问任何证人，本法另有规定者除外。[10]

28 主询问、交叉询问和再询问的顺序

除非法院另有指示：

（a）对证人进行的交叉询问不得发生在对证人进行主询问之前；以及

（b）对证人进行的再询问不得发生在准备对证人进行交叉询问的所有其他当事人进行的交叉询问之前。

29 Manner and form of questioning witnesses and their responses

(1) A party may question a witness in any way the party thinks fit, except as provided by this Chapter or as directed by the court.

(2) A court may, on its own motion or on the application of the party that called the witness, direct that the witness give evidence wholly or partly in narrative form.

(3) Such a direction may include directions about the way in which evidence is to be given in that form.

(4) Evidence may be given in the form of charts, summaries or other explanatory material if it appears to the court that the material would be likely to aid its comprehension of other evidence that has been given or is to be given.

30 Interpreters

A witness may give evidence about a fact through an interpreter unless the witness can understand and speak the English language sufficiently to enable the witness to understand, and to make an adequate reply to, questions that may be put about the fact.

31 Deaf and mute witnesses

(1) A witness who cannot hear adequately may be questioned in any appropriate way.

(2) A witness who cannot speak adequately may give evidence by any appropriate means.

(3) The court may give directions concerning either or both of the following:

(a) the way in which a witness may be questioned under subsection (1);

(b) the means by which a witness may give evidence under subsection (2).

29 对证人进行询问和证人作出回应的方式与形式

（1）当事人可以采用其认为适当的方式对证人进行询问，本章另有规定或者法院另有指示者除外。

（2）法院可以依职权或者根据传唤证人的当事人之申请，指示证人全部或者部分以叙述形式作证。

（3）上述指示可以包括以上述形式作证之方式的指示。

（4）如果在法院看来，以图表、摘要或者其他解释性材料作证，将可能帮助其理解已经提供或者将要提供的其他证据，则可以采用上述方式作证。

30 传译人员

证人可以通过传译人员就某事实作证，除非证人能理解英语、用英语说话，并足以使证人理解就该事实进行的询问和作出足够的回应。[11]

31 聋、哑证人

（1）可以以任何适当的方式对不能充分聆听的证人进行询问。

（2）不能充分言说的证人可以以任何适当的方式作证。

（3）法院可以就如下事项之一或者二者作出指示：

（a）根据（1）对证人进行询问的方式；

（b）证人根据（2）作证的方式。

(4) This section does not affect the right of a witness to whom this section applies to give evidence about a fact through an interpreter under section 30.

32 Attempts to revive memory in court

(1) A witness must not, in the course of giving evidence, use a document to try to revive his or her memory about a fact or opinion unless the court gives leave.

(2) Without limiting the matters that the court may take into account in deciding whether to give leave, it is to take into account:

   (a) whether the witness will be able to recall the fact or opinion adequately without using the document; and

   (b) whether so much of the document as the witness proposes to use is, or is a copy of, a document that:

   (i) was written or made by the witness when the events recorded in it were fresh in his or her memory; or

   (ii) was, at such a time, found by the witness to be accurate.

(3) If a witness has, while giving evidence, used a document to try to revive his or her memory about a fact or opinion, the witness may, with the leave of the court, read aloud, as part of his or her evidence, so much of the document as relates to that fact or opinion.

(4) The court is, on the request of a party, to give such directions as the court thinks fit to ensure that so much of the document as relates to the proceeding is produced to that party.

33 Evidence given by police officers

(1) Despite section 32, in any criminal proceeding, a police officer may give evidence in chief for the prosecution by reading or being led through a written statement previously made by the police officer.

（4）本条不影响本条所适用的证人根据第 30 条通过传译人员就某事实作证之权利。

32 试图当庭唤醒记忆

（1）证人在作证过程中，不得使用文件来试图唤醒其关于某事实或者意见的记忆，除非法院许可。[12]

（2）法院在决定是否作出许可时，应当虑及的事项包括但是不限于：

（a）在不使用该文件的情况下，证人是否能够充分回忆起该事实或者意见；并且

（b）证人准备使用的文件是否是下列文件或者其复制件：

（i）证人就其所记载的事件的记忆清晰时，由该证人书写或者制作的文件；或者

（ii）证人当时认定记录准确的文件。[13]

（3）如果证人在作证时使用了某文件来试图唤醒其关于某事实或者意见的记忆，经法院许可，证人可以将该文件中与该事实或者意见相关的部分朗读，作为其证言的一部分。

（4）根据当事人的请求，法院可以作出其认为适当之指示，保证该文件与程序有关的部分出示给该当事人。

33 警察作证

（1）尽管存在第 32 条，在任何刑事程序中，警察可以通过宣读以前由其制作的书面陈述或者以该陈述为引导，来为检控方提供主问证据。[14]

(2) Evidence may not be so given unless:

    (a) the statement was made by the police officer at the time of or soon after the occurrence of the events to which it refers; and

    (b) the police officer signed the statement when it was made; and

    (c) a copy of the statement had been given to the person charged or to his or her Australian legal practitioner or legal counsel a reasonable time before the hearing of the evidence for the prosecution.

(3) A reference in this section to a police officer includes a reference to a person who, at the time the statement concerned was made, was a police officer.

34 Attempts to revive memory out of court

(1) The court may, on the request of a party, give such directions as are appropriate to ensure that specified documents and things used by a witness otherwise than while giving evidence to try to revive his or her memory are produced to the party for the purposes of the proceeding.

(2) The court may refuse to admit the evidence given by the witness so far as it concerns a fact as to which the witness so tried to revive his or her memory if, without reasonable excuse, the directions have not been complied with.

35 Effect of calling for production of documents

(1) A party is not to be required to tender a document only because the party, whether under this Act or otherwise:

    (a) called for the document to be produced to the party; or

    (b) inspected it when it was so produced.

（2）警察不能采取上述形式作证，除非符合下列条件：

（a）该陈述是由警察在陈述所称事件发生之时或者之后不久制作的；并且

（b）警察在制作该陈述时进行了签名；并且

（c）在听审该检控证据之前的合理时间内，已经将该陈述的复制件送达被指控的人、其澳大利亚法律执业者或者法律顾问。

（3）本条所称警察，包括在制作有关陈述时是警察的人。

34 试图在法院外唤醒记忆

（1）如果证人在非作证时为唤醒其记忆使用了特定的文件或者物品，则根据当事人的请求，法院可以作出适当之指示，保证为程序目的将这些文件或者物品出示给该当事人。

（2）如果无正当理由，而上述指示没有被遵行，则法院可以就与证人试图恢复其记忆有关的事实，拒绝采纳该证人的证言。

35 要求出示文件的效力

（1）并不要求当事人仅仅因为根据本法或者其他规定从事了下列行为而提交某文件：

（a）要求将文件出示给该当事人；或者

（b）在出示文件时查阅了该文件。

    (2) The party who produces a document so called for is not entitled to tender it only because the party to whom it was produced, or who inspected it, fails to tender it.

36 Person may be examined without subpoena or other process

    (1) The court may order a person who:

        (a) is present at the hearing of a proceeding; and

        (b) is compellable to give evidence in the proceeding;

        to give evidence and to produce documents or things even if a subpoena or other process requiring the person to attend for that purpose has not been duly served on the person.

    (2) A person so ordered to give evidence or to produce documents or things is subject to the same penalties and liabilities as if the person had been duly served with such a subpoena or other process.

    (3) A party who inspects a document or thing produced to the court because of subsection (1) need not use the document in evidence.

Division 4—Examination in chief and re–examination

37 Leading questions

    (1) A leading question must not be put to a witness in examination in chief or in re–examination unless:

        (a) the court gives leave; or

        (b) the question relates to a matter introductory to the witness's evidence; or

        (c) no objection is made to the question and (leaving aside the party conducting the examination in chief or re–examination) each other party to the proceeding is represented by an Australian legal practitioner, legal

(2) 出示被要求出示的文件的当事人，并不仅仅因为要求出示该文件的当事人或者查阅该文件的当事人没有将其提交，而有权将其提交。[15]

36 无传证令或者其他传唤文书时可以对他人进行询问

(1) 对于符合下列情况的人员，法院可以命令其作证和出示文件或者物品，即使为该目的而要求该某人出庭的传证令或者其他文书没有被及时送达该某人：

(a) 在某程序听审时在场；并且

(b) 在程序中可以被强制作证。

(2) 上述被法院命令作证和出示文件或者物品的人员，与被及时送达上述传证令或者其他文书的人员一样，受约束于同样的处罚和责任。

(3) 查阅因（1）而出示给法院的文件或者物品的当事人，无需将该文件用作证据。

第 4 目—主询问与再询问

37 诱导性问题

(1) 在对证人的主询问和再询问中，不得提出诱导性问题，除非：

(a) 法院许可；或者

(b) 该问题与证人证言的介绍性事项有关；或者

(c) 对该问题没有异议，且（除了进行主询问或者再询问的当事人之外）程序的其他各方当事人均有澳大利亚法律执业者、法律顾问或

Section 38

counsel or prosecutor; or

    (d) the question relates to a matter that is not in dispute; or

    (e) if the witness has specialised knowledge based on the witness's training, study or experience—the question is asked for the purpose of obtaining the witness's opinion about a hypothetical statement of facts, being facts in respect of which evidence has been, or is intended to be, given.

  (2) Unless the court otherwise directs, subsection (1) does not apply in civil proceedings to a question that relates to an investigation, inspection or report that the witness made in the course of carrying out public or official duties.

  (3) Subsection (1) does not prevent a court from exercising power under rules of court to allow a written statement or report to be tendered or treated as evidence in chief of its maker.

Note: *Leading question* is defined in the Dictionary.

38 Unfavourable witnesses

  (1) A party who called a witness may, with the leave of the court, question the witness, as though the party were cross–examining the witness, about:

    (a) evidence given by the witness that is unfavourable to the party; or

    (b) a matter of which the witness may reasonably be supposed to have knowledge and about which it appears to the court the witness is not, in examination in chief, making a genuine attempt to give evidence; or

    (c) whether the witness has, at any time, made a prior inconsistent statement.

  (2) Questioning a witness under this section is taken to be cross–examination for the purposes of this Act (other than

者公诉人代理；或者

（d）该问题与不存在争议的事项有关；或者

（e）在证人基于其训练、学习或者经验而具备专
门知识的情况下，提问之目的在于就已经
就其提供证据或者准备就其提供证据的事
实，获得证人对有关假设性事实陈述的意
见。

（2）除非法院另有指示，在民事诉讼中，（1）不适用
于与证人在履行公职时所进行的调查、检查或者报
告有关的提问。

（3）（1）并不禁止法院根据法院规则行使权力来允许
提交书面陈述或者报告，或者将其视为制作人的主
答证据。【16】

注释：**诱导性问题**的定义见《术语》。

38 不利证人

（1）经法院许可，传唤证人的当事人可以如同交叉询问
一样，就下列事项对证人提问：

（a）证人作出的不利于该当事人的证言；或者

（b）可以合理地认为该证人了解，而在法院看来，
在主询问中该证人并未真正试图就其作证的
事项；或者

（c）该证人是否在任何时候曾作出先前不一致陈
述。【17】

（2）根据本条对证人的提问，视为本法所规定的交叉询

section 39).

(3) The party questioning the witness under this section may, with the leave of the court, question the witness about matters relevant only to the witness's credibility.

Note: The rules about admissibility of evidence relevant only to credibility are set out in Part 3.7.

(4) Questioning under this section is to take place before the other parties cross–examine the witness, unless the court otherwise directs.

(5) If the court so directs, the order in which the parties question the witness is to be as the court directs.

(6) Without limiting the matters that the court may take into account in determining whether to give leave or a direction under this section, it is to take into account:

(a) whether the party gave notice at the earliest opportunity of his or her intention to seek leave; and

(b) the matters on which, and the extent to which, the witness has been, or is likely to be, questioned by another party.

(7) A party is subject to the same liability to be cross–examined under this section as any other witness if:

(a) a proceeding is being conducted in the name of the party by or on behalf of an insurer or other person; and

(b) the party is a witness in the proceeding.

39 Limits on re–examination

On re–examination:

(a) a witness may be questioned about matters arising out of evidence given by the witness in cross–examination; and

(b) other questions may not be put to the witness unless the court gives leave.

问（第 39 条除外）。

（3）经法院许可，根据本条对证人提问的当事人可以就仅与证人的可信性有关的事项对证人提问。

注释：仅与可信性有关的证据的可采性规则，见第 3.7 节。

（4）根据本条进行的提问，应当在其他当事人对该证人进行交叉询问之前进行，除非法院另有指示。

（5）如果法院作出上述指示，当事人对证人提问的顺序依照法院指示进行。

（6）法院在决定是否根据本条作出许可或者指示时，应当虑及的事项包括但是不限于：

（a）当事人是否在最早时间就其寻求许可的意图进行了通知；以及

（b）另一方当事人已经或者可能向该证人询问的事项及其范围。

（7）在下列情况下，当事人像任何其他证人一样，负有接受根据本条进行的交叉询问的相同责任：

（a）程序是由保险商、其他人或者为了他们而以该当事人的名义进行的；并且

（b）该当事人是该程序中的证人。

39 对再询问的限制

就再询问而言：

（a）可以就起因于证人在交叉询问中作证的事项向其提问；并且

（b）不得向证人提出其他问题，除非法院许可。

Division 5—Cross–examination

40 Witness called in error

A party is not to cross–examine a witness who has been called in error by another party and has not been questioned by that other party about a matter relevant to a question to be determined in the proceeding.

41 Improper questions

(1) The court must disallow a question put to a witness in cross–examination, or inform the witness that it need not be answered, if the court is of the opinion that the question (referred to as a *disallowable question*):

    (a) is misleading or confusing; or

    (b) is unduly annoying, harassing, intimidating, offensive, oppressive, humiliating or repetitive; or

    (c) is put to the witness in a manner or tone that is belittling, insulting or otherwise inappropriate; or

    (d) has no basis other than a stereotype (for example, a stereotype based on the witness's sex, race, culture, ethnicity, age or mental, intellectual or physical disability).

(2) Without limiting the matters the court may take into account for the purposes of subsection (1), it is to take into account:

    (a) any relevant condition or characteristic of the witness of which the court is, or is made, aware, including age, education, ethnic and cultural background, gender, language background and skills, level of maturity and understanding and personality; and

    (b) any mental, intellectual or physical disability of which the court is, or is made, aware and to which the witness is, or appears to be, subject; and

第 5 目—交叉询问

40 错误传唤的证人

在一方当事人错误地传唤了证人的情况下，如果该方当事人并没有就与程序中待定问题有关的事项向证人提问，则另一方当事人不得对该证人进行交叉询问。

41 不适当的询问

（1）在交叉询问中，如果法院认为询问属于下列情况（简称为**不被允许的询问**），则法院不得允许对证人提出该询问，或者告知证人不需要回答该询问：

（a）误导性或者混淆性询问；或者

（b）不当地激怒、骚扰、恐吓、冒犯、逼迫、羞辱证人的询问或者重复性的询问；或者

（c）以蔑视、侮辱或者其他不适当方式或者语调对证人提出的询问；或者

（d）除了定式思维（例如以证人的性别、种族、文化、族源、年龄或者精神、智力或者身体残障为据的定式思维）之外毫无根据的询问。

（2）就（1）之目的而言，法院应当考虑的事项包括但是不限于：

（a）法院意识到的该证人的任何相关条件或者特点，包括年龄、教育程度、族源和文化背景、性别、语言背景和技能、成熟度和理解度以及个性；以及

（b）法院意识到的该证人患有或者看上去患有的任何精神、智力或者身体上的残障；以及

(c) the context in which the question is put, including:

    (i) the nature of the proceeding; and

    (ii) in a criminal proceeding—the nature of the offence to which the proceeding relates; and

    (iii) the relationship (if any) between the witness and any other party to the proceeding.

(3) A question is not a disallowable question merely because:

    (a) the question challenges the truthfulness of the witness or the consistency or accuracy of any statement made by the witness; or

    (b) the question requires the witness to discuss a subject that could be considered distasteful to, or private by, the witness.

(4) A party may object to a question put to a witness on the ground that it is a disallowable question.

(5) However, the duty imposed on the court by this section applies whether or not an objection is raised to a particular question.

(6) A failure by the court to disallow a question under this section, or to inform the witness that it need not be answered, does not affect the admissibility in evidence of any answer given by the witness in response to the question.

> Note: A person must not, without the express permission of a court, print or publish any question that the court has disallowed under this section: see section 195.

42 Leading questions

(1) A party may put a leading question to a witness in cross–examination unless the court disallows the question or directs the witness not to answer it.

(2) Without limiting the matters that the court may take into account in deciding whether to disallow the question or give such a direction, it is to take into account the extent to which:

（c）所提询问的背景，包括：

（ⅰ）程序的性质；以及

（ⅱ）在刑事程序中，与该程序有关的犯罪的性质；以及

（ⅲ）证人与程序的任何其他当事人的关系（如果存在的话）。

（3）询问并不仅仅因为下列情况而属于不被允许的询问：

（a）该询问对证人的诚实性或者证人所作任何陈述的一致性或者准确性提出了质疑；或者

（b）该询问要求证人讨论会被证人认为令人厌恶或者属于隐私的话题。

（4）当事人可以以对证人的询问属于不被允许的询问为由提出异议。

（5）然而，无论就具体的询问是否提出了异议，本条为法院设定的职责均适用。

（6）法院未能根据本条不允许某询问，或者未能告知证人不需要对此作出回答，并不影响证人针对该询问作出的任何回答的证据可采性。

注释：未经法院明确允许，任何人不得刊行或者公布法院根据本条禁止的询问：参见第 195 条。

42 诱导性问题

（1）当事人可以在交叉询问中向证人提出诱导性问题，除非法院不允许该询问或者指示证人对此不予回答。

（2）在决定是否不允许上述提问或者作出上述指示时，法院应当虑及的事项包括但是不限于：

     (a) evidence that has been given by the witness in examination in chief is unfavourable to the party who called the witness; and

     (b) the witness has an interest consistent with an interest of the cross–examiner; and

     (c) the witness is sympathetic to the party conducting the cross–examination, either generally or about a particular matter; and

     (d) the witness's age, or any mental, intellectual or physical disability to which the witness is subject, may affect the witness's answers.

(3) The court is to disallow the question, or direct the witness not to answer it, if the court is satisfied that the facts concerned would be better ascertained if leading questions were not used.

(4) This section does not limit the court's power to control leading questions.

     Note: *Leading question* is defined in the Dictionary.

43 Prior inconsistent statements of witnesses

(1) A witness may be cross–examined about a prior inconsistent statement alleged to have been made by the witness whether or not:

     (a) complete particulars of the statement have been given to the witness; or

     (b) a document containing a record of the statement has been shown to the witness.

(2) If, in cross–examination, a witness does not admit that he or she has made a prior inconsistent statement, the cross–examiner is not to adduce evidence of the statement otherwise than from the witness unless, in the

第 43 条

（a）证人在主询问中所作证言是否不利于传唤该
证人的当事人；以及

（b）证人与交叉询问者是否具有一致的利益；以
及

（c）证人在整体上或者就具体事项是否同情进行
交叉询问的当事人；以及

（d）证人的年龄、证人患有的任何精神、智力
或者身体上的残障，是否可能影响证人的
回答。

（3）如果法院确信，若不使用诱导性问题将能更好地查
明有关事实，则法院应当不允许该提问或者指示证
人对此不予回答。

（4）本条并不限制法院控制诱导性问题的权力。

注释：**诱导性问题**的定义见《术语》。

43 证人先前不一致陈述

（1）可以就所称的证人曾经作出的先前不一致陈述对证
人进行交叉询问，不论：

（a）该陈述的全部细节是否已经向证人提供；或
者

（b）包含有该陈述之记录的书证是否已经向证人
出示。

（2）在交叉询问中，如果证人不承认其曾作出先前不
一致陈述，交叉询问者不得就该陈述提出证人
之外的他人的证据，除非在交叉询问中，交叉询

cross–examination, the cross–examiner:

    (a) informed the witness of enough of the circumstances of the making of the statement to enable the witness to identify the statement; and

    (b) drew the witness's attention to so much of the statement as is inconsistent with the witness's evidence.

(3) For the purpose of adducing evidence of the statement, a party may re–open the party's case.

44 Previous representations of other persons

(1) Except as provided by this section, a cross–examiner must not question a witness about a previous representation alleged to have been made by a person other than the witness.

(2) A cross–examiner may question a witness about the representation and its contents if:

    (a) evidence of the representation has been admitted; or

    (b) the court is satisfied that it will be admitted.

(3) If subsection (2) does not apply and the representation is contained in a document, the document may only be used to question a witness as follows:

    (a) the document must be produced to the witness;

    (b) if the document is a tape recording, or any other kind of document from which sounds are reproduced—the witness must be provided with the means (for example, headphones) to listen to the contents of the document without other persons present at the cross–examination hearing those contents;

    (c) the witness must be asked whether, having examined (or heard) the contents of the document, the witness stands by the evidence that he or she has given;

    (d) neither the cross–examiner nor the witness is to identify

问者：

（a）就作出该陈述的情况对证人进行了足够的告知，使证人能够确定该陈述；并且

（b）让证人注意该陈述中所有与其证言不一致之处。

（3）为提出有关该陈述的证据之目的，当事人可以重启其案件。[18]

44 其他人的先前表述

（1）除本条另有规定者外，交叉询问者不得就所称是证人之外的人所作的先前表述对证人进行询问。

（2）在下列情况下，交叉询问者可以就该表述及其内容对证人进行询问：

（a）关于该表述的证据已经被采纳；或者

（b）法院确信该证据将会被采纳。

（3）如果（2）并不适用，并且该表述包含于某书证中，则使用该书证询问证人时，仅可采用下列方式：

（a）该书证必须出示给证人；

（b）如果该书证是磁带录制品或者任何可以重现声音的其他种类的书证，则必须向证人提供听取书证内容并使交叉询问时在场的其他人听不到这些内容的工具（例如耳机）；

（c）在证人检视（或者听取）了该书证的内容后，必须询问其是否坚持其所作证言；

（d）交叉询问者和证人均不得就该书证进行辨认

the document or disclose any of its contents.

(4) A document that is so used may be marked for identification.

45 Production of documents

(1) This section applies if a party is cross–examining or has cross–examined a witness about:

    (a) a prior inconsistent statement alleged to have been made by the witness that is recorded in a document; or

    (b) a previous representation alleged to have been made by another person that is recorded in a document.

(2) If the court so orders or if another party so requires, the party must produce:

    (a) the document; or

    (b) such evidence of the contents of the document as is available to the party;

to the court or to that other party.

(3) The court may:

    (a) examine a document or evidence that has been so produced; and

    (b) give directions as to its use; and

    (c) admit it even if it has not been tendered by a party.

(4) Subsection (3) does not permit the court to admit a document or evidence that is not admissible because of Chapter 3.

(5) The mere production of a document to a witness who is being cross–examined does not give rise to a requirement that the cross–examiner tender the document.

46 Leave to recall witnesses

(1) The court may give leave to a party to recall a witness to give evidence about a matter raised by evidence adduced by

或者披露其任何内容。

（4）对如上使用的书证可以为辨认而加以标记。

45 出示书证

（1）在当事人就下列事项正在进行或者已经对证人进行了交叉询问的情况下，适用本条：

（a）所称的由证人所作的记录在书证中的先前不一致陈述；或者

（b）所称的由其他人所作的记录在书证中的先前表述。

（2）如果法院作出了出示给法院的命令或者其他当事人提出了出示给该其他当事人的要求，则当事人必须将下列证据出示给法院或者该其他当事人：

（a）书证；或者

（b）当事人可以得到的关于该书证的内容的证据。

（3）法院可以：

（a）检视上述已经出示的书证或者证据；以及

（b）就其使用作出指示；以及

（c）采纳它，即使它还没有为一方当事人所提交。

（4）（3）并不允许法院采纳根据第 3 章不具有可采性的书证或者证据。

（5）仅仅向受到交叉询问的证人出示书证，并不产生交叉询问者应当提交该书证的要求。

46 许可再次传唤证人

（1）如果某当事人提出的证据已经被采纳，并且存在下列情况，法院可以许可另一方当事人再次传唤证

another party, being a matter on which the witness was not cross–examined, if the evidence concerned has been admitted and:

(a) it contradicts evidence about the matter given by the witness in examination in chief; or

(b) the witness could have given evidence about the matter in examination in chief.

(2) A reference in this section to a matter raised by evidence adduced by another party includes a reference to an inference drawn from, or that the party intends to draw from, that evidence.

Part 2.2—Documents

47 Definitions

(1) A reference in this Part to a *document in question* is a reference to a document as to the contents of which it is sought to adduce evidence.

(2) A reference in this Part to a copy of a document in question includes a reference to a document that is not an exact copy of the document in question but that is identical to the document in question in all relevant respects.

Note: Section 182 gives this section a wider application in relation to Commonwealth records and certain Commonwealth documents.

48 Proof of contents of documents

(1) A party may adduce evidence of the contents of a document in question by tendering the document in question or by any one or more of the following methods:

(a) adducing evidence of an admission made by another party to the proceeding as to the contents of the

人，就该某当事人提出的证据引发的且证人就此没有受到交叉询问的事项作证：

（a）上述被采纳的证据与证人在主询问中就有关事项所作证言相矛盾；或者

（b）证人本来可以在主询问中就该事项作证。

（2）本条所称因某当事人提出的证据引发的事项，包括根据该证据作出的推论，或者该某当事人意图根据该证据作出的推论。

第 2.2 节—书证

47 定义

（1）本节所称**有关书证**是指以其内容作为证据的文件。

（2）本节所称有关书证的复制件，包括虽非有关书证的精密复制件，但在所有相关方面等同于有关书证的文件。[19]

注释：就联邦记录和某些联邦文件，第 182 条赋予了本条更为广泛的适用。

48 书证内容的证明

（1）当事人可以通过提交有关书证，或者通过下列某一种或者多种方法来就有关书证的内容提出证据：[20]

（a）提出程序另一方当事人就有关书证的内容作

document in question;

(b) tendering a document that:

    (i) is or purports to be a copy of the document in question; and

    (ii) has been produced, or purports to have been produced, by a device that reproduces the contents of documents;

(c) if the document in question is an article or thing by which words are recorded in such a way as to be capable of being reproduced as sound, or in which words are recorded in a code (including shorthand writing)—tendering a document that is or purports to be a transcript of the words;

(d) if the document in question is an article or thing on or in which information is stored in such a way that it cannot be used by the court unless a device is used to retrieve, produce or collate it—tendering a document that was or purports to have been produced by use of the device;

(e) tendering a document that:

    (i) forms part of the records of or kept by a business (whether or not the business is still in existence); and

    (ii) is or purports to be a copy of, or an extract from or a summary of, the document in question, or is or purports to be a copy of such an extract or summary;

(f) if the document in question is a public document— tendering a document that is or purports to be a copy of the document in question and that is or purports to have been printed:

    (i) by the Government Printer or by the government or official printer of a State or Territory; or

    (ii) by authority of the government or administration of the

出的自认证据；

（b）提交下列书证：

　（i）有关书证的复制件或者是载明为其复制件
　　　的书证；以及

　（ii）通过复制书证内容的设备生成的书证，或
　　　者载明如此生成的书证；[21]

（c）如果有关书证是语汇得以录制且能作为声音
　　重现的物品，或者是语汇以代码形式（包括
　　速记）得以记录的物品，则提交作为该语汇
　　的笔录或者载明为其笔录的书证。

（d）如果有关书证是其存储的信息非经用于还
　　原、制作或者核对的设备则不能为法院所
　　使用的物品，则提交通过该设备生成的或
　　者是载明通过该设备生成的书证；

（e）提交下列书证：

　（i）构成业务记录一部分的书证（无论该业务
　　　是否依然存在）；以及

　（ii）是或者载明是有关书证的复制件、摘录或
　　　者概要的书证，或者是或者载明是上述摘
　　　录或者概要的复制件的书证；

（f）在有关书证是公共文件的情况下，提交由或
　　者载明由下列机构印刷的是该有关书证的复
　　制件或者载明是该有关书证的复制件的书证:

　（i）政府印务局、州或者领地的政府或者官方
　　　印务机构；或者

　（ii）联邦、州、领地或者外国的政府或者行政

Commonwealth, a State, a Territory or a foreign country; or

    (iii) by authority of an Australian Parliament, a House of an Australian Parliament, a committee of such a House or a committee of an Australian Parliament.

(2) Subsection (1) applies to a document in question whether the document in question is available to the party or not.

(3) If the party adduces evidence of the contents of a document under paragraph (1)(a), the evidence may only be used:

    (a) in respect of the party's case against the other party who made the admission concerned; or

    (b) in respect of the other party's case against the party who adduced the evidence in that way.

(4) A party may adduce evidence of the contents of a document in question that is not available to the party, or the existence and contents of which are not in issue in the proceeding, by:

    (a) tendering a document that is a copy of, or an extract from or summary of, the document in question; or

    (b) adducing from a witness evidence of the contents of the document in question.

Note 1:   Clause 5 of Part 2 of the Dictionary is about the availability of documents.

Note 2:   Section 182 gives this section a wider application in relation to Commonwealth records and certain Commonwealth documents.

49 Documents in foreign countries

No paragraph of subsection 48(1) (other than paragraph 48(1)(a)) applies to a document that is in a foreign country unless:

    (a) the party who adduces evidence of the contents of the

机构；或者

（iii）澳大利亚议会、澳大利亚议会的一院、
该院的委员会或者澳大利亚议会的委员会
的机构。

（2）不论当事人是否可以取得有关书证，（1）都适用
于该有关书证。

（3）如果当事人根据（1）（a）提出关于书证内容的证据，
该证据仅可使用于：

（a）该当事人对作出有关自认的其他当事人提起
的案件；或者

（b）其他当事人对以上述方式提出证据的当事人
提起的案件。

（4）当事人可以通过下列方式就该当事人不能取得的有
关书证的内容或者对程序中就其存在及其内容不
存在争议的有关书证提出证据：

（a）提交作为有关书证的复制件、摘录或者摘要
的书证；或者

（b）由证人作出关于有关书证的内容的证言。

注释 1：《术语》第 2 部分第 5 条规定了书证的可得性。

注释 2：就联邦记录和某些联邦文件，第 182 条赋予了本
条更为广泛的适用。

49　在外国的书证

48（1）（48（1）（a）除外）不适用于在外国的书证，除非：

（a）提出有关书证内容的证据的当事人，已在

document in question has, not less than 28 days (or such other period as may be prescribed by the regulations or by rules of court) before the day on which the evidence is adduced, served on each other party a copy of the document proposed to be tendered; or

(b) the court directs that it is to apply.

Note: Section 182 gives this section a wider application in relation to Commonwealth records and certain Commonwealth documents.

50 Proof of voluminous or complex documents

(1) The court may, on the application of a party, direct that the party may adduce evidence of the contents of 2 or more documents in question in the form of a summary if the court is satisfied that it would not otherwise be possible conveniently to examine the evidence because of the volume or complexity of the documents in question.

(2) The court may only make such a direction if the party seeking to adduce the evidence in the form of a summary has:

(a) served on each other party a copy of the summary that discloses the name and address of the person who prepared the summary; and

(b) given each other party a reasonable opportunity to examine or copy the documents in question.

(3) The opinion rule does not apply to evidence adduced in accordance with a direction under this section.

51 Original document rule abolished

The principles and rules of the common law that relate to the means of proving the contents of documents are abolished.

提出证据之日起 28 日前（或者条例或者
法院规则规定的其他期限），向每个其他
当事人送达了准备提交的书证的复制件；
或者

（b）法院指示适用该规定。

注释：就联邦记录和某些联邦文件，第 182 条赋予了本
条更为广泛的适用。

50 卷帙浩繁或者复杂书证的证明

（1）如果法院确信，由于有关书证卷帙浩繁或者复杂，
不可能以其他方式便利地检视证据，则根据当事人
申请，法院可以指示当事人可以以概要形式，提出
关于 2 件或者 2 件以上有关书证的内容的证据。[22]

（2）只有寻求以概要形式提出证据的当事人从事了下列
行为的情况下，法院才得作出上述指示：

（a）向每个其他当事人送达了披露有概要制作人
姓名和住址的概要复制件；并且

（b）给予每个其他当事人合理机会来检视或者复
制有关书证。

（3）意见规则不适用于根据本条作出的指示而提出的证
据。

51 废除原件规则

有关证明书证内容之方式的普通法原则和规则予以废
除。

> Note: Section 182 gives the provisions of this Part a wider application in relation to Commonwealth records and certain Commonwealth documents.

Part 2.3—Other evidence

52 Adducing of other evidence not affected

This Act (other than this Part) does not affect the operation of any Australian law or rule of practice so far as it permits evidence to be adduced in a way other than by witnesses giving evidence or documents being tendered in evidence.

53 Views

(1) A judge may, on application, order that a demonstration, experiment or inspection be held.

(2) A judge is not to make an order unless he or she is satisfied that:

    (a) the parties will be given a reasonable opportunity to be present; and

    (b) the judge and, if there is a jury, the jury will be present.

(3) Without limiting the matters that the judge may take into account in deciding whether to make an order, the judge is to take into account the following:

    (a) whether the parties will be present;

    (b) whether the demonstration, experiment or inspection will, in the court's opinion, assist the court in resolving issues of fact or understanding the evidence;

    (c) the danger that the demonstration, experiment or inspection might be unfairly prejudicial, might be misleading or confusing or might cause or result in undue waste of time;

    (d) in the case of a demonstration—the extent to which the

注释：就联邦记录和某些联邦文件，第 182 条赋予了本
节规定更为广泛的适用。

第 2.3 节—其他证据

52 其他证据的提出不受影响

本法（本节除外）并不影响允许以证人作证或者将书证
提交为证据的方式之外的其他方式提出证据的任何澳大
利亚法律或者法院程序规则的适用。

53 观察

（1）根据申请，法官可以命令进行演示、实验或者勘验。

（2）法官不得作出上述命令，除非其确信：

（a）当事人有在场的合理机会；并且

（b）法官以及陪审团（如果有陪审团的话）将会
在场。

（3）在决定是否作出该命令时，法官应当虑及的事项包
括但是不限于：

（a）当事人是否将会在场；

（b）在法院看来，该演示、实验或者勘验是否将
有助于法院解决事实争议或者理解证据；

（c）该演示、实验或者勘验是否存在带来不公平
的损害、误导、混淆的危险，或者可能引起
或者导致不合理的时间耗费；

（d）就演示而言，该演示在何种程度上能够适当

> demonstration will properly reproduce the conduct or event to be demonstrated;

> (e) in the case of an inspection—the extent to which the place or thing to be inspected has materially altered.

(4) The court (including, if there is a jury, the jury) is not to conduct an experiment in the course of its deliberations.

(5) This section does not apply in relation to the inspection of an exhibit by the court or, if there is a jury, by the jury.

54 Views to be evidence

The court (including, if there is a jury, the jury) may draw any reasonable inference from what it sees, hears or otherwise notices during a demonstration, experiment or inspection.

地重现被演示的行为或者事件；

(e) 就勘验而言，被勘验的地点或者物品在何种
程度上已经发生重大变化。

(4) 法院（如果有陪审团的话，还包括陪审团）不得在
其评议过程中进行实验。

(5) 本条并不适用于由法院或者在有陪审团的情况下由
陪审团对展示件进行的勘验。

54 观察作为证据

法院（如果有陪审团的话，还包括陪审团）可以根据其
在演示、实验或者勘验过程中的所看、所听或者以其他
方式进行的察觉，作出任何合理的推论。

Chapter 3—Admissibility of evidence

INTRODUCTORY NOTE

Outline of this Chapter

This Chapter is about whether evidence adduced in a proceeding is admissible.

Part 3.1 sets out the general inclusionary rule that relevant evidence is admissible.

Part 3.2 is about the exclusion of hearsay evidence, and exceptions to the hearsay rule.

Part 3.3 is about exclusion of opinion evidence, and exceptions to the opinion rule.

Part 3.4 is about admissions and the extent to which they are admissible as exceptions to the hearsay rule and the opinion rule.

Part 3.5 is about exclusion of certain evidence of judgments and convictions.

Part 3.6 is about exclusion of evidence of tendency or coincidence, and exceptions to the tendency rule and the coincidence rule.

Part 3.7 is about exclusion of evidence relevant only to credibility, and exceptions to the credibility rule.

Part 3.8 is about character evidence and the extent to which it is admissible as exceptions to the hearsay rule, the opinion rule, the tendency rule and the credibility rule.

Part 3.9 is about the requirements that must be satisfied before identification evidence is admissible.

Part 3.10 is about the various categories of privilege that may prevent evidence being adduced.

Part 3.11 provides for the discretionary and mandatory exclusion of evidence even if it would otherwise be admissible.

The following diagram shows how this Chapter applies to particular evidence:

第 3 章—证据的可采性

引言性注释

本章概要

本章就在程序中提出的证据是否具有可采性进行了规定。

第 3.1 节规定了相关证据具有可采性这一总的包容性规则。

第 3.2 节规定了传闻证据的排除，以及传闻规则的例外。

第 3.3 节规定了意见证据的排除，以及意见规则的例外。

第 3.4 节规定了自认，以及它们作为传闻规则和意见规则的例外而具有可采性的范围。

第 3.5 节规定了某些关于判决和定罪的证据的排除问题。

第 3.6 节规定了倾向和巧合证据的排除，以及倾向规则和巧合规则的例外。

第 3.7 节规定了仅与可信性有关的证据的排除，以及可信性规则的例外。

第 3.8 节规定了品性证据，以及它们作为传闻规则、意见规则、倾向规则和可信性规则的例外而具有可采性的范围。

第 3.9 节规定了辨认证据被采纳前必须要满足的要求。

第 3.10 节规定了可能阻止提出证据的各种证据特免权。

第 3.11 节规定了法院对证据的裁量性排除和强制性排除，即使证据因其他原因而具有可采性。

下列图表说明了本章是如何适用于具体证据的：

Introductory note

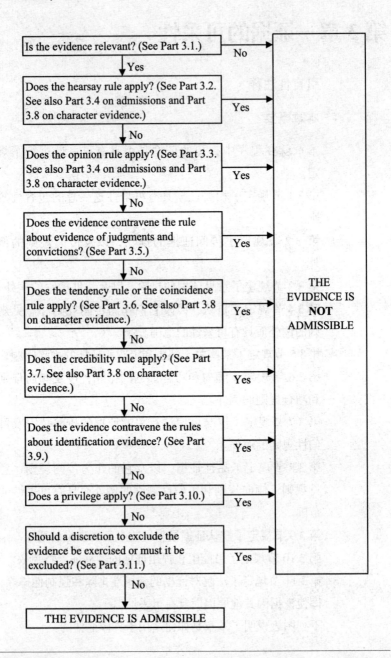

Is the evidence relevant? (See Part 3.1.) — No →

Yes ↓

Does the hearsay rule apply? (See Part 3.2. See also Part 3.4 on admissions and Part 3.8 on character evidence.) — Yes →

No ↓

Does the opinion rule apply? (See Part 3.3. See also Part 3.4 on admissions and Part 3.8 on character evidence.) — Yes →

No ↓

Does the evidence contravene the rule about evidence of judgments and convictions? (See Part 3.5.) — Yes →

No ↓

Does the tendency rule or the coincidence rule apply? (See Part 3.6. See also Part 3.8 on character evidence.) — Yes →

No ↓

Does the credibility rule apply? (See Part 3.7. See also Part 3.8 on character evidence.) — Yes →

No ↓

Does the evidence contravene the rules about identification evidence? (See Part 3.9.) — Yes →

No ↓

Does a privilege apply? (See Part 3.10.) — Yes →

No ↓

Should a discretion to exclude the evidence be exercised or must it be excluded? (See Part 3.11.) — Yes →

No ↓

THE EVIDENCE IS ADMISSIBLE

THE EVIDENCE IS NOT ADMISSIBLE

引言性注释

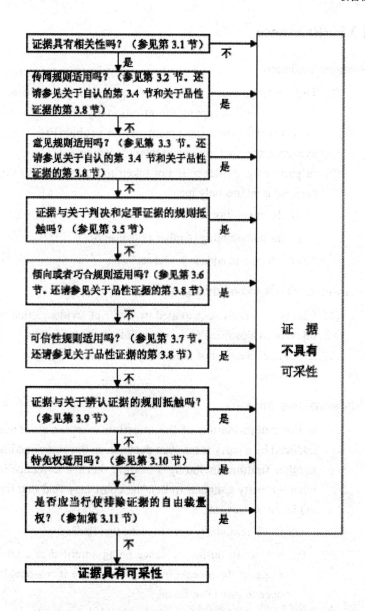

Part 3.1—Relevance

55 Relevant evidence

(1) The evidence that is relevant in a proceeding is evidence that, if it were accepted, could rationally affect (directly or indirectly) the assessment of the probability of the existence of a fact in issue in the proceeding.

(2) In particular, evidence is not taken to be irrelevant only because it relates only to:

    (a) the credibility of a witness; or

    (b) the admissibility of other evidence; or

    (c) a failure to adduce evidence.

56 Relevant evidence to be admissible

(1) Except as otherwise provided by this Act, evidence that is relevant in a proceeding is admissible in the proceeding.

(2) Evidence that is not relevant in the proceeding is not admissible.

57 Provisional relevance

(1) If the determination of the question whether evidence adduced by a party is relevant depends on the court making another finding (including a finding that the evidence is what the party claims it to be), the court may find that the evidence is relevant:

    (a) if it is reasonably open to make that finding; or

    (b) subject to further evidence being admitted at a later stage of the proceeding that will make it reasonably open to make that finding.

(2) Without limiting subsection (1), if the relevance of

第 3.1 节—相关性

55 相关证据

（1）程序中具有相关性的证据，是指如果被接受，能够
（直接或者间接地）对程序中的争议事实之存在的
可能性评估产生理性影响的证据。

（2）特别是，不能因为证据仅仅与下列事项有关而被视
为不具有相关性：

（a）证人的可信性；或者

（b）其他证据的可采性；或者

（c）未能提出证据。

56 相关证据具有可采性

（1）除本法另有规定者外，程序中具有相关性的证据在
该程序中具有可采性。

（2）程序中不具有相关性的证据不具有可采性。

57 暂定相关性[1]

（1）在下列情况下，如果确定当事人提出的证据是否具
有相关性问题，取决于法院作出的另一认定（包括
证据就是当事人所称证据的认定），则法院可以认
定该证据具有相关性：

（a）作出该另一认定是合理的；或者

（b）遵循这样的限制，即在程序以后阶段将采纳
进一步证据，这使得作出该另一认定是合理
的。[2]

（2）在不限制（1）的情况下，如果关于某人的行为的

evidence of an act done by a person depends on the court making a finding that the person and one or more other persons had, or were acting in furtherance of, a common purpose (whether to effect an unlawful conspiracy or otherwise), the court may use the evidence itself in determining whether the common purpose existed.

58 Inferences as to relevance

(1) If a question arises as to the relevance of a document or thing, the court may examine it and may draw any reasonable inference from it, including an inference as to its authenticity or identity.

(2) Subsection (1) does not limit the matters from which inferences may properly be drawn.

Part 3.2—Hearsay

Division 1—The hearsay rule

59 The hearsay rule—exclusion of hearsay evidence

(1) Evidence of a previous representation made by a person is not admissible to prove the existence of a fact that it can reasonably be supposed that the person intended to assert by the representation.

(2) Such a fact is in this Part referred to as an *asserted fact*.

(2A) For the purposes of determining under subsection (1) whether it can reasonably be supposed that the person intended to assert a particular fact by the representation, the court may have regard to the circumstances in which the representation was made.

Note: Subsection (2A) was inserted as a response to the decision of the Supreme Court of NSW in *R. v Hannes* (2000) 158 FLR 359.

证据的相关性取决于法院作出这样的认定，即该某人与一个或者多个其他人曾具有共同目的，或者曾为促进该共同目的而行动，则无论其是非法共谋还是出于其他目的，法院可以使用该证据本身来确定是否存在共同目的。[3]

58 关于相关性的推论

（1）如果就书证或者物证的相关性存在疑问，法院可进行检视并作出任何合理的推论，包括关于该证据的真实性或者同一性的推论。[4]

（2）（1）不限制法院可从中进行适当推论之事项。

第 3.2 节—传闻

第 1 目—传闻规则

59 传闻规则—传闻证据的排除

（1）某人作出的先前表述证据，不得采纳来证明存在可以合理地认为该某人旨在以该表述主张的事实。[5]

（2）在本节中，这样的事实叫作**主张的事实**。

（2A）为根据（1）确定是否可以合理地认为该某人旨在以该表述主张某具体事实，法院可以虑及作出该表述的环境。

注释：插入（2A），是为了回应新南威尔士州最高法院在 *R. v Hannes*（2000）158 FLR 359 案件中的判决。

(3) Subsection (1) does not apply to evidence of a representation contained in a certificate or other document given or made under regulations made under an Act other than this Act to the extent to which the regulations provide that the certificate or other document has evidentiary effect.

Note: Specific exceptions to the hearsay rule are as follows:

- evidence relevant for a non–hearsay purpose (section 60);

- first–hand hearsay:

  - civil proceedings, if the maker of the representation is unavailable (section 63) or available (section 64);

  - criminal proceedings, if the maker of the representation is unavailable (section 65) or available (section 66);

- contemporaneous statements about a person's health etc. (section 66A);

- business records (section 69);

- tags and labels (section 70);

- electronic communications (section 71);

- Aboriginal and Torres Strait Islander traditional laws and customs (section 72);

- marriage, family history or family relationships (section 73);

- public or general rights (section 74);

- use of evidence in interlocutory proceedings (section 75);

- admissions (section 81);

- representations about employment or authority (subsection 87(2));

- exceptions to the rule excluding evidence of judgments and convictions (subsection 92(3));

第 59 条

（3）如果条例是根据本法之外的法律制定的，并且证明
书或者其他书证是根据该条例作出或者制作的，在
该条例规定该证明书或者其他书证具有证据效力
的情况下，则（1）并不适用于关于包含在该证明
书或者其他书证中的表述证据。

注释：传闻规则的具体例外如下：

· 因非传闻目的而具有相关性的证据（第 60 条）；

· 第一手传闻：

－ 先前表述者不能到庭的民事程序（第 63 条）
或者先前表述者到庭的民事程序（第 64 条）；

－ 先前表述者不能到庭的刑事程序（第 65 条）
或者先前表述者到庭的刑事程序（第 66 条）；

· 关于某人健康状况等的即时陈述（第 66A 条）

· 业务记录（第 69 条）；

· 标牌和标签（第 70 条）；

· 电子通信（第 71 条）；

· 原住民和 Torres 海峡岛民传统法律与习俗（第 72
条）；

· 婚姻、家史或者家庭关系（第 73 条）；

· 公共或者一般权利（第 74 条）；

· 在中间程序中使用证据（第 75 条）；

· 自认（第 81 条）；

· 关于雇佣或者授权的表述（87（2））；

· 排除判决和定罪证据之规则的例外（92（3））；

- character of and expert opinion about accused persons (sections 110 and 111).

Other provisions of this Act, or of other laws, may operate as further exceptions.

Examples:

(1) D is the defendant in a sexual assault trial. W has made a statement to the police that X told W that X had seen D leave a night club with the victim shortly before the sexual assault is alleged to have occurred. Unless an exception to the hearsay rule applies, evidence of what X told W cannot be given at the trial.

(2) P had told W that the handbrake on W's car did not work. Unless an exception to the hearsay rule applies, evidence of that statement cannot be given by P, W or anyone else to prove that the handbrake was defective.

(3) W had bought a video cassette recorder and written down its serial number on a document. Unless an exception to the hearsay rule applies, the document is inadmissible to prove that a video cassette recorder later found in D's possession was the video cassette recorder bought by W.

60 Exception: evidence relevant for a non–hearsay purpose

(1) The hearsay rule does not apply to evidence of a previous representation that is admitted because it is relevant for a purpose other than proof of an asserted fact.

(2) This section applies whether or not the person who made the representation had personal knowledge of the asserted fact (within the meaning of subsection 62(2)).

Note: Subsection (2) was inserted as a response to the decision of the High Court of Australia in *Lee v The Queen* (1998) 195 CLR 594.

第 60 条

· 关于被指控者的品性和专家意见 （第 110 条和第
111 条）。

本法或者其他法律的其他规定，可能规定有进一步
的例外。

示例：

（1）D 是性侵犯审判中的被告。W 曾向警方陈述
说，X 告诉 W 说在诉称的性侵犯发生之前不久，
X 看到 D 和被害人离开了夜总会。在审判时 W
不能就 X 所述作证，除非适用传闻规则的某个
例外。

（2）P 曾告诉 W 说 W 的汽车的手刹失灵了。P、
W 或者其他人不能就该陈述作证来证明手刹失
灵，除非适用传闻规则的某个例外。

（3）W 购买了一台盒带式录像机，并在某个书证上
写下了其序列号。该书证不能采纳来证明此后
发现的 D 持有的录像机就是 W 购买的录像机，
除非适用传闻规则的某个例外。

60 例外：因非传闻目的而具有相关性的证据

（1）如果先前表述证据之所以被采纳，是因为其就证明
主张的事实之外之目的具有相关性，则该先前表述
证据不适用传闻规则。[6]

（2）无论作出该表述的人就主张的事实是否有亲身知识
（其含义见 62（2）），本条都适用。

注释：插入（2），是为了回应澳大利亚最高法院在 *Lee v
The Queen*（1998）195 CLR 594 案件中的判决。

(3) However, this section does not apply in a criminal proceeding to evidence of an admission.

> Note: The admission might still be admissible under section 81 as an exception to the hearsay rule if it is "first–hand" hearsay: see section 82.

61 Exceptions to the hearsay rule dependent on competency

(1) This Part does not enable use of a previous representation to prove the existence of an asserted fact if, when the representation was made, the person who made it was not competent to give evidence about the fact because of subsection 13(1).

(2) This section does not apply to a contemporaneous representation made by a person about his or her health, feelings, sensations, intention, knowledge or state of mind.

> Note: For the admissibility of such contemporaneous representations, see section 66A.

(3) For the purposes of this section, it is presumed, unless the contrary is proved, that when the representation was made the person who made it was competent to give evidence about the asserted fact.

Division 2—First–hand hearsay

62 Restriction to "first–hand" hearsay

(1) A reference in this Division (other than in subsection (2)) to a previous representation is a reference to a previous representation that was made by a person who had personal knowledge of an asserted fact.

(2) A person has personal knowledge of the asserted fact if his or her knowledge of the fact was, or might reasonably be supposed to have been, based on something that the person

（3）然而，本条并不适用于刑事程序中的自认证据。[7]

> 注释：自认如果是"第一手"传闻，仍可根据第 81 条作为
> 传闻规则的例外而被采纳：参见第 82 条。

61 取决于证人能力的传闻规则例外

（1）在某人作出先前表述时，如果该某人因 13（1）无能力就事实作证，则本节并不能够使得可以使用该先前表述来证明所主张的事实的存在。[8]

（2）本条并不适用于该某人就其健康、感觉、情感、意图、知识或者心态所作的即时表述。[9]

> 注释：就上述即时表述的可采性，参见第 66A 条。

（3）就本条目的而言，应当推定该某人在作出表述时就所主张的事实有作证能力，除非证明相反。

第 2 目—第一手传闻

62 对"第一手"传闻的限定

（1）本目（（2）除外）所称先前表述，是指对所主张的事实有亲身知识之人所作的先前表述。[10]

（2）如果某人对事实的知识是基于或者可以合理地被认为是基于其所见、所听或者以其他方式感知的事物，而非基于其他人对该事实作出的先前表述，则

saw, heard or otherwise perceived, other than a previous representation made by another person about the fact.

(3) For the purposes of section 66A, a person has personal knowledge of the asserted fact if it is a fact about the person's health, feelings, sensations, intention, knowledge or state of mind at the time the representation referred to in that section was made.

63 Exception: civil proceedings if maker not available

(1) This section applies in a civil proceeding if a person who made a previous representation is not available to give evidence about an asserted fact.

(2) The hearsay rule does not apply to:

(a) evidence of the representation that is given by a person who saw, heard or otherwise perceived the representation being made; or

(b) a document so far as it contains the representation, or another representation to which it is reasonably necessary to refer in order to understand the representation.

Note 1: Section 67 imposes notice requirements relating to this subsection.

Note 2: Clause 4 of Part 2 of the Dictionary is about the availability of persons.

64 Exception: civil proceedings if maker available

(1) This section applies in a civil proceeding if a person who made a previous representation is available to give evidence about an asserted fact.

(2) The hearsay rule does not apply to:

(a) evidence of the representation that is given by a person who saw, heard or otherwise perceived the representation being made; or

该某人对其所主张的事实有亲身知识。

（3）就第 66A 条目的而言，如果主张的事实是某人在作出该条所称表述时的健康、感觉、情感、意图、知识或者心态之事实，则该某人对其所主张的事实有亲身知识。

63 例外：先前表述者不能到庭的民事程序

（1）本条适用于作出先前表述之人不能到庭就所主张的事实作证的民事程序。

（2）传闻规则并不适用于：

（a）以所见、所听或者以其他方式感知到作出该表述的情况的人所作出的表述证据；或者

（b）包含该表述的书证，或者包含为理解该表述而有参考之合理需要的其他表述的书证。[11]

注释 1：第 67 条就本款规定了通知要求。

注释 2：《术语》第 2 部分的第 4 条就人员的到庭作了规定。

64 例外：先前表述者到庭的民事程序

（1）本条适用于作出先前表述之人能够到庭就所主张的事实作证的民事程序。

（2）如果传唤作出表述之人作证将导致不合理的费用或者迟延，或者不具合理可行性，则传闻规则并不适用于：

（a）以所见、所听或者以其他方式感知到作出该表述情况的人所作出的表述证据；或者

    (b) a document so far as it contains the representation, or another representation to which it is reasonably necessary to refer in order to understand the representation;

if it would cause undue expense or undue delay, or would not be reasonably practicable, to call the person who made the representation to give evidence.

Note: Section 67 imposes notice requirements relating to this subsection. Section 68 is about objections to notices that relate to this subsection.

(3) If the person who made the representation has been or is to be called to give evidence, the hearsay rule does not apply to evidence of the representation that is given by:

    (a) that person; or

    (b) a person who saw, heard or otherwise perceived the representation being made.

(4) A document containing a representation to which subsection (3) applies must not be tendered before the conclusion of the examination in chief of the person who made the representation, unless the court gives leave.

Note: Clause 4 of Part 2 of the Dictionary is about the availability of persons.

65 Exception: criminal proceedings if maker not available

(1) This section applies in a criminal proceeding if a person who made a previous representation is not available to give evidence about an asserted fact.

(2) The hearsay rule does not apply to evidence of a previous representation that is given by a person who saw, heard or otherwise perceived the representation being made, if the representation:

    (a) was made under a duty to make that representation or to

（b）包含该表述的书证，或者包含为理解该表述而有参考之合理需要的其他表述的书证。【12】

注释：第 67 条规定了与本款有关的通知要求。第 68 条规定了与本款有关的通知异议问题。

（3）如果作出表述之人已经或者将由法院传唤作证，则传闻规则不适用于下列人员作出的表述证据：

（a）作出该表述之人；或者

（b）以所见、所听或者以其他方式感知到作出该表述的情况的人。【13】

（4）在对作出表述之人的主询问结束之前，不得提交包含适用（3）的表述的书证，除非法院作出许可。【14】

注释：《术语》第 2 部分的第 4 条就有关人员的到庭作了规定。

65 例外：先前表述者不能到庭的刑事程序

（1）本条适用于作出先前表述之人不能到庭就其所主张的事实作证的刑事程序。

（2）如果先前表述属于下列情况，则传闻规则并不适用于某人就其所见、所听或者以其他方式感知到的该表述作出情况所作出的先前表述证据：

（a）该表述是根据作出该表述或者作出此类表述

make representations of that kind; or

(b) was made when or shortly after the asserted fact occurred and in circumstances that make it unlikely that the representation is a fabrication; or

(c) was made in circumstances that make it highly probable that the representation is reliable; or

(d) was:

(i) against the interests of the person who made it at the time it was made; and

(ii) made in circumstances that make it likely that the representation is reliable.

Note: Section 67 imposes notice requirements relating to this subsection.

(3) The hearsay rule does not apply to evidence of a previous representation made in the course of giving evidence in an Australian or overseas proceeding if, in that proceeding, the defendant in the proceeding to which this section is being applied:

(a) cross–examined the person who made the representation about it; or

(b) had a reasonable opportunity to cross–examine the person who made the representation about it.

Note: Section 67 imposes notice requirements relating to this subsection.

(4) If there is more than one defendant in the criminal proceeding, evidence of a previous representation that:

(a) is given in an Australian or overseas proceeding; and

(b) is admitted into evidence in the criminal proceeding because of subsection (3);

cannot be used against a defendant who did not cross–examine, and did not have a reasonable opportunity to cross–examine,

的职责作出的；或者

（b）该表述是在所主张的事实发生当时或者发生后不久，在不可能捏造该表述的情形下作出的；或者

（c）该表述是在该表述具有高度可靠性的情形下作出的；或者

（d）该表述是：

（i）作出该表述当时不利于该作出表述之人的；并且

（ii）在该表述可能具有可靠性的环境中作出的。[15]

注释：第 67 条就本款规定了通知要求。

（3）如果在澳大利亚或者海外进行的程序中，适用本条规定的程序中的被告符合下列情形，则传闻规则不适用于在上述程序中作证时作出的先前表述证据：

（a）该被告就该表述对作出该表述的人进行了交叉询问；或者

（b）该被告有合理的机会就该表述对作出该表述的人进行交叉询问。

注释：第 67 条就本款规定了通知要求。

（4）如果在刑事程序中有一个以上的被告，关于下列先前表述的证据不能用于反对没有或者没有合理机会就该表述对该某人进行交叉询问的被告：

（a）该表述是在澳大利亚或者海外程序中作出的；并且

（b）根据（3）该表述在刑事程序中被采纳为了证据。

the person about the representation.

(5) For the purposes of subsections (3) and (4), a defendant is taken to have had a reasonable opportunity to cross–examine a person if the defendant was not present at a time when the cross–examination of a person might have been conducted but:

    (a) could reasonably have been present at that time; and

    (b) if present could have cross–examined the person.

(6) Evidence of the making of a representation to which subsection (3) applies may be adduced by producing a transcript, or a recording, of the representation that is authenticated by:

    (a) the person to whom, or the court or other body to which, the representation was made; or

    (b) if applicable, the registrar or other proper officer of the court or other body to which the representation was made; or

    (c) the person or body responsible for producing the transcript or recording.

(7) Without limiting paragraph (2)(d), a representation is taken for the purposes of that paragraph to be against the interests of the person who made it if it tends:

    (a) to damage the person's reputation; or

    (b) to show that the person has committed an offence for which the person has not been convicted; or

    (c) to show that the person is liable in an action for damages.

(8) The hearsay rule does not apply to:

    (a) evidence of a previous representation adduced by a defendant if the evidence is given by a person who saw, heard or otherwise perceived the representation being

（5）就（3）和（4）之目的而言，如果被告在本可以对某人进行交叉询问时不在场，但是存在下列情形，则应视为被告有合理的机会对该某人进行交叉询问：

（a）在交叉询问时本可合理在场；并且

（b）如果其在场本可以对该某人进行交叉询问。

（6）关于作出了适用（3）的表述的证据，可以通过提供经过下列人员验真的表述笔录或者录制品来提出：

（a）听取该表述的人员、法院或者其他机构；或者

（b）如果可行的话，法院或者其他机构听取该陈述的登记官或者其他适当的官员；或者

（c）负责生成上述笔录或者录制品的人员或者机构。[16]

（7）在并不限制（2）（d）的情况下，如果表述存在下列情况，则就该项目的而言，该表述被认为是该某人作出的于己不利的陈述：

（a）倾向于损害该某人的声望；或者

（b）倾向于表明该某人实施了还没有被定罪的犯罪；或者

（c）倾向于表明该某人在损害赔偿之诉中负有责任。

（8）传闻规则并不适用于：

（a）被告提出的由看到、听到或者以其他方式感知到先前表述作出情况的人作出的先前表述

made; or

(b) a document tendered as evidence by a defendant so far as it contains a previous representation, or another representation to which it is reasonably necessary to refer in order to understand the representation.

Note: Section 67 imposes notice requirements relating to this subsection.

(9) If evidence of a previous representation about a matter has been adduced by a defendant and has been admitted, the hearsay rule does not apply to evidence of another representation about the matter that:

(a) is adduced by another party; and

(b) is given by a person who saw, heard or otherwise perceived the other representation being made.

Note: Clause 4 of Part 2 of the Dictionary is about the availability of persons.

66 Exception: criminal proceedings if maker available

(1) This section applies in a criminal proceeding if a person who made a previous representation is available to give evidence about an asserted fact.

(2) If that person has been or is to be called to give evidence, the hearsay rule does not apply to evidence of the representation that is given by:

(a) that person; or

(b) a person who saw, heard or otherwise perceived the representation being made;

if, when the representation was made, the occurrence of the asserted fact was fresh in the memory of the person who made the representation.

(2A) In determining whether the occurrence of the asserted fact was

证据；或者

（b）被告作为证据提交的包含有先前表述或者为
理解该表述而有参考之合理需要的其他表述
的书证。[17]

注释：第 67 条就本款规定了通知要求。

（9）如果有关某事项的先前表述证据已经被被告提出并
被采纳为证据，则传闻规则并不适用于符合下列情
况的关于有关该某事项的另一表述证据；

（a）该证据是另一方当事人提出的；并且

（b）该证据是看到、听到或者以其他方式感知到
作出该另一表述情况的人作出的。

注释：《术语》第 2 部分的第 4 条就人员的到庭作了规定。

66 例外：先前表述者能够到庭的刑事程序

（1）本条适用于作出先前表述之人能够到庭就其所主张
的事实作证的刑事程序。

（2）如果作出先前表述之人已经或者将由法院传唤作
证，并且如果其在作出表述之时该某人对所主张
事实之发生记忆犹新，则传闻规则不适用于下列
人员所作出的表述证据：

（a）该作出表述之人；或者

（b）看到、听到或者以其他方式感知到该表述作
出情况之人。

（2A）在确定所主张事实之发生当时在某人的记忆中是

fresh in the memory of a person, the court may take into account all matters that it considers are relevant to the question, including:

(a) the nature of the event concerned; and

(b) the age and health of the person; and

(c) the period of time between the occurrence of the asserted fact and the making of the representation.

Note: Subsection (2A) was inserted as a response to the decision of the High Court of Australia in *Graham v The Queen* (1998) 195 CLR 606.

(3) If a representation was made for the purpose of indicating the evidence that the person who made it would be able to give in an Australian or overseas proceeding, subsection (2) does not apply to evidence adduced by the prosecutor of the representation unless the representation concerns the identity of a person, place or thing.

(4) A document containing a representation to which subsection (2) applies must not be tendered before the conclusion of the examination in chief of the person who made the representation, unless the court gives leave.

Note: Clause 4 of Part 2 of the Dictionary is about the availability of persons.

66A Exception: contemporaneous statements about a person's health etc.

The hearsay rule does not apply to evidence of a previous representation made by a person if the representation was a contemporaneous representation about the person's health, feelings, sensations, intention, knowledge or state of mind.

67 Notice to be given

(1) Subsections 63(2), 64(2) and 65(2), (3) and (8) do not

否清新时，法院可以虑及它认为与该问题有关的所有事项，包括：

（a）有关事件的性质；以及

（b）该某人的年龄和健康；以及

（c）在发生主张的事实与作出陈述之间的时间间隔。

注释：插入（2A），是为了回应澳大利亚最高法院在 *Graham v The Queen*（1998）195 CLR 606 案件中作出的判决。

（3）如果作出某表述之目的在于言明这样的证言，即作出该表述的人将能够在澳大利亚或者海外程序中作出的证言，则（2）不适用于公诉人就该表述提出的证据，除非该表述涉及某人员、地点或者物品的身份。[18]

（4）在对作出表述之人的主询问结束之前，不得提交包含（2）所适用的表述的书证，除非法院许可。

注释：《术语》第 2 部分的第 4 条就人员不能到庭作了规定。

66A 例外：关于某人健康状况等的即时陈述

如果先前表述证据是某人就其健康、感觉、情感、意图、知识或者心态所作的即时表述，则不适用传闻规则。

67 进行通知

（1）63（2）、64（2）、65（2）、（3）和（8）并不

apply to evidence adduced by a party unless that party has given reasonable notice in writing to each other party of the party's intention to adduce the evidence.

(2) Notices given under subsection (1) are to be given in accordance with any regulations or rules of court made for the purposes of this section.

(3) The notice must state:

   (a) the particular provisions of this Division on which the party intends to rely in arguing that the hearsay rule does not apply to the evidence; and

   (b) if subsection 64(2) is such a provision—the grounds, specified in that provision, on which the party intends to rely.

(4) Despite subsection (1), if notice has not been given, the court may, on the application of a party, direct that one or more of those subsections is to apply despite the party's failure to give notice.

(5) The direction:

   (a) is subject to such conditions (if any) as the court thinks fit; and

   (b) in particular, may provide that, in relation to specified evidence, the subsection or subsections concerned apply with such modifications as the court specifies.

68 Objections to tender of hearsay evidence in civil proceedings if maker available

(1) In a civil proceeding, if the notice discloses that it is not intended to call the person who made the previous representation concerned because it:

   (a) would cause undue expense or undue delay; or

   (b) would not be reasonably practicable;

a party may, not later than 21 days after notice has been given,

适用于当事人提出的证据，除非该当事人就其提出
该证据的意图对所有其他当事人进行了合理的书
面通知。

（2）根据（1）作出的通知，应遵照为本条目的制定的
条例或者法院规则进行。

（3）该通知必须载明：

（a）当事人为主张传闻规则不适用于某证据而准
备依据的本节的具体规定；以及

（b）如果 64（2）是其准备依据的规定，则必须
载明当事人准备依据的该规定中列举的理由。

（4）尽管有（1），如果通知还没有作出，则根据当事
人的申请，法院可以指示适用这些款中的一个或者
多个，尽管当事人未能作出通知。

（5）该指示：

（a）应遵守法院认为适当的条件（如果有任何条
件的话）；并且

（b）特别是，就特定的证据而言，可以规定有关
条款的适用要遵守法院就具体规定所进行的
修改。

68 在表述者到庭的民事程序中就提交传闻证据提出异议

（1）在民事程序中，如果通知表明当事人因下列原因而
不准备传唤作出先前表述的的人，其他当事人可以
在通知发送之日后不迟于 21 日内，反对提交该证
据或者该证据的特定部分：

（a）将会导致不合理的费用或者迟延；或者

（b）将不具有合理的可行性。

object to the tender of the evidence, or of a specified part of the evidence.

(2) The objection is to be made by giving to each other party a written notice setting out the grounds on which the objection is made.

(3) The court may, on the application of a party, determine the objection at or before the hearing.

(4) If the objection is unreasonable, the court may order that, in any event, the party objecting is to bear the costs (ascertained on a solicitor and client basis) incurred by another party:

(a) in relation to the objection; and

(b) in calling the person who made the representation to give evidence.

Note: Subsection (4) differs from subsection 68(4) of the NSW Act.

Division 3—Other exceptions to the hearsay rule

69 Exception: business records

(1) This section applies to a document that:

(a) either:

(i) is or forms part of the records belonging to or kept by a person, body or organisation in the course of, or for the purposes of, a business; or

(ii) at any time was or formed part of such a record; and

(b) contains a previous representation made or recorded in the document in the course of, or for the purposes of, the business.

(2) The hearsay rule does not apply to the document (so far as it contains the representation) if the representation was made:

（2）就上述异议，应当向每个其他当事人发出书面通知，列明异议所依据的理由

（3）根据当事人的申请，法院可以在听审之时或者之前就该异议作出决定。

（4）如果该异议是不合理的，法院在任何情况下都可以命令提出异议的当事人承担其他当事人所发生的如下费用（根据一个律师与委托人加以确定）：

（a）与异议有关的费用；以及

（b）传唤作出表述的人作证所产生的费用。

注释：（4）不同于《新南威尔士州证据法》之 68（4）。

第 3 目—传闻规则的其他例外

69 例外：业务记录

（1）本条适用于下列书证：

（a）该书证

（i）或者属于某人、某机构或者组织的业务记录，或者其在业务活动过程中保存的或者为业务目而保存的业务记录，或者是该业务记录的一部分；或者

（ii）在任何时候曾经是上述业务记录或者是该业务记录的一部分；并且

（b）该书证包含有在业务活动中或者为业务目的而制作或者记录在书证中的先前表述。

（2）如果表述符合下列情形的，则传闻规则不适用于该书证（就其包括该表述而论）：

     (a) by a person who had or might reasonably be supposed to have had personal knowledge of the asserted fact; or

     (b) on the basis of information directly or indirectly supplied by a person who had or might reasonably be supposed to have had personal knowledge of the asserted fact.

(3) Subsection (2) does not apply if the representation:

     (a) was prepared or obtained for the purpose of conducting, or for or in contemplation of or in connection with, an Australian or overseas proceeding; or

     (b) was made in connection with an investigation relating or leading to a criminal proceeding.

(4) If:

     (a) the occurrence of an event of a particular kind is in question; and

     (b) in the course of a business, a system has been followed of making and keeping a record of the occurrence of all events of that kind;

the hearsay rule does not apply to evidence that tends to prove that there is no record kept, in accordance with that system, of the occurrence of the event.

(5) For the purposes of this section, a person is taken to have had personal knowledge of a fact if the person's knowledge of the fact was or might reasonably be supposed to have been based on what the person saw, heard or otherwise perceived (other than a previous representation made by a person about the fact).

Note 1:   Sections 48, 49, 50, 146, 147 and subsection 150(1) are relevant to the mode of proof, and authentication, of business records.

Note 2:   Section 182 gives this section a wider application in relation to Commonwealth records.

（a）该表述是由对所主张的事实有或者可以合理
地认为有亲身知识的人作出的；或者

（b）该表述是以直接或者间接地由对所主张的事
实有或者可以合理地认为有亲身知识的人提
供的信息为基础的。[19]

（3）如果表述属于下列情形，则（2）不适用：

（a）该表述是为进行或者准备进行澳大利亚或者
海外程序而制作或者获得的，或者是与这些
程序有关；或者

（b）该表述是在与刑事程序有关或者导致该程序
的调查中作出的。

（4）在下列情况下，传闻法则不适用于倾向于证明在遵
循了某种制度的情况下，就某事件的发生没有保存
记录的证据：

（a）就某一具体类型的事件发生存在争议；并且

（b）在业务活动过程中，已遵循该制度，就所有
此类事件的发生加以记录并予以保存。

（5）就本条目的而言，如果某人对事实的知识是或者
可以合理地认为是基于该某人所见、所听或者以
其他方式感知的事实（而不是基于某人就该事实
所作出的先前表述），则认为该某人对该事实有
亲身知识。

注释 1：第 48 条、第 49 条、第 50 条、第 146 条、第 147
条和 150（1）都与业务记录的证明模式以及验真
有关。

注释 2：就联邦记录，第 182 条赋予了本条更为广泛的适用。

70 Exception: contents of tags, labels and writing

(1) The hearsay rule does not apply to a tag or label attached to, or writing placed on, an object (including a document) if the tag or label or writing may reasonably be supposed to have been so attached or placed:

    (a) in the course of a business; and

    (b) for the purpose of describing or stating the identity, nature, ownership, destination, origin or weight of the object, or of the contents (if any) of the object.

Note: Section 182 gives this subsection a wider application in relation to Commonwealth records.

(2) This section, and any provision of a law of a State or Territory that permits the use in evidence of such a tag, label or writing as an exception to a rule of law restricting the admissibility or use of hearsay evidence, does not apply to:

    (a) a Customs prosecution within the meaning of Part XIV of the Customs Act 1901; or

    (b) an Excise prosecution within the meaning of Part XI of the Excise Act 1901.

Note 1: Subsection (2) does not appear in section 70 of the NSW Act.

Note 2: Section 5 extends the application of this subsection to proceedings in all Australian courts.

71 Exception: electronic communications

The hearsay rule does not apply to a representation contained in a document recording an electronic communication so far as the representation is a representation as to:

    (a) the identity of the person from whom or on whose

70 例外：标牌、标签和写字纸的内容

（1）如果可以合理地认为物品（包括书证）上所附的标牌、标签或者写字纸是在下列情况下附着或者置放的，则传闻规则并不适用于这些标牌、标签或者写字纸：

（a）这些标牌、标签或者写字纸是在业务过程中附着或者置放的；并且

（b）其目的是描述或者说明物品的身份、性质、所有权、目的地、原产地或者重量，或者是物品的内容（如果有的话）。

注释：就联邦记录，第 182 条赋予了本款更为广泛的适用。

（2）本条以及州法或者领地法允许将标牌、标签和写字纸用作限定传闻证据可采性或者运用的法律规则之例外的任何规定，不适用于：

（a）《1901 年海关法》第 14 章规定的关税检控；或者

（b）《1901 年税收法》第 11 章规定的税务检控。

注释 1：（2）并没有出现在《新南威尔士州证据法》第 70 条中。

注释 2：第 5 条将本款扩展适用于所有澳大利亚法院的程序。

71 例外：电子通信

传闻规则并不适用于记录电子通信的书证中所包含的表述，只要该表述是关于下列情况的表述：

（a）信息发送人或者代表其进行信息发送的人的

behalf the communication was sent; or

(b) the date on which or the time at which the communication was sent; or

(c) the destination of the communication or the identity of the person to whom the communication was addressed.

Note 1: Division 3 of Part 4.3 contains presumptions about electronic communications.

Note 2: Section 182 gives this section a wider application in relation to Commonwealth records.

Note 3: *Electronic communication* is defined in the Dictionary.

72 Exception: Aboriginal and Torres Strait Islander traditional laws and customs

The hearsay rule does not apply to evidence of a representation about the existence or non-existence, or the content, of the traditional laws and customs of an Aboriginal or Torres Strait Islander group.

73 Exception: reputation as to relationships and age

(1) The hearsay rule does not apply to evidence of reputation concerning:

(a) whether a person was, at a particular time or at any time, a married person; or

(b) whether a man and a woman cohabiting at a particular time were married to each other at that time; or

(c) a person's age; or

(d) family history or a family relationship.

(2) In a criminal proceeding, subsection (1) does not apply to evidence adduced by a defendant unless:

身份；或者

（b）信息发送的日期或者时间；或者

（c）信息的目的地或者信息接收人的身份。

注释 1：第 4.3 节第 3 目包含有关于电子通信的推定。

注释 2：就联邦记录，第 182 条赋予了本条更为广泛的适用。

注释 3：**电子通信**的定义见《术语》。

72 例外：土著民和 Torres 海峡岛民的传统法律与习俗

传闻规则并不适用于有关土著民和 Torres 海峡岛民群体的传统法律与习俗存在与否或者其内容的表述证据。

73 例外：关于关系和年龄的声望

（1）传闻规则并不适用于关于下列事项的声望证据：

（a）在某具体时间或者在任何时间，某人是否已婚；或者

（b）在某具体时间共同生活的某男和某女在当时是否已经彼此结婚；或者

（c）某人的年龄；或者

（d）家史或者家庭关系。

（2）在刑事程序中，（1）并不适用于被告提出的证据，除非：

（a）该证据倾向对已被采纳的（1）所称证据进行

> (a) it tends to contradict evidence of a kind referred to in subsection (1) that has been admitted; or
>
> (b) the defendant has given reasonable notice in writing to each other party of the defendant's intention to adduce the evidence.

(3) In a criminal proceeding, subsection (1) does not apply to evidence adduced by the prosecutor unless it tends to contradict evidence of a kind referred to in subsection (1) that has been admitted.

74 Exception: reputation of public or general rights

(1) The hearsay rule does not apply to evidence of reputation concerning the existence, nature or extent of a public or general right.

(2) In a criminal proceeding, subsection (1) does not apply to evidence adduced by the prosecutor unless it tends to contradict evidence of a kind referred to in subsection (1) that has been admitted.

75 Exception: interlocutory proceedings

In an interlocutory proceeding, the hearsay rule does not apply to evidence if the party who adduces it also adduces evidence of its source.

Part 3.3—Opinion

76 The opinion rule

(1) Evidence of an opinion is not admissible to prove the existence of a fact about the existence of which the opinion was expressed.

(2) Subsection (1) does not apply to evidence of an opinion

反驳；或者

（b）被告已经就其提出该证据的意图以书面形式
向每个其他当事人进行了合理通知。

（3）在刑事程序中，（1）不适用于公诉人提出的证据，
除非该证据倾向对已被采纳的（1）所称证据进行
反驳。

74 例外：关于公共或者一般权利的声望

（1）传闻规则不适用于有关公共权利或者一般权利的存
在、性质或者范围的声望证据。

（2）在刑事程序中，（1）不适用于公诉人提出的证据，
除非该证据倾向对已被采纳的（1）所称证据进行
反驳。

75 例外：中间程序

在中间程序中，如果提出某证据的当事人也提出了关
于其来源的证据，则传闻规则并不适用于该证据。[20]

第 3.3 节—意见

76 意见规则

（1）不得采纳意见证据来证明就其存在而表达意见的事
实之存在。

（2）对于根据本法之外的其他法律制定的条例颁发或者
制作的证明书或者其他书证，如果这些条例规定该

contained in a certificate or other document given or made under regulations made under an Act other than this Act to the extent to which the regulations provide that the certificate or other document has evidentiary effect.

Note: Specific exceptions to the opinion rule are as follows:

- summaries of voluminous or complex documents (subsection 50(3));
- evidence relevant otherwise than as opinion evidence (section 77);
- lay opinion (section 78);
- Aboriginal and Torres Strait Islander traditional laws and customs (section 78A);
- expert opinion (section 79);
- admissions (section 81);
- exceptions to the rule excluding evidence of judgments and convictions (subsection 92(3));
- character of and expert opinion about accused persons (sections 110 and 111).

Other provisions of this Act, or of other laws, may operate as further exceptions.

Examples:

(1) P sues D, her doctor, for the negligent performance of a surgical operation. Unless an exception to the opinion rule applies, P's neighbour, W, who had the same operation, cannot give evidence of his opinion that D had not performed the operation as well as his own.

(2) P considers that electrical work that D, an electrician, has done for her is unsatisfactory. Unless an exception to the opinion rule applies, P cannot give evidence of her opinion that D does not have the necessary skills to do electrical work.

第76条

证明书或者其他书证具有证据效力，则（1）并不适用于包含在这些证明书或者其他书证中的意见证据。

注释：意见规则的具体例外如下：

· 卷帙浩繁或者复杂文件的摘要（50（3））；

· 因意见证据之外之目的而具有相关性的证据（第77条）；

· 外行意见（第78条）；

· 土著民和Torres海峡岛民的传统法律与习俗（第78A条）；

· 专家意见（第79条）；

· 自认（第81条）；

· 排除判决与定罪证据之规则的例外（92（3））；

· 关于被指控者的品性和专家意见（第110条和第111条）。

本法或者其他法律的其他规定，可能规定有进一步的例外。

示例：

（1）P因外科手术过失起诉了其医生D。P的邻居W也接受了同样的手术。W不能就D做的这个手术没有像给他做的手术那样好提供意见证据，除非适用意见规则的某个例外。

（2）P认为电工D为其所做的电工工作令人不满意。P不能就D并不具备从事电工工作所必需的技能提供意见证据，除非适用意见规则的某个例外。

77 Exception: evidence relevant otherwise than as opinion evidence

The opinion rule does not apply to evidence of an opinion that is admitted because it is relevant for a purpose other than proof of the existence of a fact about the existence of which the opinion was expressed.

78 Exception: lay opinions

The opinion rule does not apply to evidence of an opinion expressed by a person if:

(a) the opinion is based on what the person saw, heard or otherwise perceived about a matter or event; and

(b) evidence of the opinion is necessary to obtain an adequate account or understanding of the person's perception of the matter or event.

78A Exception: Aboriginal and Torres Strait Islander traditional laws and customs

The opinion rule does not apply to evidence of an opinion expressed by a member of an Aboriginal or Torres Strait Islander group about the existence or non–existence, or the content, of the traditional laws and customs of the group.

79 Exception: opinions based on specialised knowledge

(1) If a person has specialised knowledge based on the person's training, study or experience, the opinion rule does not apply to evidence of an opinion of that person that is wholly or substantially based on that knowledge.

(2) To avoid doubt, and without limiting subsection (1):

(a) a reference in that subsection to specialised knowledge includes a reference to specialised knowledge of child development and child behaviour (including specialised

77 例外：因意见证据之外之目的而具有相关性的证据

如果意见证据之所以被采纳，是因为其因证明就其存在而表达意见的事实之存在之外之目的而具有相关性，则意见规则不适用于该意见证据。

78 例外：外行意见

在下列情况下，意见规则并不适用于某人表达的意见证据：

（a）该意见是建立在该某人对某事项或者事件的所见、所听或者其他方式的感知基础上的；并且

（b）该意见证据为足够说明或者理解该某人关于该某事项或者事件的感知所必需。

78A 例外：土著民和 Torres 海峡岛民的传统法律与习俗

意见规则并不适用于土著民和 Torres 海峡岛民群体成员就该群体的传统法律与习俗存在与否或者其内容所作的意见证据。

79 例外：基于专门知识的意见

（1）如果某人基于其训练、学习或者经验而具有专门知识，则意见规则并不适用于关于该某人完全或者主要基于该知识所表达的意见证据。

（2）为避免疑义，且在并不限制（1）的情况下：

（a）该款所称专门知识，包括关于儿童成长和儿童行为的专门知识（包括关于性侵犯对儿童

knowledge of the impact of sexual abuse on children and their development and behaviour during and following the abuse); and

(b) a reference in that subsection to an opinion of a person includes, if the person has specialised knowledge of the kind referred to in paragraph (a), a reference to an opinion relating to either or both of the following:

(i) the development and behaviour of children generally;

(ii) the development and behaviour of children who have been victims of sexual offences, or offences similar to sexual offences.

80 Ultimate issue and common knowledge rules abolished

Evidence of an opinion is not inadmissible only because it is about:

(a) a fact in issue or an ultimate issue; or

(b) a matter of common knowledge.

Part 3.4—Admissions

Note: *Admission* is defined in the Dictionary.

81 Hearsay and opinion rules: exception for admissions and related representations

(1) The hearsay rule and the opinion rule do not apply to evidence of an admission.

(2) The hearsay rule and the opinion rule do not apply to evidence of a previous representation:

(a) that was made in relation to an admission at the time the admission was made, or shortly before or after that time; and

(b) to which it is reasonably necessary to refer in order to

的影响，以及对性侵犯期间和之后儿童成长

和行为的影响的专门知识）；以及

（b）在某人具有（a）所称的专门知识的情况下，

该款所称该某人的意见，包括与下列二者或

者二者之一有关的意见：

（i）一般性的儿童成长和行为；

（ii）作为性侵犯或者与性侵犯类似的犯罪的受

害人的成长和行为。【21】

80 废除最终争点与常识规则

关于意见的证据不得仅因其有关下列事项而不可采：

（a）争议事实或者最终争点；或者

（b）常识事项。

第 3.4 节—自认

注释：**自认的定义见《术语》。**

81 传闻和意见规则：自认和相关表述的例外

（1）传闻规则和意见规则并不适用于自认证据。【22】

（2）传闻规则和意见规则并不适用于下列先前表述证

据：

（a）作出自认时或者作出自认前后不久作出的与

自认有关的先前表述；以及

（b）为理解自认而有参考之合理必要的先前表述。

understand the admission.

Note: Specific exclusionary rules relating to admissions are as follows:

- evidence of admissions that is not first–hand (section 82);
- use of admissions against third parties (section 83);
- admissions influenced by violence etc. (section 84);
- unreliable admissions of accused persons (section 85);
- records of oral questioning of accused persons (section 86).

   Example: D admits to W, his best friend, that he sexually assaulted V. In D's trial for the sexual assault, the prosecution may lead evidence from W:

   (a) that D made the admission to W as proof of the truth of that admission; and

   (b) that W formed the opinion that D was sane when he made the admission.

82 Exclusion of evidence of admissions that is not first–hand

Section 81 does not prevent the application of the hearsay rule to evidence of an admission unless:

(a) it is given by a person who saw, heard or otherwise perceived the admission being made; or

(b) it is a document in which the admission is made.

Note: Section 60 does not apply in a criminal proceeding to evidence of an admission.

注释：与自认有关的具体排除规则如下：

· 关于自认的非第一手的证据（第 82 条）；

· 使用自认来反对第三方（第 83 条）；

· 受暴力等影响的自认（第 84 条）；

· 被指控者的不可靠自认（第 85 条）；

· 对被指控者的口头询问所作的记录（第 86 条）。

示例：D 向其最好的朋友 W 自认说，他对 V 进行
了性侵犯。在因该性侵犯而对 D 进行的审判
中，检控方可以：

（a）从 W 那里引导出 D 向 W 作了自认的
证据，来证明该自认的真实性；以及

（b）从 W 那里引导出这样的证据，即 W
形成了这样的意见：D 在作出自认时精
神健全

82 非第一手自认证据的排除

第 81 条并不禁止就自认证据适用传闻规则，除非：

（a）该自认证据是由看到、听到或者以其他方
式感知到自认作出过程的人员作出的；或
者

（b）该自认证据是作出自认的书证。[23]

注释：第 60 条并不适用于刑事程序中的自认证据。

83 Exclusion of evidence of admissions as against third parties

(1) Section 81 does not prevent the application of the hearsay rule or the opinion rule to evidence of an admission in respect of the case of a third party.

(2) The evidence may be used in respect of the case of a third party if that party consents.

(3) Consent cannot be given in respect of part only of the evidence.

(4) In this section:

third party means a party to the proceeding concerned, other than the party who:

(a) made the admission; or

(b) adduced the evidence.

84 Exclusion of admissions influenced by violence and certain other conduct

(1) Evidence of an admission is not admissible unless the court is satisfied that the admission, and the making of the admission, were not influenced by:

(a) violent, oppressive, inhuman or degrading conduct, whether towards the person who made the admission or towards another person; or

(b) a threat of conduct of that kind.

(2) Subsection (1) only applies if the party against whom evidence of the admission is adduced has raised in the proceeding an issue about whether the admission or its making were so influenced.

85 Criminal proceedings: reliability of admissions by defendants

(1) This section applies only in a criminal proceeding and only to evidence of an admission made by a defendant:

83 反对第三方的自认证据的排除

（1）第81条并不禁止就第三方的案件，对自认证据适用传闻规则或者意见规则。

（2）如果第三方同意，可以就该第三方的案件使用该证据。

（3）不得仅就该证据的一部分作出同意。

（4）在本条中：

第三方是指有关程序的当事人，但是下列当事人除外：

（a）作出了自认的当事人；或者

（b）提出该证据的当事人。[24]

84 受到暴力和某些其他行为影响的自认的排除

（1）自认证据不具有可采性，除非法院确信该自认以及自认的过程没有受到下列因素的影响：

（a）暴力、胁迫、不人道或者有损人的尊严的行为，

不论该行为是针对作出自认的人还是其他人；

或者

（b）采取上述行为的威胁。

（2）仅在受到提出的自认证据所反对的当事人在程序中就该自认或者自认的过程是否受到上述影响提出争议的情况下，才适用（1）。[25]

85 刑事程序：被告自认的可靠性

（1）本条仅适用于刑事程序，仅适用于被告在下列情况下所作的自认证据：

(a) to, or in the presence of, an investigating official who at that time was performing functions in connection with the investigation of the commission, or possible commission, of an offence; or

(b) as a result of an act of another person who was, and who the defendant knew or reasonably believed to be, capable of influencing the decision whether a prosecution of the defendant should be brought or should be continued.

Note: Subsection (1) was inserted as a response to the decision of the High Court of Australia in *Kelly v The Queen* (2004) 218 CLR 216.

(2) Evidence of the admission is not admissible unless the circumstances in which the admission was made were such as to make it unlikely that the truth of the admission was adversely affected.

(3) Without limiting the matters that the court may take into account for the purposes of subsection (2), it is to take into account:

(a) any relevant condition or characteristic of the person who made the admission, including age, personality and education and any mental, intellectual or physical disability to which the person is or appears to be subject; and

(b) if the admission was made in response to questioning:

(i) the nature of the questions and the manner in which they were put; and

(ii) the nature of any threat, promise or other inducement made to the person questioned.

86 Exclusion of records of oral questioning

(1) This section applies only in a criminal proceeding and only if an oral admission was made by a defendant to an

第 86 条

（a）对在当时履行与犯罪或者可能的犯罪之调查有关的职责的调查人员作出的，或者是在该调查人员在场情况下作出的；或者

（b）是被告知道或者合理地认为能够对是否对被告提起检控或者该检控是否继续进行下去的决定产生影响的其他人的行为之结果。

注释：插入（1），是为了回应澳大利亚最高法院在 *Kelly v The Queen*（2004）218 CLR 216 案件中作出的判决。

（2）关于自认的证据不可采，除非自认是在其真实性不可能受到不利影响的情况下所作出的。

（3）就（2）之目的而言，法院应当虑及的事项包括但是不限于：

（a）作出自认的人的任何相关条件或者特点，包括年龄、个性和教育程度，以及患有或者看上去患有任何精神、智力或者身体上的残障；以及

（b）如果自认是针对询问所作的回应：

（i）问题的性质和提问的方式；以及

（ii）对被询问人所进行的威胁、承诺或者其他诱惑的性质。

86 口头询问记录的排除

（1）本条仅适用于刑事程序，仅适用于被告对调查人员的询问或者表述作出回应时所作的口头自认。

investigating official in response to a question put or a representation made by the official.

(2) A document prepared by or on behalf of the official is not admissible to prove the contents of the question, representation or response unless the defendant has acknowledged that the document is a true record of the question, representation or response.

(3) The acknowledgment must be made by signing, initialling or otherwise marking the document.

(4) In this section:

document does not include:

   (a) a sound recording, or a transcript of a sound recording; or

   (b) a recording of visual images and sounds, or a transcript of the sounds so recorded.

87 Admissions made with authority

(1) For the purpose of determining whether a previous representation made by a person is also taken to be an admission by a party, the court is to admit the representation if it is reasonably open to find that:

   (a) when the representation was made, the person had authority to make statements on behalf of the party in relation to the matter with respect to which the representation was made; or

   (b) when the representation was made, the person was an employee of the party, or had authority otherwise to act for the party, and the representation related to a matter within the scope of the person's employment or authority; or

   (c) the representation was made by the person in furtherance of a common purpose (whether lawful or not) that the person had with the party or one or more

（2）调查人员或者其代表制作的书证，不能采纳来证
明询问、表述或者回应的内容，除非被告已经承认
该书证是对询问、表述或者回应的真实记录。

（3）该承认必须通过签名、缩写签名或者其他在书证上
作记号的方式作出。[27]

（4）在本条中：

书证并不包括：

（a）声音录制品，或者声音录制品的笔录；或者

（b）音像录制品，或者音像录制品中声音的笔录。

87 经授权作出的自认

（1）为确定某人作出的先前表述是否也可以视为当事人
的自认，法院如果合理地发现存在下列情形，则应
当采纳该表述：

（a）在该表述作出时，该某人有权代表当事人就
作出表述有关事项作出陈述；或者

（b）在作出该表述时，该某人是当事人的雇员，或
者因其他原因有权为当事人行动，并且该表
述与其雇用或者授权范围内的事项有关；或
者

（c）该某人作出该表述，是为了促进该某人与当
事人或者包括当事人在内的人的共同目的（无
论合法与否）。

persons including the party.

(2) For the purposes of this section, the hearsay rule does not apply to a previous representation made by a person that tends to prove:

   (a) that the person had authority to make statements on behalf of another person in relation to a matter; or

   (b) that the person was an employee of another person or had authority otherwise to act for another person; or

   (c) the scope of the person's employment or authority.

88 Proof of admissions

For the purpose of determining whether evidence of an admission is admissible, the court is to find that a particular person made the admission if it is reasonably open to find that he or she made the admission.

89 Evidence of silence

(1) In a criminal proceeding, an inference unfavourable to a party must not be drawn from evidence that the party or another person failed or refused:

   (a) to answer one or more questions; or

   (b) to respond to a representation;

   put or made to the party or other person by an investigating official who at that time was performing functions in connection with the investigation of the commission, or possible commission, of an offence.

(2) Evidence of that kind is not admissible if it can only be used to draw such an inference.

(3) Subsection (1) does not prevent use of the evidence to

（2）就本条目的而言，传闻规则并不适用于某人所作的
倾向于证明下列事项的先前表述：

（a）该某人有权代表他人就某事项作出陈述；或
者

（b）该某人是他人的雇员，或者有权力为他人而
行动；或者

（c）该某人的雇佣或者授权范围。

88 自认的证明

为确定关于自认的证据是否可采，如果法院能合理地认
定具体的人员作出了自认，则应当判定该某人作出了自
认。[28]

89 关于沉默的证据

（1）在刑事程序中，如果提问或者表述是由在当时履行
与犯罪或者可能的犯罪之调查有关的职责的调查
人员对当事人或者其他人作出的，则不得从该当事
人或者其他人未能或者拒绝进行下列行为的证据，
作出不利于当事人的推论：

（a）回答提问；或者

（b）对某个表述作出回应。[29]

（2）上述证据如果仅用于作出上述推论，则该证据不具
有可采性。

（3）如果当事人或者其他人未能或者拒绝回答提问或者

prove that the party or other person failed or refused to answer the question or to respond to the representation if the failure or refusal is a fact in issue in the proceeding.

(4) In this section:

inference includes:

(a) an inference of consciousness of guilt; or

(b) an inference relevant to a party's credibility.

90 Discretion to exclude admissions

In a criminal proceeding, the court may refuse to admit evidence of an admission, or refuse to admit the evidence to prove a particular fact, if:

(a) the evidence is adduced by the prosecution; and

(b) having regard to the circumstances in which the admission was made, it would be unfair to a defendant to use the evidence.

Note: Part 3.11 contains other exclusionary discretions that are applicable to admissions.

Part 3.5—Evidence of judgments and convictions

91 Exclusion of evidence of judgments and convictions

(1) Evidence of the decision, or of a finding of fact, in an Australian or overseas proceeding is not admissible to prove the existence of a fact that was in issue in that proceeding.

(2) Evidence that, under this Part, is not admissible to prove the existence of a fact may not be used to prove that fact even if it is relevant for another purpose.

Note: Section 178 (Convictions, acquittals and other judicial proceedings) provides for certificate evidence of decisions.

对表述作出回应是程序中的争议事实，则（1）并不禁止使用该证据来证明上述事项。

（4）在本条中：

推论包括：

（a）意识到有罪的推论；或者

（b）与当事人的可信性有关的推论。

90 排除自认的自由裁量权

在刑事程序中，在下列情况下，法院可以拒绝采纳自认证据，或者拒绝采纳该证据来证明具体事实：

（a）该证据是检控方提出的；并且

（b）虑及作出自认的环境，使用该证据对于被告不公平。[30]

注释：第 3.11 节包含有适用于自认的其他排除性自由裁量权。

第 3.5 节—判决与定罪证据

91 判决与定罪证据的排除

（1）关于在澳大利亚或者海外程序中作出的裁决或者事实认定的证据，不得采纳来证明在该程序中的争议事实的存在。

（2）根据本节不能采纳来证明某事实之存在的证据，即使因其他目的具有相关性，也不得用于证明该事实。[31]

注释：第 178 条（定罪、无罪开释和其他司法程序）就关于裁决的证明书证据作出了规定。

Section 94

92 Exceptions

(1) Subsection 91(1) does not prevent the admission or use of evidence of the grant of probate, letters of administration or a similar order of a court to prove:

    (a) the death, or date of death, of a person; or

    (b) the due execution of a testamentary document.

(2) In a civil proceeding, subsection 91(1) does not prevent the admission or use of evidence that a party, or a person through or under whom a party claims, has been convicted of an offence, not being a conviction:

    (a) in respect of which a review or appeal (however described) has been instituted but not finally determined; or

    (b) that has been quashed or set aside; or

    (c) in respect of which a pardon has been given.

(3) The hearsay rule and the opinion rule do not apply to evidence of a kind referred to in this section.

93 Savings

This Part does not affect the operation of:

    (a) a law that relates to the admissibility or effect of evidence of a conviction tendered in a proceeding (including a criminal proceeding) for defamation; or

    (b) a judgment in rem; or

    (c) the law relating to res judicata or issue estoppel.

Part 3.6—Tendency and coincidence

94 Application

(1) This Part does not apply to evidence that relates only to the

92 例外

（1）91（1）并不禁止采纳和使用关于法院作出的遗嘱
检验决定书、遗产管理书或者类似命令的证据，来
证明下列事项：

（a）某人的死亡或者死亡期日；或者

（b）遗嘱文件的妥当签立。

（2）在民事程序中，91（1）并不禁止采纳和使用关于当
事人或者当事人通过其提出主张的人已经因某犯罪
被定罪，但是该定罪并非属于下列情况的证据：

（a）关于该定罪的复审或者上诉（无论如何表述）
已经启动但是还没有最后确定；或者

（b）该定罪已经被取消或者撤销；或者

（c）该定罪已经被赦免。[32]

（3）传闻规则和意见规则并不适用于本条所称的此类证
据。

93 保留

本节并不影响下列法律或者判决的运作：

（a）与因诽谤提起的程序（包括刑事程序）中提
交的定罪证据的可采性和效力有关的法律；
[33]或者

（b）对物判决；或者

（c）与既判力或者争议点禁止反言有关的法律。

第 3.6 节—倾向与巧合

94 适用

（1）本节并不适用于仅仅与证人的可信性有关的证据。

credibility of a witness.

(2) This Part does not apply so far as a proceeding relates to bail or sentencing.

(3) This Part does not apply to evidence of:

   (a) the character, reputation or conduct of a person; or

   (b) a tendency that a person has or had;

   if that character, reputation, conduct or tendency is a fact in issue.

95 Use of evidence for other purposes

(1) Evidence that under this Part is not admissible to prove a particular matter must not be used to prove that matter even if it is relevant for another purpose.

(2) Evidence that under this Part cannot be used against a party to prove a particular matter must not be used against the party to prove that matter even if it is relevant for another purpose.

96 Failure to act

A reference in this Part to doing an act includes a reference to failing to do that act.

97 The tendency rule

(1) Evidence of the character, reputation or conduct of a person, or a tendency that a person has or had, is not admissible to prove that a person has or had a tendency (whether because of the person's character or otherwise) to act in a particular way, or to have a particular state of mind unless:

   (a) the party seeking to adduce the evidence gave reasonable notice in writing to each other party of the party's intention to adduce the evidence; and

   (b) the court thinks.0 that the evidence will, either by itself or having regard to other evidence adduced or to be

（2）本节并不适用于与保释或者量刑有关的程序。

（3）在品性、声望、行为或者倾向是争议事实的情况下，本节并不适用于关于下列情况的证据：

（a）某人的品性、声望或者行为；或者

（b）某人的倾向或者曾有的倾向。

95 为其他目的使用证据

（1）根据本节不能采纳来证明某具体事项的证据，即使就其他目的而相关，也不得用来证明该某具体事项

（2）根据本节不能通过证明某具体事项来反对一方当事人的证据，即使就其他目的而相关，也不得用来证明该某事项来反对该当事人。

96 不作为

本节所称作为，包括不作为。

97 倾向规则

（1）在下列情况下，关于某人的品性、声望或者行为的证据，或者关于某人的倾向或者曾有的倾向的证据，不得采纳来证明该某人有或者曾有以具体方式行为的倾向（不论是因该某人的品性还是因为其他），或者有具体的心态，除非：

（a）试图提出该证据的当事人就其提出该证据的意图，对每个其他当事人以书面形式进行了合理的通知；并且

（b）法院认为根据该证据本身，或者虑及试图提出该证据的当事人所提出的或者将要提出的

adduced by the party seeking to adduce the evidence, have significant probative value.

(2) Paragraph (1)(a) does not apply if:

    (a) the evidence is adduced in accordance with any directions made by the court under section 100; or

    (b) the evidence is adduced to explain or contradict tendency evidence adduced by another party.

Note: The tendency rule is subject to specific exceptions concerning character of and expert opinion about accused persons (sections 110 and 111). Other provisions of this Act, or of other laws, may operate as further exceptions.

98 The coincidence rule

(1) Evidence that 2 or more events occurred is not admissible to prove that a person did a particular act or had a particular state of mind on the basis that, having regard to any similarities in the events or the circumstances in which they occurred, or any similarities in both the events and the circumstances in which they occurred, it is improbable that the events occurred coincidentally unless:

    (a) the party seeking to adduce the evidence gave reasonable notice in writing to each other party of the party's intention to adduce the evidence; and

    (b) the court thinks that the evidence will, either by itself or having regard to other evidence adduced or to be adduced by the party seeking to adduce the evidence, have significant probative value.

Note: One of the events referred to in subsection (1) may be an event the occurrence of which is a fact in issue in the proceeding.

(2) Paragraph (1)(a) does not apply if:

其他证据，该证据具有重大证明价值。

（2）在下列情况下，（1）（a）并不适用：

（a）该证据是遵照法院根据第 100 条作出的任何
指示而提出的；或者

（b）提出该证据用于解释或者反驳其他当事人提
出的倾向证据。

注释：倾向规则要遵守关于被指控者的品性和意见证据的
例外的限制（第 110 条和第 111 条）。本法或者其
他法律的其他规定，可能规定了进一步的例外。

98 巧合规则

（1）就 2 个或者 2 个以上已经发生的事件证据，不得因
为虑及这些事件或者这些事件的发生环境具有类
似性，或者在这些事件及其发生环境方面都有类似
性，认为这些事件是不可能巧合发生的，而采纳
来证明一个人从事了具体行为或者曾有具体心态，
除非：

（a）试图提出该证据的当事人就其提出该证据的
意图，对每个其他当事人以书面形式进行了
合理的通知；并且

（b）法院认为根据该证据本身，或者虑及试图提
出该证据的当事人所提出的或者将要提出的
其他证据，该证据具有重大证明价值。

注释：（1）所称的事件之一，可能是其发生乃程序中的争
议事实的事件。

（2）在下列情况下，（1）（a）并不适用：

(a) the evidence is adduced in accordance with any directions made by the court under section 100; or

(b) the evidence is adduced to explain or contradict coincidence evidence adduced by another party.

Note: Other provisions of this Act, or of other laws, may operate as exceptions to the coincidence rule.

99 Requirements for notices

Notices given under section 97 or 98 are to be given in accordance with any regulations or rules of court made for the purposes of this section.

100 Court may dispense with notice requirements

(1) The court may, on the application of a party, direct that the tendency rule is not to apply to particular tendency evidence despite the party's failure to give notice under section 97.

(2) The court may, on the application of a party, direct that the coincidence rule is not to apply to particular coincidence evidence despite the party's failure to give notice under section 98.

(3) The application may be made either before or after the time by which the party would, apart from this section, be required to give, or to have given, the notice.

(4) In a civil proceeding, the party's application may be made without notice of it having been given to one or more of the other parties.

(5) The direction:

(a) is subject to such conditions (if any) as the court thinks fit; and

(b) may be given either at or before the hearing.

(6) Without limiting the court's power to impose conditions

（a）该证据是遵照法院根据第 100 条作出的任何指示而提出的；或者

（b）提出该证据用于解释或者反驳其他当事人提出的巧合证据。

注释：本法或者其他法律的其他条款，可能就巧合规则规定了例外。

99 通知要求

根据第 97 条和第 98 条发送的通知，应当依据为本条目的制定的任何条例或者法院规则进行。

100 法院可以免除通知要求

（1）根据当事人的申请，法院可以指示倾向规则并不适用于具体倾向证据，尽管该当事人未能根据第 97 条发出通知。

（2）根据当事人的申请，法院可以指示巧合规则并不适用于具体巧合证据，尽管该当事人未能根据第 98 条发出通知。

（3）该申请可以在当事人除了本条之外被要求发出通知或者已经发出通知的时间之前或者之后提出。

（4）在民事程序中，当事人可以提出申请，而不就此通知其他一方或者多方当事人。

（5）该指示：

（a）应当符合法院认为适当的条件（如果有的话）；并且

（b）可以在听审之前或者之后作出。

（6）在不限制法院根据本条设定条件的权力的情况下，

under this section, those conditions may include one or more of the following:

(a) a condition that the party give notice of its intention to adduce the evidence to a specified party, or to each other party other than a specified party;

(b) a condition that the party give such notice only in respect of specified tendency evidence, or all tendency evidence that the party intends to adduce other than specified tendency evidence;

(c) a condition that the party give such notice only in respect of specified coincidence evidence, or all coincidence evidence that the party intends to adduce other than specified coincidence evidence.

101 Further restrictions on tendency evidence and coincidence evidence adduced by prosecution

(1) This section only applies in a criminal proceeding and so applies in addition to sections 97 and 98.

(2) Tendency evidence about a defendant, or coincidence evidence about a defendant, that is adduced by the prosecution cannot be used against the defendant unless the probative value of the evidence substantially outweighs any prejudicial effect it may have on the defendant.

(3) This section does not apply to tendency evidence that the prosecution adduces to explain or contradict tendency evidence adduced by the defendant.

(4) This section does not apply to coincidence evidence that the prosecution adduces to explain or contradict coincidence evidence adduced by the defendant.

这些条件可以包括下列一个或者数个：

（a）当事人就其提出证据的意图向指定当事人发出通知，或者向指定当事人之外的每个其他当事人发出通知；

（b）当事人仅就指定的倾向证据发出上述通知，或者仅就当事人意图提出的指定的倾向证据之外的所有倾向证据发出上述通知；

（c）当事人仅就指定的巧合证据发出上述通知，或者仅就当事人意图提出的指定的巧合证据之外的所有巧合证据发出上述通知。

101 对检控方提出的倾向证据和巧合证据的进一步限定

（1）本条仅适用于刑事程序，其适用为对第 97 条和第 98 条之补充。

（2）检控方提出的关于被告的倾向证据或者关于被告的巧合证据，不能用于反对被告，除非上述证据的证明价值严重超过了其可能给被告造成的任何损害后果。[34]

（3）本条并不适用于检控方为解释或者反驳被告提出的倾向证据而提出的倾向证据。

（4）本条并不适用于检控方为解释或者反驳被告提出的巧合证据而提出的巧合证据。

Part 3.7—Credibility

Division 1—Credibility evidence

101A Credibility evidence

Credibility evidence, in relation to a witness or other person, is evidence relevant to the credibility of the witness or person that:

(a) is relevant only because it affects the assessment of the credibility of the witness or person; or

(b) is relevant:

(i) because it affects the assessment of the credibility of the witness or person; and

(ii) for some other purpose for which it is not admissible, or cannot be used, because of a provision of Parts 3.2 to 3.6.

Note 1:   Sections 60 and 77 will not affect the application of paragraph (b), because they cannot apply to evidence that is yet to be admitted.

Note 2:   Section 101A was inserted as a response to the decision of the High Court of Australia in *Adam* The Queen (2001) 207 CLR 96.

Division 2—Credibility of witnesses

102 The credibility rule

Credibility evidence about a witness is not admissible.

Note 1:   Specific exceptions to the credibility rule are as follows:

• evidence adduced in cross–examination (sections 103 and 104);

• evidence in rebuttal of denials (section 106);

第 3.7 节—可信性

第 1 目—可信性证据

101A 可信性证据

就证人或者其他人而言，**可信性证据**是指与证人或者其他人的可信性有关的下列证据：

（a）仅仅因为它会影响对证人或者其他人的可信性的评估而具有相关性；或者

（b）因下列情况具有相关性：

（i）它会影响对证人或者其他人的可信性的评估；并且

（ii）因第 3.2 节至第 3.6 节之规定，出于某些其他目的而不可采，或者不能使用。【35】

注释 1：第 60 条和第 77 条将不会影响（b）的适用，因为它们不能适用于还未被采纳的证据。

注释 2：插入第 101A 条，是为了回应澳大利亚最高法院在 *Adam v The Queen*（2001）207 *CLR* 96 案件中的判决。

第 2 目—证人的可信性

102 可信性规则

关于证人可信性的证据不具有可采性。

注释 1：可信性规则的具体例外如下：

· 交叉询问中提出的证据（第 103 条和第 104 条）；

· 驳斥否认的证据（第 106 条）；

> * evidence to re–establish credibility (section 108);
>
> * evidence of persons with specialised knowledge (section 108C);
>
> * character of accused persons (section 110).
>
> Other provisions of this Act, or of other laws, may operate as further exceptions.
>
> Note 2: Sections 108A and 108B deal with the admission of credibility evidence about a person who has made a previous representation but who is not a witness.

103 Exception: cross–examination as to credibility

(1) The credibility rule does not apply to evidence adduced in cross–examination of a witness if the evidence could substantially affect the assessment of the credibility of the witness.

(2) Without limiting the matters to which the court may have regard for the purposes of subsection (1), it is to have regard to:

    (a) whether the evidence tends to prove that the witness knowingly or recklessly made a false representation when the witness was under an obligation to tell the truth; and

    (b) the period that has elapsed since the acts or events to which the evidence relates were done or occurred.

104 Further protections: cross–examination of accused

(1) This section applies only to credibility evidence in a criminal proceeding and so applies in addition to section 103.

(2) A defendant must not be cross–examined about a matter that is relevant to the assessment of the defendant's credibility, unless the court gives leave.

(3) Despite subsection (2), leave is not required for cross–examination by the prosecutor about whether the defendant:

·重建可信性的证据（第 108 条）；

·具有专门知识的人的证言（第 108C 条）；

·被指控者的品性（第 110 条）。

本法或者其他法律的其他规定，可能规定了进一步的例外。

注释 2：第 108A 条和第 108B 条就与作出了先前表述的但不是证人的人的可信性有关的证据的采纳问题作了规定。

103 例外：关于可信性的交叉询问

（1）在对证人进行交叉询问中提出的证据，如果该证据会严重影响对证人可信性的评估，则可信性规则不适用于该证据。[36]

（2）就（1）之目的而言，法院应当虑及的事项包括但是不限于：

（a）该证据是否倾向于证明证人在有义务说实话时故意或者过失作了不实表述；以及

（b）与该证据有关的行为或者事件做出或者发生后所经历的期间。

104 进一步保护：对被指控者的交叉询问

（1）本条仅适用于刑事程序中的可信性证据，其适用为对第 103 条之补充。

（2）不得就仅仅与被告的可信性有关的事项对被告进行交叉询问，除非法院许可。

（3）尽管有（2），公诉人就下列事项对被告进行交叉询问不需要得到许可：

Section 106

(a) is biased or has a motive to be untruthful; or

(b) is, or was, unable to be aware of or recall matters to which his or her evidence relates; or

(c) has made a prior inconsistent statement.

(4) Leave must not be given for cross–examination by the prosecutor under subsection (2) unless evidence adduced by the defendant has been admitted that:

(a) tends to prove that a witness called by the prosecutor has a tendency to be untruthful; and

(b) is relevant solely or mainly to the witness's credibility.

(5) A reference in subsection (4) to evidence does not include a reference to evidence of conduct in relation to:

(a) the events in relation to which the defendant is being prosecuted; or

(b) the investigation of the offence for which the defendant is being prosecuted.

(6) Leave is not to be given for cross–examination by another defendant unless:

(a) the evidence that the defendant to be cross–examined has given includes evidence adverse to the defendant seeking leave to cross–examine; and

(b) that evidence has been admitted.

106 Exception: rebutting denials by other evidence

(1) The credibility rule does not apply to evidence that is relevant to a witness's credibility and that is adduced otherwise than from the witness if:

(a) in cross–examination of the witness:

(i) the substance of the evidence was put to the witness; and

第 106 条

（a）被告是否具有偏见，或者有不诚实的动机；
或者

（b）被告是否不能或者曾经不能意识到或者回忆
起与其陈述有关的事项；或者

（c）被告是否作出过先前不一致陈述。

（4）不得许可公诉人根据（2）进行交叉询问，除非被
告提出的已经被采纳的证据：

（a）倾向于证明公诉人传唤的证人具有不诚实的
倾向；并且

（b）仅仅或者主要与证人的可信性有关。

（5）（4）所称证据，并不包括与下列情况有关的行为
证据：

（a）被告正在被检控的事件；或者

（b）对被告正在被检控的犯罪进行的调查。

（6）不得许可其他被告进行交叉询问，除非：

（a）被交叉询问的被告已经作出的证言包含有对
寻求得到交叉询问许可的被告不利的证据；
并且

（b）该证据已经被采纳。

106 例外：以其他证据对否认进行反驳

（1）在下列情况下，可信性规则并不适用于与证人的可
信性有关，且并非自证人提出的证据：

（a）在对证人的交叉询问中：

（i）已经向证人提示该证据之要旨；并且

(ii) the witness denied, or did not admit or agree to, the substance of the evidence; and

(b) the court gives leave to adduce the evidence.

(2) Leave under paragraph (1)(b) is not required if the evidence tends to prove that the witness:

(a) is biased or has a motive for being untruthful; or

(b) has been convicted of an offence, including an offence against the law of a foreign country; or

(c) has made a prior inconsistent statement; or

(d) is, or was, unable to be aware of matters to which his or her evidence relates; or

(e) has knowingly or recklessly made a false representation while under an obligation, imposed by or under an Australian law or a law of a foreign country, to tell the truth.

108 Exception: re–establishing credibility

(1) The credibility rule does not apply to evidence adduced in re–examination of a witness.

(3) The credibility rule does not apply to evidence of a prior consistent statement of a witness if:

(a) evidence of a prior inconsistent statement of the witness has been admitted; or

(b) it is or will be suggested (either expressly or by implication) that evidence given by the witness has been fabricated or re–constructed (whether deliberately or otherwise) or is the result of a suggestion;

and the court gives leave to adduce the evidence of the prior consistent statement.

（ii）证人否认、不承认或者不同意该证据的要旨；并且

（b）法院准许提出该证据。

（2）如果证据倾向于证明证人存在下列情况，则并不要求得到（1）（b）所规定的准许：

（a）具有偏见，或者有不诚实的动机；或者

（b）曾被判有罪，包括违反外国法律的犯罪；或者

（c）曾作出过先前不一致陈述；或者

（d）不能或者曾经不能意识到与其证言有关的事项；或者

（e）根据澳大利亚法律或者外国法律的规定，有如实陈述义务，但是因故意或者过失进行了不实表述。

108 例外：可信性的重建

（1）可信性规则并不适用于在对证人进行再询问时提出的证据。

（3）如果存在下列情况，并且法院许可提出证人先前一致陈述证据，则可信性规则并不适用于该先前一致陈述证据：

（a）证人的先前不一致陈述证据已经被采纳；或者

（b）有人提出或者将会提出（无论明示还是默示）证人所作证言系捏造或者已经被重构（无论是故意还是出于其他原因），或者是暗示的结果。

Division 3—Credibility of persons who are not witnesses

108A Admissibility of evidence of credibility of person who has made a previous representation

(1) If:

    (a) evidence of a previous representation has been admitted in a proceeding; and

    (b) the person who made the representation has not been called, and will not be called, to give evidence in the proceeding;

    credibility evidence about the person who made the representation is not admissible unless the evidence could substantially affect the assessment of the person's credibility.

(2) Without limiting the matters to which the court may have regard for the purposes of subsection (1), it is to have regard to:

    (a) whether the evidence tends to prove that the person who made the representation knowingly or recklessly made a false representation when the person was under an obligation to tell the truth; and

    (b) the period that elapsed between the doing of the acts or the occurrence of the events to which the representation related and the making of the representation.

108B Further protections: previous representations of an accused who is not a witness

(1) This section applies only in a criminal proceeding and so applies in addition to section 108A.

(2) If the person referred to in that section is a defendant, the credibility evidence is not admissible unless the court gives leave.

第 3 目—不是证人之人的可信性

108A 关于曾作出先前表述之人的可信性证据的可采性

（1）如果存在下列情况，关于作出先前表述之人的可信性证据不具有可采性，除非该证据能够严重影响到对该某人可信性的评估：

（a）该先前表述证据在程序中已经被采纳；并且

（b）作出该表述的人没有被传唤，也将不会被传唤在程序中作证。[37]

（2）就（1）之目的而言，法院应当考虑的事项包括但是不限于：

（a）该证据是否倾向于证明作出该先前表述之人在有如实陈述义务时，故意或者过失作了不实表述；并且

（b）与该表述有关的行为或者事件做出或者发生后到作出该表述时所经历的期间。

108B 进一步保护：不是证人的被指控者的先前表述

（1）本条仅适用于刑事程序，其适用为对第 108A 条之补充。

（2）如果该条所称之人是被告，可信性证据不可采，除非法院许可。

(3) Despite subsection (2), leave is not required if the evidence is about whether the defendant:

  (a) is biased or has a motive to be untruthful; or

  (b) is, or was, unable to be aware of or recall matters to which his or her previous representation relates; or

  (c) has made a prior inconsistent statement.

(4) The prosecution must not be given leave under subsection (2) unless evidence adduced by the defendant has been admitted that:

  (a) tends to prove that a witness called by the prosecution has a tendency to be untruthful; and

  (b) is relevant solely or mainly to the witness's credibility.

(5) A reference in subsection (4) to evidence does not include a reference to evidence of conduct in relation to:

  (a) the events in relation to which the defendant is being prosecuted; or

  (b) the investigation of the offence for which the defendant is being prosecuted.

(6) Another defendant must not be given leave under subsection (2) unless the previous representation of the defendant that has been admitted includes evidence adverse to the defendant seeking leave.

Division 4—Persons with specialised knowledge

108C Exception: evidence of persons with specialised knowledge

(1) The credibility rule does not apply to evidence given by a person concerning the credibility of another witness if:

  (a) the person has specialised knowledge based on the person's training, study or experience; and

（3）尽管有（2），如果证据所涉及的是被告是否有下列情况，则不需要得到许可：

（a）被告是否具有偏见，或者有不诚实的动机；或者

（b）被告是否不能或者曾经不能意识到或者回忆起与其先前陈述有关的事项；或者

（c）被告是否作出过先前不一致陈述。

（4）不得根据（2）对检控方作出许可，除非已经被采纳的被告所提出的证据：

（a）倾向于证明检控方传唤的证人具有不诚实倾向；并且

（b）仅仅或者主要与证人的可信性相关。

（5）（4）所称证据并不包括关于下列情况的行为证据：

（a）被告正在受到检控的事件；或者

（b）对被告正在受到检控的犯罪的调查。

（6）不得根据（2）对其他被告作出许可，除非已经被采纳的被告的先前表述包括有不利于寻求准许的被告的证据。

第 4 目—有专门知识的人

108C 例外：有专门知识的人的证言

（1）在下列情况下，可信性规则并不适用于某人就另一证人的可信性所作的证言：

（a）该某人因其训练、学习或者经验而具有专门知识；并且

(b) the evidence is evidence of an opinion of the person that:

   (i) is wholly or substantially based on that knowledge; and

   (ii) could substantially affect the assessment of the credibility of a witness; and

(c) the court gives leave to adduce the evidence.

(2) To avoid doubt, and without limiting subsection (1):

(a) a reference in that subsection to specialised knowledge includes a reference to specialised knowledge of child development and child behaviour (including specialised knowledge of the impact of sexual abuse on children and their behaviour during and following the abuse); and

(b) a reference in that subsection to an opinion of a person includes, if the person has specialised knowledge of that kind, a reference to an opinion relating to either or both of the following:

   (i) the development and behaviour of children generally;

   (ii) the development and behaviour of children who have been victims of sexual offences, or offences similar to sexual offences.

Part 3.8—Character

109 Application

This Part applies only in a criminal proceeding.

110 Evidence about character of accused persons

(1) The hearsay rule, the opinion rule, the tendency rule and the credibility rule do not apply to evidence adduced by a defendant to prove (directly or by implication) that the defendant is, either generally or in a particular respect, a

（b）该证言是该某人作出的属下列情况的意见证据：

（i）完全或者主要基于该知识；并且

（ii）能够对证人可信性评估产生重大影响；并且

（c）法院准许提出该证言。

（2）为避免疑义，且在并不限制（1）的情况下：

（a）该款所称专门知识，包括关于儿童成长和儿童行为的专门知识（包括关于性侵犯对儿童的影响，以及对性侵犯期间和之后儿童成长和行为的影响的专门知识）；以及

（b）在某人具有上述专门知识的情况下，该款所称某人的意见，包括与下列二者或者二者之一有关的意见：

（i）一般性的儿童成长和行为；

（ii）作为性侵犯或者与性侵犯类似的犯罪的受害人的成长和行为。

第 3.8 节—品性

109 适用

本节仅适用于刑事程序。

110 关于被指控者的品性的证据

（1）传闻规则、意见规则、倾向规则和可信性规则并不适用于被告提出的用于证明（直接或者暗示）被告在总体上或者具体方面是一个具有良好品性之人

Section 112

person of good character.

(2) If evidence adduced to prove (directly or by implication) that a defendant is generally a person of good character has been admitted, the hearsay rule, the opinion rule, the tendency rule and the credibility rule do not apply to evidence adduced to prove (directly or by implication) that the defendant is not generally a person of good character.

(3) If evidence adduced to prove (directly or by implication) that a defendant is a person of good character in a particular respect has been admitted, the hearsay rule, the opinion rule, the tendency rule and the credibility rule do not apply to evidence adduced to prove (directly or by implication) that the defendant is not a person of good character in that respect.

111 Evidence about character of co-accused

(1) The hearsay rule and the tendency rule do not apply to evidence of a defendant's character if:

    (a) the evidence is evidence of an opinion about the defendant adduced by another defendant; and

    (b) the person whose opinion it is has specialised knowledge based on the person's training, study or experience; and

    (c) the opinion is wholly or substantially based on that knowledge.

(2) If such evidence has been admitted, the hearsay rule, the opinion rule and the tendency rule do not apply to evidence adduced to prove that that evidence should not be accepted.

112 Leave required to cross-examine about character of accused or co-accused

A defendant must not be cross-examined about matters

的证据。[38]

（2）如果提出用于证明（直接或者暗示）被告总体上是一个具有良好品性的人的证据被采纳了，传闻规则、意见规则、倾向规则和可信性规则并不适用于提出的用于证明（直接或者暗示）被告不是一个总体上具有良好品性的人的证据。

（3）如果提出用于证明（直接或者暗示）被告在具体方面是一个具有良好品性的人的证据被采纳了，传闻规则、意见规则、倾向规则和可信性规则并不适用于提出的用于证明（直接或者暗示）被告不是一个在该方面具有良好品性的人的证据。

111 关于共同被指控者的品性的证据

（1）在下列情况下，传闻规则和倾向规则并不适用于关于某被告的品性的证据：

（a）该证据是其他被告提出的关于该某被告的意见证据；并且

（b）表达该意见的人基于其训练、学习或者经验而拥有专门知识；并且

（c）该意见完全或者主要基于该知识。[39]

（2）如果上述证据已经被采纳，传闻规则、意见规则和倾向规则并不适用于提出用于证明该证据不应当被采纳的证据。

112 就被指控者或者共同被指控者的品性进行交叉询问需要得到许可

不得就起因于本节所称证据的事项，对被告进行交叉询

arising out of evidence of a kind referred to in this Part unless the court gives leave.

Part 3.9—Identification evidence

Note: Identification evidence is defined in the Dictionary.

113 Application of Part

This Part applies only in a criminal proceeding.

114 Exclusion of visual identification evidence

(1) In this section:

visual identification evidence means identification evidence relating to an identification based wholly or partly on what a person saw but does not include picture identification evidence.

(2) Visual identification evidence adduced by the prosecutor is not admissible unless:

(a) an identification parade that included the defendant was held before the identification was made; or

(b) it would not have been reasonable to have held such a parade; or

(c) the defendant refused to take part in such a parade;

and the identification was made without the person who made it having been intentionally influenced to identify the defendant.

(3) Without limiting the matters that may be taken into account by the court in determining whether it was reasonable to hold an identification parade, it is to take into account:

(a) the kind of offence, and the gravity of the offence, concerned; and

问，除非法院许可。

第 3.9 节—辨认证据

注释：辨认证据 的定义见《术语》。

113 本节的适用

本节仅适用于刑事程序。

114 视像辨认证据的排除

（1）在本条中：

视像辨认证据是指与完全或者部分根据一个人所见而进行的辨认有关的辨认证据，但并不包括图片辨认证据。

（2）公诉人提出的视像辨认证据不具有可采性，除非存在下列情况，并且在进行辨认时，进行辨认的人没有受到要去指认被告的故意影响：

（a）在辨认之前，进行了包括被告在内的排队辨认；或者

（b）进行这样的排队辨认本不合理；或者

（c）被告拒绝参加上述排队辨认。[40]

（3）法院在确定进行排队辨认是否合理时，应当虑及的事项包括但是不限于：

（a）有关犯罪的种类和严重性；以及

(b) the importance of the evidence; and

(c) the practicality of holding an identification parade having regard, among other things:

    (i) if the defendant failed to cooperate in the conduct of the parade—to the manner and extent of, and the reason (if any) for, the failure; and

    (ii) in any case—to whether the identification was made at or about the time of the commission of the offence; and

(d) the appropriateness of holding an identification parade having regard, among other things, to the relationship (if any) between the defendant and the person who made the identification.

(4) It is presumed that it would not have been reasonable to have held an identification parade if it would have been unfair to the defendant for such a parade to have been held.

(5) If:

(a) the defendant refused to take part in an identification parade unless an Australian legal practitioner or legal counsel acting for the defendant, or another person chosen by the defendant, was present while it was being held; and

(b) there were, at the time when the parade was to have been conducted, reasonable grounds to believe that it was not reasonably practicable for such an Australian legal practitioner or legal counsel or person to be present;

it is presumed that it would not have been reasonable to have held an identification parade at that time.

(6) In determining whether it was reasonable to have held an identification parade, the court is not to take into account the availability of pictures or photographs that could be

第 114 条

（b）证据的重要性；以及

（c）除了其他因素以外，虑及下列情况时，进行
排队辨认的可行性：

（i）在被告未能在排队辨认中合作的情况下，
该未能合作的方式、范围以及原因（如果
有的话）；以及

（ii）在任何情况下，辨认是否是在犯罪当时或
者不久后进行的；以及

（d）除了其他因素以外，虑及被告与进行辨认的
人的关系（如果有的话）时，进行排队辨认
的适当性。

（4）如果对于被告而言，进行的上述排队辨认本不公平，
则应当推定进行这样的排队辨认不合理。

（5）在下列情况下，应当推定在当时进行这样的排队辨
认本不合理：

（a）被告拒绝参加排队辨认，除非代理被告的澳
大利亚法律执业者、法律顾问或者被告选定
的其他人在进行排队辨认时在场；并且

（b）在进行排队辨认时，有合理根据认为上述澳
大利亚律师、法律顾问或者其他人在场具有
合理的不可行性。

（6）在确定进行排队辨认是否合理时，法院不得考
虑本可以在辨认中使用的图片或者照片的可得

used in making identifications.

115 Exclusion of evidence of identification by pictures

(1) In this section:

picture identification evidence means identification evidence relating to an identification made wholly or partly by the person who made the identification examining pictures kept for the use of police officers.

(2) Picture identification evidence adduced by the prosecutor is not admissible if the pictures examined suggest that they are pictures of persons in police custody.

(3) Subject to subsection (4), picture identification evidence adduced by the prosecutor is not admissible if:

    (a) when the pictures were examined, the defendant was in the custody of a police officer of the police force investigating the commission of the offence with which the defendant has been charged; and

    (b) the picture of the defendant that was examined was made before the defendant was taken into that police custody.

(4) Subsection (3) does not apply if:

    (a) the defendant's appearance had changed significantly between the time when the offence was committed and the time when the defendant was taken into that custody; or

    (b) it was not reasonably practicable to make a picture of the defendant after the defendant was taken into that custody.

(5) Picture identification evidence adduced by the prosecutor is not admissible if, when the pictures were examined, the defendant was in the custody of a police officer of the police force investigating the commission of the offence with which the defendant has been charged, unless:

性。【41】

115 图片辨认证据的排除

（1）在本条中：

图片辨认证据是指与进行辨认的人通过完全或者部分检视保存供警察使用的图片而进行的辨认有关的辨认证据。

（2）如果公诉人提出的被检视的图片表明，它们是处于警方监禁中的人的图片，则该图片辨认证据不具有可采性。

（3）在遵守（4）的情况下，如果存在下列情况，公诉人提出的图片辨认证据不具有可采性：

（a）在对图片检视时，被告处于对被告被控犯罪进行调查的警察机构的监禁中；并且

（b）被检视的被告的图片是在被告被警方监禁前制作的。

（4）在下列情况下，（3）并不适用：

（a）被告在犯罪时的外貌与被采取监禁措施时的外貌相比，已经发生了重大变化；或者

（b）在被告被采取监禁措施后制作被告的图片，具有合理的不可行性。

（5）如果在图片被检视时，被告处于对被告被控犯罪进行调查的警察机构警察的监禁中，则公诉人提出的图片辨认证据不具有可采性，除非：

      (a) the defendant refused to take part in an identification parade; or

      (b) the defendant's appearance had changed significantly between the time when the offence was committed and the time when the defendant was taken into that custody; or

      (c) it would not have been reasonable to have held an identification parade that included the defendant.

(6) Subsections 114(3), (4), (5) and (6) apply in determining, for the purposes of paragraph (5)(c) of this section, whether it would have been reasonable to have held an identification parade.

(7) If picture identification evidence adduced by the prosecutor is admitted into evidence, the judge must, on the request of the defendant:

      (a) if the picture of the defendant was made after the defendant was taken into that custody—inform the jury that the picture was made after the defendant was taken into that custody; or

      (b) otherwise—warn the jury that they must not assume that the defendant has a criminal record or has previously been charged with an offence.

Note: Sections 116 and 165 also deal with warnings about identification evidence.

(8) This section does not render inadmissible picture identification evidence adduced by the prosecutor that contradicts or qualifies picture identification evidence adduced by the defendant.

(9) This section applies in addition to section 114.

(10) In this section:

      (a) a reference to a picture includes a reference to a

第 115 条

　　　　（a）被告拒绝参加排队辨认；或者

　　　　（b）被告在犯罪时的外貌与被采取监禁措施时的
　　　　　　外貌相比，已经发生了重大变化；或者

　　　　（c）在当时进行包括被告在内的排队辨认，具有
　　　　　　合理的不可行性。

（6）就本条（5）（c）之目的而言，114（3）、（4）、
　　　（5）和（6）适用于确定当时进行排队辨认是否
　　合理。

（7）如果公诉人提出的图片辨认证据被采纳为证据，根
　　　据被告的请求，法官：

　　　　（a）在被告的图片是在被告被监禁后制作的情况
　　　　　　下，必须告知陪审团该图片是在被告被监禁
　　　　　　后制作的；或者

　　　　（b）在其他情况下，必须警告陪审团他们不得
　　　　　　认为被告有刑事犯罪记录，或者以前曾受
　　　　　　过犯罪指控。

　　　注释：第 116 条和第 165 条也规定了关于辨认证据的警告
　　　　　问题。

（8）就公诉人为反驳或者限定被告提出的图片辨认证据
　　　而提出的图片辨认证据而言，本条并不导致其不可
　　采。

（9）本条之适用，是对第 114 条的补充。

（10）在本条中：

　　　　（a）所称图片包括照片；并且

photograph; and

(b) a reference to making a picture includes a reference to taking a photograph.

116 Directions to jury

(1) If identification evidence has been admitted, the judge is to inform the jury:

(a) that there is a special need for caution before accepting identification evidence; and

(b) of the reasons for that need for caution, both generally and in the circumstances of the case.

(2) It is not necessary that a particular form of words be used in so informing the jury.

Part 3.10—Privileges

Division 1—Client legal privilege

117 Definitions

(1) In this Division:

client includes the following:

(a) a person or body who engages a lawyer to provide legal services or who employs a lawyer (including under a contract of service);

(b) an employee or agent of a client;

(c) an employer of a lawyer if the employer is:

(i) the Commonwealth or a State or Territory; or

(ii) a body established by a law of the Commonwealth or a State or Territory;

(d) if, under a law of a State or Territory relating to persons

（b）所称制作图片包括进行照相。

116 对陪审团的指示

（1）如果辨认证据已经被采纳，法官应当告知陪审团：

（a）在接受辨认证据之前，特别需要谨慎；并且

（b）需要谨慎的一般性理由以及个案中的理由。

（2）在如此告知陪审团时，使用具体形式的词语并非必需。

第 3.10 节—特免权

第 1 目—委托人法律建议特免权

117 定义

（1）在本目中：

委托人包括下列人员：

（a）聘请律师提供法律服务或者雇佣律师的自然人或者机构（包括依服务合同进行的雇佣）；

（b）委托人的雇员或者代理人；

（c）下列情况下的律师的雇主：

（i）联邦、州或者领地；或者

（ii）根据联邦、州或者领地法律设立的机构；

（d）在根据有关精神不健全之人的州法律或者领

of unsound mind, a manager, committee or person (however described) is for the time being acting in respect of the person, estate or property of a client—a manager, committee or person so acting;

(e) if a client has died—a personal representative of the client;

(f) a successor to the rights and obligations of a client, being rights and obligations in respect of which a confidential communication was made.

confidential communication means a communication made in such circumstances that, when it was made:

(a) the person who made it; or

(b) the person to whom it was made;

was under an express or implied obligation not to disclose its contents, whether or not the obligation arises under law.

confidential document means a document prepared in such circumstances that, when it was prepared:

(a) the person who prepared it; or

(b) the person for whom it was prepared;

was under an express or implied obligation not to disclose its contents, whether or not the obligation arises under law.

lawyer means:

(a) an Australian lawyer; and

(b) an Australian–registered foreign lawyer; and

(c) an overseas–registered foreign lawyer or a natural person who, under the law of a foreign country, is permitted to engage in legal practice in that country; and

(d) an employee or agent of a lawyer referred to in paragraph (a), (b) or (c).

party includes the following:

(a) an employee or agent of a party;

地法律，管理人、委员会或者个人（无论是如何规定的）目前正在就委托人的人身或者财产进行代理的情况下，从事该代理活动的管理人、委员会或者个人；

(e) 委托人已经死亡情况下的委托人的个人代表；

(f) 委托人权利和义务（就这些权利和义务发生了秘密交流）的继承人。

秘密交流是指下列情况下进行的交流，即在该交流进行时，下列人员负有不披露该交流的内容之明示或者默示的义务，无论该义务是否为法律义务：

(a) 作出交流的人；或者

(b) 该交流所针对的人。

秘密文件是指下列情况下准备的文件，即在制作该文件时，下列人员负有不披露该文件的内容之明示或者默示的义务，无论该义务是否为法律义务：

(a) 制作该文件的人；或者

(b) 制作该文件所针对的人。

律师是指：

(a) 澳大利亚律师；以及

(b) 在澳大利亚注册的外国律师；以及

(c) 根据外国法律，准许在该国从事法律业务的在海外注册的外国律师或者自然人；以及

(d) (a)、(b) 和 (c) 所称律师的雇员或者代理人

当事人包括下列人员：

(a) 当事人的雇员或者代理人；

(b) if, under a law of a State or Territory relating to persons of unsound mind, a manager, committee or person (however described) is for the time being acting in respect of the person, estate or property of a party—a manager, committee or person so acting;

(c) if a party has died—a personal representative of the party;

(d) a successor to the rights and obligations of a party, being rights and obligations in respect of which a confidential communication was made.

(2) A reference in this Division to the commission of an act includes a reference to a failure to act.

118 Legal advice

Evidence is not to be adduced if, on objection by a client, the court finds that adducing the evidence would result in disclosure of:

(a) a confidential communication made between the client and a lawyer; or

(b) a confidential communication made between 2 or more lawyers acting for the client; or

(c) the contents of a confidential document (whether delivered or not) prepared by the client, lawyer or another person;

for the dominant purpose of the lawyer, or one or more of the lawyers, providing legal advice to the client.

119 Litigation

Evidence is not to be adduced if, on objection by a client, the court finds that adducing the evidence would result in disclosure of:

（b）在根据有关精神不健全之人的州法律或者领
地法律，管理人、委员会或者个人（无论是
如何规定的）目前正在就委托人的人身或者
财产进行代理的情况下，从事该代理活动的
管理人、委员会或者个人；

（c）委托人已经死亡情况下的委托人的个人代表；

（d）委托人权利和义务（就这些权利和义务发生
了秘密交流）的继承人。

（2）本目所称作为，包括不作为。

118 法律建议

如果根据委托人的异议，法院判定提出证据将会导致披
露下列因为一个或者多个律师向委托人提供法律建议之
主要目的而进行的交流或者制作的文件的内容，则不得
提出该证据：

（a）委托人与律师之间的秘密交流；或者

（b）为委托人而行动的 2 个或者 2 个以上律师之
间的秘密交流；或者

（c）委托人、律师或者他人所制作的秘密文件的
内容（无论是否已经交发）。[42]

119 诉讼

对于下列秘密交流或者文件而言，如果进行该交流或者
文件制作活动的主要目的，是为了使委托人能够就其是、
可能是、已经是或者可能已经是当事人的澳大利亚或者
海外程序（包括法院前的程序），或者预期的或者未决

    (a) a confidential communication between the client and another person, or between a lawyer acting for the client and another person, that was made; or

    (b) the contents of a confidential document (whether delivered or not) that was prepared;

for the dominant purpose of the client being provided with professional legal services relating to an Australian or overseas proceeding (including the proceeding before the court), or an anticipated or pending Australian or overseas proceeding, in which the client is or may be, or was or might have been, a party.

120 Unrepresented parties

(1) Evidence is not to be adduced if, on objection by a party who is not represented in the proceeding by a lawyer, the court finds that adducing the evidence would result in disclosure of:

    (a) a confidential communication between the party and another person; or

    (b) the contents of a confidential document (whether delivered or not) that was prepared, either by or at the direction or request of, the party;

for the dominant purpose of preparing for or conducting the proceeding.

121 Loss of client legal privilege: generally

(1) This Division does not prevent the adducing of evidence relevant to a question concerning the intentions, or competence in law, of a client or party who has died.

(2) This Division does not prevent the adducing of evidence if,

第 121 条

的澳大利亚或者海外程序得到职业法律服务，则在委托人提出反对的情况下，如果法院认定提出有关证据将导致披露下列交流或者文件的内容，则不得提出该有关证据：

（a）委托人与其他人，或者代理委托人的律师与其他人进行的秘密交流；或者

（b）所制作的秘密文件的内容（无论是否已经交发）。【43】

120 没有代理律师的当事人

（1）对于下列秘密交流或者文件的内容而言，如果进行该交流或者文件制作活动的主要目的是为了准备或者进行程序活动，则在该程序中无律师代理的当事人提出反对的情况下，如果法院认为提出有关证据将导致披露下列秘密交流或者文件的内容，则该有关证据不得提出：

（a）该当事人与其他人员的秘密交流；或者

（b）根据该当事人的指示或者要求所制作的秘密文件（无论是否已经提交）的内容。

121 委托人法律建议特免权的丧失：一般规定

（1）本目并不禁止提出与死亡的委托人或者当事人的意图或者法律上的能力问题有关的证据。

（2）在如果不提出某证据，将会或者可以合理地预期将

were the evidence not adduced, the court would be prevented, or it could reasonably be expected that the court would be prevented, from enforcing an order of an Australian court.

(3) This Division does not prevent the adducing of evidence of a communication or document that affects a right of a person.

122 Loss of client legal privilege: consent and related matters

(1) This Division does not prevent the adducing of evidence given with the consent of the client or party concerned.

(2) Subject to subsection (5), this Division does not prevent the adducing of evidence if the client or party concerned has acted in a way that is inconsistent with the client or party objecting to the adducing of the evidence because it would result in a disclosure of a kind referred to in section 118, 119 or 120.

(3) Without limiting subsection (2), a client or party is taken to have so acted if:

(a) the client or party knowingly and voluntarily disclosed the substance of the evidence to another person; or

(b) the substance of the evidence has been disclosed with the express or implied consent of the client or party.

(4) The reference in paragraph (3)(a) to a knowing and voluntary disclosure does not include a reference to a disclosure by a person who was, at the time of the disclosure, an employee or agent of the client or party or of a lawyer of the client or party unless the employee or agent was authorised by the client, party or lawyer to make the disclosure.

(5) A client or party is not taken to have acted in a manner inconsistent with the client or party objecting to the adducing of the evidence merely because:

(a) the substance of the evidence has been disclosed:

会妨害法院执行澳大利亚法院的命令的情况下，本目并不禁止提出该证据。

（3）本目并不禁止提出关于影响某人的权利的交流或者书证的证据。

122 委托人法律建议特免权的丧失：同意与相关事项

（1）本目并不禁止提出经委托人或者有关当事人同意的证据。

（2）在遵守（5）的情况下，如果该委托人或者有关当事人的行为方式将导致第 118 条、第 119 条或者第 120 条所称的披露，而与其反对提出证据不一致，则本目并不禁止提出该证据。

（3）在不限制（2）的情况下，委托人或者当事人的下列行为被视为上述行为：

（a）委托人或者当事人故意或者自愿向他人披露证据之要旨；或者

（b）证据之要旨的披露，已经得到委托人或者当事人的明示或者默示同意。

（4）（3）（a）所称的故意或者自愿披露，并不包括披露当时是委托人、当事人或者他们的律师的雇员或者代理人的人进行的披露，除非该雇员或者代理人经委托人、当事人或者律师授权进行该披露。

（5）委托人或者当事人并不仅仅因为下列情况，而被视为其行为方式与其反对提出证据不一致：

（a）证据要旨的披露：

(i) in the course of making a confidential communication or preparing a confidential document; or

(ii) as a result of duress or deception; or

(iii) under compulsion of law; or

(iv) if the client or party is a body established by, or a person holding an office under, an Australian law— to the Minister, or the Minister of the Commonwealth, the State or Territory, administering the law, or part of the law, under which the body is established or the office is held; or

(b) of a disclosure by a client to another person if the disclosure concerns a matter in relation to which the same lawyer is providing, or is to provide, professional legal services to both the client and the other person; or

(c) of a disclosure to a person with whom the client or party had, at the time of the disclosure, a common interest relating to the proceeding or an anticipated or pending proceeding in an Australian court or a foreign court.

(6) This Division does not prevent the adducing of evidence of a document that a witness has used to try to revive the witness's memory about a fact or opinion or has used as mentioned in section 32 (Attempts to revive memory in court) or 33 (Evidence given by police officers).

123 Loss of client legal privilege: defendants

In a criminal proceeding, this Division does not prevent a defendant from adducing evidence unless it is evidence of:

(a) a confidential communication made between an

第 123 条

（ⅰ）发生在秘密交流或者制作秘密文件的过程中；或者

（ⅱ）是胁迫或者欺骗的结果；或者

（ⅲ）出于法律的强制；或者

（ⅳ）在委托人或者当事人是依照澳大利亚法律设立的机构，或者是依照澳大利亚法律居于某公职的人的情况下，是对执行该机构得以设立或者该公职得以设立的法律或者部分法律的部长或者联邦、州或者领地的部长所进行的披露；或者

（b）因为涉及同一律师正在为或者将要为委托人及他人提供职业法律服务的事项，而由委托人对该他人进行的披露；或者

（c）因为委托人或者当事人在进行披露之时，与某人就澳大利亚法院或者外国法院的程序、预期程序或者未决程序具有共同利益，而对该某人进行的披露。

（6）本目并不禁止引入证人已用于试图唤醒其关于某事实或者意见之记忆的书证，或者已用于第 32 条（试图当庭唤醒记忆）、第 33 条（警察作证）所提及活动的书证。

123 法律建议特免权的丧失：被告

在刑事程序中，本目并不禁止被告提出证据，除非该证据是关于下列情况的证据：

（a）关联被告与代理该关联被告的律师进行的

associated defendant and a lawyer acting for that person in connection with the prosecution of that person; or

(b) the contents of a confidential document prepared by an associated defendant or by a lawyer acting for that person in connection with the prosecution of that person.

Note: *Associated defendant* is defined in the Dictionary.

124 Loss of client legal privilege: joint clients

(1) This section only applies to a civil proceeding in connection with which 2 or more parties have, before the commencement of the proceeding, jointly retained a lawyer in relation to the same matter.

(2) This Division does not prevent one of those parties from adducing evidence of:

(a) a communication made by any one of them to the lawyer; or

(b) the contents of a confidential document prepared by or at the direction or request of any one of them;

in connection with that matter.

125 Loss of client legal privilege: misconduct

(1) This Division does not prevent the adducing of evidence of:

(a) a communication made or the contents of a document prepared by a client or lawyer (or both), or a party who is not represented in the proceeding by a lawyer, in furtherance of the commission of a fraud or an offence or the commission of an act that renders a person liable to a civil penalty; or

(b) a communication or the contents of a document that the client or lawyer (or both), or the party, knew or ought

关于对该关联被告的检控的秘密交流；或
者

（b）关联被告或者代理该关联被告的律师制作的
关于对该被告的检控的秘密文件的内容。

注释：**关联被告**的定义见《术语》。

124 委托人法律建议特免权的丧失：共同委托人

（1）本条仅适用于 2 名或者 2 名以上当事人在程序开始
之前，就同一事项已共同聘请同一律师的民事程
序。

（2）本目并不禁止这些当事人之一提出有关下列事项的
证据：

（a）其中任一当事人同该律师进行的与该事项有
关的交流；或者

（b）其中任一当事人制作的或者根据其中任一当
事人的指示或者请求制作的与该事项有关的
秘密文件的内容。

125 委托人法律建议特免权的丧失：不端行为

（1）本目并不禁止提出关于下列事项的证据：

（a）委托人、律师（或者二者）或者在程序中没
有代理律师的当事人，为促进欺诈、犯罪或
者致使某人承担民事处罚之作为的实施，而
进行的交流或者制作的文件的内容；或者

（b）委托人、律师（或者二者）或者当事人知道

reasonably to have known was made or prepared in furtherance of a deliberate abuse of a power.

(2) For the purposes of this section, if the commission of the fraud, offence or act, or the abuse of power, is a fact in issue and there are reasonable grounds for finding that:

(a) the fraud, offence or act, or the abuse of power, was committed; and

(b) a communication was made or document prepared in furtherance of the commission of the fraud, offence or act or the abuse of power;

the court may find that the communication was so made or the document so prepared.

(3) In this section:

power means a power conferred by or under an Australian law.

126 Loss of client legal privilege: related communications and documents

If, because of the application of section 121, 122, 123, 124 or 125, this Division does not prevent the adducing of evidence of a communication or the contents of a document, those sections do not prevent the adducing of evidence of another communication or document if it is reasonably necessary to enable a proper understanding of the communication or document.

Note:

Example: A lawyer advises his client to understate her income for the previous year to evade taxation because of her potential tax liability "as set out in my previous letter to you dated 11 August 1994". In proceedings against the taxpayer for tax evasion, evidence of the contents of the letter dated 11 August 1994 may be admissible (even if that letter would

或者合理地应当已经知道为促进故意滥用权
力而进行的交流或者制作的文件的内容。

（2）就本条目的而言，如果欺诈、犯罪、作为或者权力
滥用的实施系争议事实，并且有合理的理由认定下
列情况，则法院可以判定进行了上述交流或者制作
了上述文件：

（a）已经实施了该欺诈、犯罪、作为或者权力滥
用；并且

（b）为促进该欺诈、犯罪、作为或者权力滥用的
实施，进行了某交流或者制作了某文件。

（3）在本条中：

权力是指澳大利亚法律所赋予或者根据澳大利亚法
律享有的权力。

126 委托人法律建议特免权的丧失：相关的交流和书证

在因适用本法第121条、第122条、第123条、第124
条或者第125条，本目并不禁止提出关于某交流或者书
证内容的证据的情况下，如果为适当理解该交流或者书
证所合理必需，则上述条文并不禁止提出关于另一交流
或者书证的证据。

注释：

示例：律师建议其委托人瞒报上一年度收入以逃税，因为
该委托人可能的纳税责任"列明于我以前给你的日
期为1994年8月11日的信函中"了。在因逃税而
对该纳税人提起的程序中，关于该日期为1994年8
月11日的信函的内容的证据可以被采纳（即使该信
函本来受特免权保护），以便对第二封信作出更适

otherwise be privileged) to enable a proper understanding of
the second letter.

Division 1A—Journalists' privilege

126G Definitions

(1) In this Division:

informant means a person who gives information to a
journalist in the normal course of the journalist's work in the
expectation that the information may be published in a news
medium.

journalist means a person who is engaged and active in the
publication of news and who may be given information by
an informant in the expectation that the information may
be published in a news medium.

news medium means any medium for the dissemination to the
public or a section of the public of news and observations on news.

126H Protection of journalists' sources

(1) If a journalist has promised an informant not to disclose
the informant's identity, neither the journalist nor his or
her employer is compellable to answer any question or
produce any document that would disclose the identity of
the informant or enable that identity to be ascertained.

(2) The court may, on the application of a party, order that
subsection (1) is not to apply if it is satisfied that, having
regard to the issues to be determined in that proceeding, the
public interest in the disclosure of evidence of the identity
of the informant outweighs:

(a) any likely adverse effect of the disclosure on the
informant or any other person; and

当的理解。

第 1A 目—记者特免权

126G 定义

（1）在本目中：

报信人是指在记者的通常工作中向其提供信息，期待新闻媒体公布该信息的人。

记者是指从事新闻公布活动，报信人向其提供信息，期待新闻媒体公布该信息的人。

新闻媒体是指将新闻和新闻评论传播给公众或者某部分公众的任何媒体。

126H 保护记者的信息来源

（1）如果记者曾向报信人承诺不披露报信人的身份，则就记者及其雇主而言，均不得被强制来回答将披露报信人的身份或者使该身份被确知的提问，或者出示将披露报信人的身份或者使该身份被确知的书证。

（2）如果法院确信，虑及该程序中所要确定的问题，披露报信人身份证据的公共利益超过了下列情况，则根据当事人的申请，法院可以命令（1）并不适用：

（a）披露对报信人或者任何其他人的可能不利影响；以及

       (h) the public interest in the communication of facts and opinion to the public by the news media and, accordingly also, in the ability of the news media to access sources of facts.

  (3) An order under subsection (2) may be made subject to such terms and conditions (if any) as the court thinks fit.

Division 2—Other privileges

127 Religious confessions

  (1) A person who is or was a member of the clergy of any church or religious denomination is entitled to refuse to divulge that a religious confession was made, or the contents of a religious confession made, to the person when a member of the clergy.

  (2) Subsection (1) does not apply if the communication involved in the religious confession was made for a criminal purpose.

  (3) This section applies even if an Act provides:

       (a) that the rules of evidence do not apply or that a person or body is not bound by the rules of evidence; or

       (b) that a person is not excused from answering any question or producing any document or other thing on the ground of privilege or any other ground.

  (4) In this section:

religious confession means a confession made by a person to a member of the clergy in the member's professional capacity according to the ritual of the church or religious denomination concerned.

128 Privilege in respect of self-incrimination in other proceedings

  (1) This section applies if a witness objects to giving particular evidence, or evidence on a particular matter, on the ground

（b）通过新闻媒体将事实和意见传播给公众所具

有的公共利益，以及与此相应的新闻媒体获

得事实来源的能力所具有的公共利益。

（3）根据（2）作出的命令，可以受制于法院认为适当

的条件（如果有的话）。

第 2 目—其他特免权

127 宗教自白

（1）身为或者曾为任何教堂或者教派之神职人员的人

员，有权拒绝披露在该某人是神职人员之时，有人

曾向其作出宗教自白，或者该宗教自白的内容。【44】

（2）如果宗教自白中所涉及的交流是为犯罪目的所作出

的，则（1）并不适用。

（3）即使某部法律规定了下列事项，本条仍然适用：

（a）证据规则并不适用或者某人或者某机构不受

证据规则约束；或者

（b）某人不得基于特免权或者任何其他理由免于

回答任何问题、出示任何文件或者其他物品。

（4）在本条中：

宗教自白是指某人根据有关教堂或者教派之仪轨向

以职业身份出现的神职人员所作的自白。

128 其他程序中的反对被迫自我归罪特免权

（1）在证人反对作出具体证言或者关于具体事项的证言，

是因为该证言可能倾向于证明该证人存在下列情

that the evidence may tend to prove that the witness:

(a) has committed an offence against or arising under an Australian law or a law of a foreign country; or

(b) is liable to a civil penalty.

(2) The court must determine whether or not there are reasonable grounds for the objection.

(3) If the court determines that there are reasonable grounds for the objection, the court is to inform the witness:

(a) that the witness need not give the evidence unless required by the court to do so under subsection (4); and

(b) that the court will give a certificate under this section if:

(i) the witness willingly gives the evidence without being required to do so under subsection (4); or

(ii) the witness gives the evidence after being required to do so under subsection (4); and

(c) of the effect of such a certificate.

(4) The court may require the witness to give the evidence if the court is satisfied that:

(a) the evidence does not tend to prove that the witness has committed an offence against or arising under, or is liable to a civil penalty under, a law of a foreign country; and

(b) the interests of justice require that the witness give the evidence.

(5) If the witness either willingly gives the evidence without being required to do so under subsection (4), or gives it after being required to do so under that subsection, the court must cause the witness to be given a certificate under this section in respect of the evidence.

(6) The court is also to cause a witness to be given a certificate

形的情况下，适用本条：

(a) 实施了违反或者起因于澳大利亚法律或者外国法律的犯罪；或者

(b) 应当对民事处罚承担责任。

(2) 法院必须确定该异议是否有合理根据。

(3) 如果法院确定该异议存在合理根据，则应当告知证人：

(a) 证人不需要作证，除非法院根据 (4) 要求其作证；并且

(b) 在下列情况下，法院将根据本条赋予其证明书：

(i) 证人未经法院根据 (4) 提出要求而情愿作证；或者

(ii) 法院根据 (4) 要求其作证后，证人作了证；以及

(c) 该证明书的效力。

(4) 如果法院确信存在下列情况，则法院可以要求证人作证：

(a) 有关证据并不倾向于证明该证人实施了违反或者起因于外国法律的犯罪，或者根据外国法律应当对民事处罚承担责任；并且

(b) 正义利益要求证人作证。

(5) 如果证人未经法院根据 (4) 提出要求而情愿作证，或者在法院根据该规定提出要求后作了证，法院必须根据本条就该证言促成赋予证人以证明书。

(6) 在下列情况下，法院作也应当就促成根据本条赋予

under this section if:

    (a) the objection has been overruled; and

    (b) after the evidence has been given, the court finds that there were reasonable grounds for the objection.

(7) In any proceeding in an Australian court:

    (a) evidence given by a person in respect of which a certificate under this section has been given; and

    (b) evidence of any information, document or thing obtained as a direct or indirect consequence of the person having given evidence;

cannot be used against the person. However, this does not apply to a criminal proceeding in respect of the falsity of the evidence.

> Note: Subsection 128(7) differs from subsection 128(7) of the NSW Act. The NSW provision refers to a NSW Court instead of an Australian Court.

(8) Subsection (7) has effect despite any challenge, review, quashing or calling into question on any ground of the decision to give, or the validity of, the certificate concerned.

(9) If a defendant in a criminal proceeding for an offence is given a certificate under this section, subsection (7) does not apply in a proceeding that is a retrial of the defendant for the same offence or a trial of the defendant for an offence arising out of the same facts that gave rise to that offence.

(10) In a criminal proceeding, this section does not apply in relation to the giving of evidence by a defendant, being evidence that the defendant:

    (a) did an act the doing of which is a fact in issue; or

    (b) had a state of mind the existence of which is a fact in issue.

(11) A reference in this section to doing an act includes a

证人以证明书：

（a）异议已经被驳回；并且

（b）在作证之后，法院认定异议有合理根据。

（7）在澳大利亚法院的任何程序中，下列证据不得用于反对根据本条被赋予证明书的人：

（a）根据本条被赋予证明书的人所作的证言；以及

（b）作为该某人作证的直接或者间接结果而获得的关于任何信息、书证或者物证的证据。

然而，这并不适用于关于证据造假行为的刑事程序。

注释：第 128（7）不同于《新南威尔士州证据法》128（7）。《新南威尔士州证据法》的规定所称的是新南威尔士州法院而不是澳大利亚法院。

（8）无论对赋予有关证明书的决定的根据或者是该证明书的有效性提出何种质疑、审查、撤销或者疑问，（7）均有效。

（9）如果在刑事程序中，根据本条就某犯罪赋予了被告以证明书，（7）并不适用于对被告就同一犯罪进行重新审判的程序，或者起因于该犯罪的同样事实的犯罪的审判程序。

（10）在刑事程序中，本条并不适用于被告提供的关于下列情形的证言：

（a）被告从事了系本案争议事实的作为；或者

（b）被告曾存有系本案争议事实的心态。

（11）本条所称作为，包括不作为。

reference to failing to act.

(12) If a person has been given a certificate under a prescribed State or Territory provision in respect of evidence given by the person in a proceeding in a State or Territory court, the certificate has the same effect, in a proceeding to which this subsection applies, as if it had been given under this section.

(13) The following are prescribed State or Territory provisions for the purposes of subsection (12):

 (a) section 128 of the Evidence Act 1995 of New South Wales;

 (b) a provision of a law of a State or Territory declared by the regulations to be a prescribed State or Territory provision for the purposes of subsection (12).

(14) Subsection (12) applies to:

 (a) a proceeding in relation to which this Act applies because of section 4; and

 (b) a proceeding for an offence against a law of the Commonwealth or for the recovery of a civil penalty under a law of the Commonwealth, other than a proceeding referred to in paragraph (a).

(15) Until the day fixed under subsection 4(6), subsection (12) applies to a proceeding for an offence against a law of the Australian Capital Territory or for the recovery of a civil penalty under such a law, other than a proceeding referred to in paragraph (14)(a).

 Note 1: Bodies corporate cannot claim this privilege: see section 187.

 Note 2: Clause 3 of Part 2 of the Dictionary sets out what is a civil penalty.

 Note 3: The NSW Act does not contain provisions corresponding to subsections (12) to (15).

（12）如果一个人就其在州或者领地法院的程序中所作
的证言，根据规定的州或者领地之规定被赋予了证
明书，则在适用本款的程序中，该证明书具有本条
所赋予的同等效力。

（13）就第（12）款目的而言，下列是规定的州或者领
地之规定：

（a）《新南威士州 1995 年证据法》第 128 条；

（b）由条例为第（12）款之目的宣布为规定
的州或者领地规定的州或者领地的法律规
定。

（14）（12）适用于：

（a）因第 4 条而适用本法的程序；以及

（b）（a）所称程序之外的追究违反联邦法律的犯
罪的程序，或者是根据联邦法律提起的民事
处罚追缴程序。

（15）在 4（6）确定的期日之前，（12）适用于就违反
澳大利亚首都领地法律的犯罪而提起的程序，或者
根据该法律提起的民事处罚追缴程序，（14）（a）
所称的程序除外。【45】

注释 1：法人不能主张该特免权：参见第 187 条。

注释 2：《术语》第 2 部分第 3 条规定了什么是民事处罚。

注释 3：《新南威士州证据法》并不包含与（12）至（15）
相对应的规定。

Note 4: Subsections (8) and (9) were inserted as a response to the decision of the High Court of Australia in *Cornwell v The Queen* [2007] HCA 12 (22 March 2007).

128A Privilege in respect of self–incrimination—exception for certain orders etc

(1) In this section:

disclosure order means an order made by a federal court or an ACT court in a civil proceeding requiring a person to disclose information, as part of, or in connection with a freezing or search order, but does not include an order made by a court under the *Proceeds of Crime Act 2002*.

relevant person means a person to whom a disclosure order is directed.

(2) If a relevant person objects to complying with a disclosure order on the grounds that some or all of the information required to be disclosed may tend to prove that the person:

(a) has committed an offence against or arising under an Australian law or a law of a foreign country; or

(b) is liable to a civil penalty;

the person must:

(c) disclose so much of the information required to be disclosed to which no objection is taken; and

(d) prepare an affidavit containing so much of the information required to be disclosed to which objection is taken (the *privilege affidavit*) and deliver it to the court in a sealed envelope; and

(e) file and serve on each other party a separate affidavit setting out the basis of the objection.

(3) The sealed envelope containing the privilege affidavit must not be opened except as directed by the court.

第 128A 条

注释 4：插入（8）和（9），是为了回应澳大利亚最高法
院 在 *Cornwell v The Queen* [2007] HCA 12 （22
March 2007）案件中的判决。

128A 反对被迫自我归罪特免权——对某些命令等的例外

（1）在本条中：

> **披露命令**是指联邦法院或者澳大利亚首都领地法
> 院在民事程序中，作为冻结命令或者搜查命令的
> 一部分，或者与之相关联，而作出的要求某人披
> 露信息的命令，但是并不包括法院根据《2002 年
> 犯罪收益法》作出的命令。
>
> **相关人员**是指对其发出披露命令的人员。

（2）如果相关人员反对遵行披露命令，根据是要求披露
的某些或者全部信息可能倾向于证明该某人：

> （a）犯有违反或者起因于澳大利亚法律或者外国
> 法律的罪行；或者
>
> （b）要对民事处罚承担责任；
>
> 则该某人必须：
>
> （c）披露要求其披露且未就此提出异议的信息；
> 并且
>
> （d）准备一份包含有就其提出异议的被要求披露
> 的信息的宣誓陈述书（**特免权宣誓陈述书**），
> 将其密封在信封中送交法院；并且
>
> （e）提交并向每个其他当事人送达单独的宣誓陈
> 述书，说明提出异议的根据。

（3）装有特免权宣誓陈述书的密封信封，非经法院指示
不得开启。

(4) The court must determine whether or not there are reasonable grounds for the objection.

(5) Subject to subsection (6), if the court finds that there are reasonable grounds for the objection, the court must not require the information contained in the privilege affidavit to be disclosed and must return it to the relevant person.

(6) If the court is satisfied that:

    (a) any information disclosed in the privilege affidavit may tend to prove that the relevant person has committed an offence against or arising under, or is liable to a civil penalty under, an Australian law; and

    (b) the information does not tend to prove that the relevant person has committed an offence against or arising under, or is liable to a civil penalty under, a law of a foreign country; and

    (c) the interests of justice require the information to be disclosed;

    the court may make an order requiring the whole or any part of the privilege affidavit containing information of the kind referred to in paragraph (a) to be filed and served on the parties.

(7) If the whole or any part of the privilege affidavit is disclosed (including by order under subsection (6)), the court must cause the relevant person to be given a certificate in respect of the information as referred to in paragraph (6)(a).

(8) In any proceeding in an Australian court:

    (a) evidence of information disclosed by a relevant person in respect of which a certificate has been given under this section; and

    (b) evidence of any information, document or thing

第 128A 条

（4）法院必须确定该异议是否存在合理根据。

（5）在遵守（6）的情况下，如果法院判定异议有合理根据，法院不得要求披露包含在特免权宣誓陈述书中的信息，必须将其交还相关人员。

（6）如果法院确信存在下列情况，法院可以作出命令，要求包含有（a）所称的信息的特免权宣誓陈述书的全部或者部分提交并送达当事人：

　　（a）特免权宣誓陈述书中披露的信息，可能倾向于证明相关人员犯有违反或者起因于澳大利亚法律的罪行，或者根据澳大利亚法律应就民事处罚承担责任；并且

　　（b）信息并不倾向于证明相关人员犯有违反或者起因于外国法律的罪行，或者根据外国法律应就民事处罚承担责任；并且

　　（c）正义利益要求披露该信息。

（7）如果披露了特免权宣誓陈述书的全部或者部分（包括根据（6）作出的命令而进行的披露），法院必须就（6）（a）所称信息，促成为相关人员赋予一份证明书。

（8）在澳大利亚法院的任何程序中，下列证据不能用于反对相关人员：

　　（a）相关人员披露的根据本条赋予了证明书的信息证据；以及

　　（b）作为相关人员披露上述信息的直接结果或

obtained as a direct result or indirect consequence of the relevant person having disclosed that information;

cannot be used against the person. However, this does not apply to a criminal proceeding in respect of the falsity of the evidence concerned.

(9) Subsection (8) does not prevent the use against the relevant person of any information disclosed by a document:

    (a) that is an annexure or exhibit to a privilege affidavit prepared by the person in response to a disclosure order; and

    (b) that was in existence before the order was made.

(10) Subsection (8) has effect despite any challenge, review, quashing or calling into question on any ground of the decision to give, or the validity of, the certificate concerned.

Division 3—Evidence excluded in the public interest

129 Exclusion of evidence of reasons for judicial etc. decisions

(1) Evidence of the reasons for a decision made by a person who is:

    (a) a judge in an Australian or overseas proceeding; or

    (b) an arbitrator in respect of a dispute that has been submitted to the person, or to the person and one or more other persons, for arbitration;

or the deliberations of a person so acting in relation to such a decision, must not be given by the person, or a person who was, in relation to the proceeding or arbitration, under the direction or control of that person.

者间接后果的任何信息、书证或者物证证
据。

然而，这并不适用于关于就证据造假的刑事程
序。

（9）（8）并不禁止使用下列文件披露的任何信息来反
对相关人员：

（a）该某人就披露命令而制作的特免权宣誓陈述
书的附件或者展示件；以及

（b）在披露命令作出之前已经存在的书证

（10）无论对赋予有关证明书的决定的根据或者是该证
明书的有效性提出何种质疑、审查、撤销或者疑问，
（8）均有效。

第3目—为公共利益而排除的证据

129 排除关于司法等裁决理由的证据

（1）下列人员，或者受该某人员指挥或者控制的与该程
序或者仲裁有关的人员，不得就该某人员作出裁决
的原因的或者就该裁决的评议情况作证：

（a）澳大利亚或者海外程序的法官；或者

（b）将某一争议提交其仲裁的的仲裁人员。

(2) Such evidence must not be given by tendering as evidence a document prepared by such a person.

(3) This section does not prevent the admission or use, in a proceeding, of published reasons for a decision.

(4) In a proceeding, evidence of the reasons for a decision made by a member of a jury in another Australian or overseas proceeding, or of the deliberations of a member of a jury in relation to such a decision, must not be given by any of the members of that jury.

(5) This section does not apply in a proceeding that is:

    (a) a prosecution for one or more of the following offences:

        (i) an offence against or arising under Part III of the *Crimes Act 1914*;

        (ii) embracery;

        (iii) attempting to pervert the course of justice;

        (iv) an offence connected with an offence mentioned in subparagraph (i), (ii) or (iii), including an offence of conspiring to commit such an offence; or

    (b) in respect of a contempt of a court; or

    (c) by way of appeal from, or judicial review of, a judgment, decree, order or sentence of a court; or

    (d) by way of review of an arbitral award; or

    (e) a civil proceeding in respect of an act of a judicial officer or arbitrator that was, and that was known at the time by the judicial officer or arbitrator to be, outside the scope of the matters in relation to which the judicial officer or arbitrator had authority to act.

Note: Paragraph (5)(a) differs from paragraph 129(5)(a) of the NSW Act.

（2）上述证据不得以提交上述人员所制作的文件的形式提出。

（3）本条并不禁止在程序中采纳或者使用已经公布的裁决理由。

（4）在程序中，关于在澳大利亚或者海外的其他程序中，陪审员作出裁断的理由的证据，或者与该裁断有关的陪审团成员的评议活动的证据，不得由该陪审团的任何成员提出。

（5）本条并不适用于下列程序：

（a）对下列一个或者数个犯罪的公诉：

（i）违反或者起因于《1914 年犯罪法》第 III 章的犯罪；[46]

（ii）贿赂陪审员；

（iii）试图妨害司法；

（iv）与（i）、（ii）或者（iii）所提及的犯罪相关联的犯罪，包括共谋实施上述犯罪的犯罪；或者

（b）有关藐视法院的程序；或者

（c）对法院的判决、裁定、命令或者量刑提起的上诉或者司法审查程序；或者

（d）对仲裁裁决的审查程序；或者

（e）就司法人员或者仲裁员做出的其在行为当时明知超出其权限范围的行为提起的民事程序。

注释：（5）（a）不同于《新南威尔士州证据法》之 129（5）（a）。

130 Exclusion of evidence of matters of state

(1) If the public interest in admitting into evidence information or a document that relates to matters of state is outweighed by the public interest in preserving secrecy or confidentiality in relation to the information or document, the court may direct that the information or document not be adduced as evidence.

(2) The court may give such a direction either on its own initiative or on the application of any person (whether or not the person is a party).

(3) In deciding whether to give such a direction, the court may inform itself in any way it thinks fit.

(4) Without limiting the circumstances in which information or a document may be taken for the purposes of subsection (1) to relate to matters of state, the information or document is taken for the purposes of that subsection to relate to matters of state if adducing it as evidence would:

   (a) prejudice the security, defence or international relations of Australia; or

   (b) damage relations between the Commonwealth and a State or between 2 or more States; or

   (c) prejudice the prevention, investigation or prosecution of an offence; or

   (d) prejudice the prevention or investigation of, or the conduct of proceedings for recovery of civil penalties brought with respect to, other contraventions of the law; or

   (e) disclose, or enable a person to ascertain, the existence or identity of a confidential source of information relating to the enforcement or administration of a law of the Commonwealth or a State; or

130 因国家事项而排除证据

（1）就有关国家事务的信息或者文件而言，如果保守有
关机密或者秘密的公共利益超过了将其采纳为证
据的公共利益，则法院可以指示该上述信息或者文
件不得作为证据提出。

（2）法院可以自行或者根据任何人员（无论该某人是否
是当事人）的申请而作出上述指示。

（3）在决定是否作出上述指示时，法院可以采取其认为
适当的任何方式了解情况。

（4）就（1）目的而言，如果将信息或者文件作为证据
提出将会出现但是不限于下列情形，则该信息或者
文件视为与国家事务有关：

（a）有损于澳大利亚的安全、国防或者国际关系
的；或者

（b）破坏联邦与州或者州与州之间的关系的；或
者

（c）有损于对犯罪的预防、调查或者检控的；或
者

（d）有损于对其他违法行为的预防、调查或者就
该违法行为所提起的民事处罚之追缴程序进
行的；或者

（e）将披露或者使人确知与联邦或者州之执法或
者司法有关的秘密信息来源的存在或者身份
的；或者

(f) prejudice the proper functioning of the government of the Commonwealth or a State.

(5) Without limiting the matters that the court may take into account for the purposes of subsection (1), it is to take into account the following matters:

(a) the importance of the information or the document in the proceeding;

(b) if the proceeding is a criminal proceeding—whether the party seeking to adduce evidence of the information or document is a defendant or the prosecutor;

(c) the nature of the offence, cause of action or defence to which the information or document relates, and the nature of the subject matter of the proceeding;

(d) the likely effect of adducing evidence of the information or document, and the means available to limit its publication;

(e) whether the substance of the information or document has already been published;

(f) if the proceeding is a criminal proceeding and the party seeking to adduce evidence of the information or document is a defendant—whether the direction is to be made subject to the condition that the prosecution be stayed.

(6) A reference in this section to a State includes a reference to a Territory.

131 Exclusion of evidence of settlement negotiations

(1) Evidence is not to be adduced of:

(a) a communication that is made between persons in dispute, or between one or more persons in dispute and

（f）有损于联邦政府或者州政府的适当运作的。

（5）为（1）目的而考虑时，法院应当虑及的事项包括但是不限于：

（a）有关信息或者文件在该程序中的重要性；

（b）在该程序是刑事程序的情况下，寻求将该信息或者文件提出作为证据的当事人是被告还是公诉人；

（c）与该信息或者文件有关的犯罪、诉因或者辩护的性质；以及该程序标的的性质；

（d）将该信息或者文件作为证据提出的可能效果，以及能够限制其被公布的手段；

（e）该信息或者文件的要旨是否已经被公布；

（f）如果该程序是刑事程序，并且要求将该信息或者文件作为证据提出的是被告，是否可以以延缓起诉为条件作出该指示。

（6）本条所称的州（国家），包括领地。

131 排除和解谈判证据

（1）下列情况下的交流或者书证不得作为证据提出：

（a）存在争议的人之间，或者是存在争议的人与第三方之间，试图以谈判方式解决该争议时

    a third party, in connection with an attempt to negotiate a settlement of the dispute; or

 (b) a document (whether delivered or not) that has been prepared in connection with an attempt to negotiate a settlement of a dispute.

(2) Subsection (1) does not apply if:

 (a) the persons in dispute consent to the evidence being adduced in the proceeding concerned or, if any of those persons has tendered the communication or document in evidence in another Australian or overseas proceeding, all the other persons so consent; or

 (b) the substance of the evidence has been disclosed with the express or implied consent of all the persons in dispute; or

 (c) the substance of the evidence has been partly disclosed with the express or implied consent of the persons in dispute, and full disclosure of the evidence is reasonably necessary to enable a proper understanding of the other evidence that has already been adduced; or

 (d) the communication or document included a statement to the effect that it was not to be treated as confidential; or

 (e) the evidence tends to contradict or to qualify evidence that has already been admitted about the course of an attempt to settle the dispute; or

 (f) the proceeding in which it is sought to adduce the evidence is a proceeding to enforce an agreement between the persons in dispute to settle the dispute, or a proceeding in which the making of such an agreement is in issue; or

 (g) evidence that has been adduced in the proceeding, or an inference from evidence that has been adduced in

所进行的交流；或者

（b）试图以谈判方式解决争议时所制作的书证（无论是否已经送交）。

（2）在下列情况下，（1）并不适用：

（a）发生争议的人员同意在有关程序中提出该证据，或者在任何上述人员已经在其他澳大利亚或者海外程序中将交流或者书证提交为证据的情况下，所有其他人员表示同意的；或者

（b）经发生争议的所有人员的明示或者默示同意，证据的要旨已经被披露的；或者

（c）在经发生争议的人员的明示或者默示同意，证据的部分内容已经被披露的情况下，全面披露证据为对其他已经提出的证据作出适当理解所合理必需的；或者

（d）该交流或者书证中包含有使其不被视为具有秘密性的陈述；或者

（e）该证据倾向于反驳或者限定已经被采纳的关于试图解决争议的过程的证据；或者

（f）试图提出证据的程序是执行发生争议人员之间的争议和解协议的程序，或者是就是否达成了上述协议存在争议的程序；或者

（g）在程序中已经提出的证据，或者根据在程序

the proceeding, is likely to mislead the court unless evidence of the communication or document is adduced to contradict or to qualify that evidence; or

(h) the communication or document is relevant to determining liability for costs; or

(i) making the communication, or preparing the document, affects a right of a person; or

(j) the communication was made, or the document was prepared, in furtherance of the commission of a fraud or an offence or the commission of an act that renders a person liable to a civil penalty; or

(k) one of the persons in dispute, or an employee or agent of such a person, knew or ought reasonably to have known that the communication was made, or the document was prepared, in furtherance of a deliberate abuse of a power.

(3) For the purposes of paragraph (2)(j), if commission of the fraud, offence or act is a fact in issue and there are reasonable grounds for finding that:

(a) the fraud, offence or act was committed; and

(b) a communication was made or a document was prepared in furtherance of the commission of the fraud, offence or act;

the court may find that the communication was so made or the document so prepared.

(4) For the purposes of paragraph (2)(k), if:

(a) the abuse of power is a fact in issue; and

(b) there are reasonable grounds for finding that a communication was made or a document was prepared in furtherance of the abuse of power;

中已经提出的证据进行的推论，有可能误导
法院，除非提出关于交流或者书证的证据以
反驳或者限定该证据；或者

（h）该交流或者书证与费用责任的确定有关；或者

（i）进行该交流或者制作该书证，影响了某人的
权利；或者

（j）进行该交流或者制作该书证，是为了促进实
施欺诈、犯罪或者导致某人就民事处罚承担
责任的作为；或者

（k）发生争议的人员一方或者其雇员或者代理人，知
道或者合理地应当已经知道，进行该交流或者
制作该书证之目的，是为了促进故意滥用权力。

（3）就（2）（j）目的而言，如果欺诈、犯罪或者作为的
实施系争议事实，并有合理根据认定下列事项，则
法院可以判定已经进行了上述交流或者制作了上
述书证：

（a）已经实施欺诈、犯罪或者作为；并且

（b）为促进该欺诈、犯罪或者作为的实施，进行
了该交流或者制作了文件。

（4）就（2）（k）目的而言，如果存在下列情形，则法院可
以判定有关交流已经作出或者有关书证已经制作：

（a）滥用权力系争议事实；并且

（b）有合理根据认定为促进滥用权力而进行了交
流或者制作了书证。

the court may find that the communication was so made or the document was so prepared.

(5) In this section:

    (a) a reference to a dispute is a reference to a dispute of a kind in respect of which relief may be given in an Australian or overseas proceeding; and

    (b) a reference to an attempt to negotiate the settlement of a dispute does not include a reference to an attempt to negotiate the settlement of a criminal proceeding or an anticipated criminal proceeding; and

    (c) a reference to a communication made by a person in dispute includes a reference to a communication made by an employee or agent of such a person; and

    (d) a reference to the consent of a person in dispute includes a reference to the consent of an employee or agent of such a person, being an employee or agent who is authorised so to consent; and

    (e) a reference to commission of an act includes a reference to a failure to act.

(6) In this section:

power means a power conferred by or under an Australian law.

Division 4—General

131A Extended application of Division 1A

(1) This section applies if, in response to a disclosure requirement, a person claims that they are not compellable to answer any question or produce any document that would disclose the identity of the informant (within the meaning of section 126H)

（5）在本条中：

（a）争议是指就此可以在澳大利亚或者海外程序
中获得救济的争议；以及

（b）试图以谈判方式解决争议，不包括试图就刑
事程序或者准备进行的刑事程序进行和解谈
判；以及

（c）某人在争议中所作的交流，包括该某人的雇
员或者代理人所作的交流；以及

（d）发生争议的人员的同意，包括该某人的雇员
或者代理人经授权作出的同意；以及

（e）作为包括不作为。

（6）在本条中：

权力，是指澳大利亚法律所赋予或者规定的权力。

第 4 目——一般规定

131A 第 1A 目的扩展适用

（1）如果针对披露要求，某人主张其不能被强制回答任
何问题，或者出示任何书证将披露报信人（含义见
第 126H 条）的身份，或者使得该身份被确知，则

or enable that identity to be ascertained.

(1A) A party that seeks disclosure pursuant to a disclosure requirement may apply to the court for an order, under section 126H, that subsection 126H(1) does not apply in relation to the information or document.

(2) In this section, *disclosure requirement* means a court process or court order that requires the disclosure of information or a document and includes the following:

(a) a summons or subpoena to produce documents or give evidence;

(b) pre–trial discovery;

(c) non–party discovery;

(d) interrogatories;

(e) a notice to produce;

(f) a request to produce a document under Division 1 of Part 4.6.

131B Extended application of Division 1A etc. to all proceedings for Commonwealth offences

In addition to their application under section 4 to all proceedings in a federal court or an ACT court, Division 1A and section 131A apply to all proceedings in any other Australian court for an offence against a law of the Commonwealth, including proceedings that:

(a) relate to bail; or

(b) are interlocutory proceedings or proceedings of a similar kind; or

(c) are heard in chambers; or

(d) relate to sentencing.

适用本条。

（1A）依据第 126H 条规定的披露要求寻求披露的当事

人，可以向法院提出申请，请求法院命令 126H（1）

并不适用于有关信息或者书证。

（2）在本条中，**披露要求**是指要求披露信息或者书证的

法院文书或者法院命令，包括以下：

（a）要求出示证据或者作证的传票或者传证令；

（b）审前案情先悉；

（c）非当事人案情先悉；

（d）询问；

（e）出示证据通知；

（f）根据第 4.6 节第 1 目要求出示某文件。

131B 第 1A 目等对联邦犯罪所有程序的扩展适用

除了根据第 4 条适用于联邦法院和澳大利亚首都领地法

院的所有程序之外，第 1A 目和第 131A 条适用于任何其

他澳大利亚法院审理违反联邦法律的犯罪的所有程序，

包括下列程序：

（a）与保释有关的程序；或者

（b）中间程序或者类似程序；或者

（c）在法官办公室听审的程序；或者

（d）与量刑有关的程序。

132 Court to inform of rights to make applications and objections

If it appears to the court that a witness or a party may have grounds for making an application or objection under a provision of this Part, the court must satisfy itself (if there is a jury, in the absence of the jury) that the witness or party is aware of the effect of that provision.

133 Court may inspect etc. documents

If a question arises under this Part in relation to a document, the court may order that the document be produced to it and may inspect the document for the purpose of determining the question.

134 Inadmissibility of evidence that must not be adduced or given

Evidence that, because of this Part, must not be adduced or given in a proceeding is not admissible in the proceeding.

Part 3.11—Discretionary and mandatory exclusions

135 General discretion to exclude evidence

The court may refuse to admit evidence if its probative value is substantially outweighed by the danger that the evidence might:

(a) be unfairly prejudicial to a party; or

(b) be misleading or confusing; or

(c) cause or result in undue waste of time.

136 General discretion to limit use of evidence

The court may limit the use to be made of evidence if there is a danger that a particular use of the evidence might:

(a) be unfairly prejudicial to a party; or

132 法院应当就提出申请或者异议的权利进行告知

如果在法院看来，证人或者当事人可能有理由根据本节之规定提出申请或者反对，则法院必须自己确信（如果有陪审团，则在陪审团不在场的情况下）证人或者当事人知道该规定的效力。

133 法院可以查阅文件

如果根据本节对某文件产生了疑问，则法院可以命令向其出示该文件，并可以为就该疑问作出决定而查阅该文件。

134 不得提出或者作出的证据不具有可采性

根据本节而不得在程序中提出或者作出的证据，在该程序中不得采纳。

第 3.11 节—裁量性排除与强制性排除

135 排除证据的一般自由裁量权

如果证据的证明价值将会为下列危险所严重超过，则法院可以拒绝采纳该证据：

(a) 该证据可能给一方当事人造成不公平的损害；或者

(b) 该证据可能具有误导性或者迷惑性；或者

(c) 该证据可能导致或者造成不合理的时间耗费。[47]

136 有限使用证据的一般自由裁量权

如果证据的具体使用可能造成下列危险，则法院可以对其使用进行限制：

(a) 给一方当事人造成不公平的损害；或者

(b) be misleading or confusing.

137 Exclusion of prejudicial evidence in criminal proceedings

In a criminal proceeding, the court must refuse to admit evidence adduced by the prosecutor if its probative value is outweighed by the danger of unfair prejudice to the defendant.

138 Discretion to exclude improperly or illegally obtained evidence

(1) Evidence that was obtained:

    (a) improperly or in contravention of an Australian law; or

    (b) in consequence of an impropriety or of a contravention of an Australian law;

is not to be admitted unless the desirability of admitting the evidence outweighs the undesirability of admitting evidence that has been obtained in the way in which the evidence was obtained.

(2) Without limiting subsection (1), evidence of an admission that was made during or in consequence of questioning, and evidence obtained in consequence of the admission, is taken to have been obtained improperly if the person conducting the questioning:

    (a) did, or omitted to do, an act in the course of the questioning even though he or she knew or ought reasonably to have known that the act or omission was likely to impair substantially the ability of the person being questioned to respond rationally to the questioning; or

    (b) made a false statement in the course of the questioning even though he or she knew or ought reasonably to have known that the statement was false and that making the false statement was likely to cause the person who was being questioned to make an admission.

（b）具有误导性或者迷惑性。

137 刑事程序中有害证据的排除

在刑事程序中，法院必须拒绝采纳公诉人提出的给被告带来的不公平的损害超过其证明价值的证据。

138 排除不当或者非法取得的证据的自由裁量权

（1）下列证据不得被采纳，除非采纳下列方式获得的证据的可取性大于其不可取性：

（a）不当获得或者违反澳大利亚法律获得的证据；或者

（b）作为不当行为或者违反澳大利亚法律的结果而获得的证据。

（2）在不限制（1）的情况下，关于被告在询问过程中作出的或者因询问而作出的自认的证据，或者因自认之结果而获得的证据，如果询问人存在下列情形，则这些证据被视为是不当获得的证据：

（a）在询问过程中作为或者不作为，尽管他知道或者合理地应当知道该作为或者不作为可能严重损害正在被询问的人对询问作出理性回答的能力；或者

（b）在询问过程中作出了不实陈述，尽管他知道或者合理地应当知道该陈述是不实的，作出该不实陈述将可能导致正在被询问的人作出自认。

(3) Without limiting the matters that the court may take into account under subsection (1), it is to take into account:

(a) the probative value of the evidence; and

(b) the importance of the evidence in the proceeding; and

(c) the nature of the relevant offence, cause of action or defence and the nature of the subject–matter of the proceeding; and

(d) the gravity of the impropriety or contravention; and

(e) whether the impropriety or contravention was deliberate or reckless; and

(f) whether the impropriety or contravention was contrary to or inconsistent with a right of a person recognised by the International Covenant on Civil and Political Rights; and

(g) whether any other proceeding (whether or not in a court) has been or is likely to be taken in relation to the impropriety or contravention; and

(h) the difficulty (if any) of obtaining the evidence without impropriety or contravention of an Australian law.

Note: The International Covenant on Civil and Political Rights is set out in Schedule 2 to the *Australian Human Rights Commission Act* 1986.

139 Cautioning of persons

(1) For the purposes of paragraph 138(1)(a), evidence of a statement made or an act done by a person during questioning is taken to have been obtained improperly if:

(a) the person was under arrest for an offence at the time; and

(b) the questioning was conducted by an investigating

（3）法院根据（1）所虑及的事项，包括但是不限于：

（a）该证据的证明价值；以及

（b）该证据在程序中的重要性；以及

（c）相关犯罪、诉因或者抗辩的性质以及程序标的的性质；以及

（d）不当行为或者违法的严重性；以及

（e）该不当行为或者违法行为是故意的还是疏忽造成的；以及

（f）该不当行为或者违法行为是否违反了《公民和政治权利国际公约》所认可的人的权利或者与此不一致；以及

（g）是否就不当行为或者违法行为已经提起或者可能提起任何其他程序（无论是否为法院程序）；以及

（h）在不从事不当行为或者违反澳大利亚法律行为的情况下获得证据的难度（如果有的话）。【48】

注释：《1986 年澳大利亚人权委员会法》的附录 2 载明了《公民和政治权利国际公约》。

139 对相关人员的警告

（1）就 138（1）（a）之目的而言，在下列情况下，关于某人在询问活动中所为的陈述或者行为的证据被视为不当获得的证据：

（a）该某人因为当时的犯罪而被逮捕；并且

（b）询问活动是由因其所任公职而在当时有权逮

official who was at the time empowered, because of the office that he or she held, to arrest the person; and

(c) before starting the questioning the investigating official did not caution the person that the person does not have to say or do anything but that anything the person does say or do may be used in evidence.

(2) For the purposes of paragraph 138(1)(a), evidence of a statement made or an act done by a person during questioning is taken to have been obtained improperly if:

(a) the questioning was conducted by an investigating official who did not have the power to arrest the person; and

(b) the statement was made, or the act was done, after the investigating official formed a belief that there was sufficient evidence to establish that the person has committed an offence; and

(c) the investigating official did not, before the statement was made or the act was done, caution the person that the person does not have to say or do anything but that anything the person does say or do may be used in evidence.

(3) The caution must be given in, or translated into, a language in which the person is able to communicate with reasonable fluency, but need not be given in writing unless the person cannot hear adequately.

(4) Subsections (1), (2) and (3) do not apply so far as any Australian law requires the person to answer questions put by, or do things required by, the investigating official.

(5) A reference in subsection (1) to a person who is under arrest includes a reference to a person who is in the company of an investigating official for the purpose of being questioned, if:

捕该某人的调查人员进行的；并且

（c）在开始询问之前，调查人员没有警告该某人说，该某人不必为任何陈述或者行为，但是该某人所为的任何陈述或者行为都可能被用作证据。

（2）就138（1）（a）之目的而言，在下列情况下，关于某人在询问中所为的陈述或者行为的证据被视为不当获得的证据：

（a）询问活动是由无权逮捕该某人的调查人员进行的；并且

（b）该某人在询问活动中的陈述或者行为，是在调查人员形成了有足够的证据证明该某人实施了犯罪的信念之后所为的；并且

（c）在该某人为陈述或者行为之前，调查人员没有警告该某人说，该某人不必为任何陈述或者行为，但是该某人所为的任何陈述或者行为都可能被用作证据。

（3）上述警告必须采用或者翻译成该某人能够合理地进行流畅交流的语言，但是并不需要采用书面形式，除非该某人不能充分聆听。

（4）如果任何澳大利亚法律要求该某人回答调查人员提出的问题或者做出调查人员要求的行为，则不适用于（1）、（2）和（3）。

（5）在下列情况下，（1）所称被逮捕的人，包括为询问目的而由调查人员陪伴的人：

    (a) the official believes that there is sufficient evidence to establish that the person has committed an offence that is to be the subject of the questioning; or

    (b) the official would not allow the person to leave if the person wished to do so; or

    (c) the official has given the person reasonable grounds for believing that the person would not be allowed to leave if he or she wished to do so.

(6) A person is not treated as being under arrest only because of subsection (5) if:

    (a) the official is performing functions in relation to persons or goods entering or leaving Australia and the official does not believe the person has committed an offence against a law of the Commonwealth; or

    (b) the official is exercising a power under an Australian law to detain and search the person or to require the person to provide information or to answer questions.

（a）调查人员认为有足够的证据证实该某人实施了作为询问内容的犯罪；或者

（b）在该某人希望离去的情况下，调查人员不允许该某人离去；或者

（c）在该某人希望离去的情况下，调查人员向该某人说明了认为不得允许该某人离去的合理根据。

（6）在下列情况下，不得仅因第（5）款而将某人视为被逮捕：

（a）调查人员就进出澳大利亚的人员或者货物履行职能，并且不认为该某人实施了违反联邦法律的犯罪；或者

（b）调查人员正在根据澳大利亚法律行使扣留和搜查该某人的权力，或者要求该某人提供信息或者回答问题的权力。

Chapter 4—Proof

INTRODUCTORY NOTE

Outline of this Chapter

This Chapter is about the proof of matters in a proceeding.

Part 4.1 is about the standard of proof in civil proceedings and in criminal proceedings.

Part 4.2 is about matters that do not require proof in a proceeding.

Part 4.3 makes easier the proof of the matters dealt with in that Part.

Part 4.4 is about requirements that evidence be corroborated.

Part 4.5 requires judges to warn juries about the potential unreliability of certain kinds of evidence.

Part 4.6 sets out procedures for proving certain other matters.

Part 4.1—Standard of proof

140 Civil proceedings: standard of proof

(1) In a civil proceeding, the court must find the case of a party proved if it is satisfied that the case has been proved on the balance of probabilities.

(2) Without limiting the matters that the court may take into account in deciding whether it is so satisfied, it is to take into account:

    (a) the nature of the cause of action or defence; and

    (b) the nature of the subject—matter of the proceeding; and

第 4 章—证明

引言性注释

本章概要

本章对程序中的事项证明进行了规定。

第 4.1 节规定了刑事程序和民事程序中的证明标准。

第 4.2 节规定了程序中不需要加以证明的事项。

第 4.3 节对该节规定的事项的证明进行了简化。

第 4.4 节是关于证据补强的要求。

第 4.5 节要求法官要就某些种类的证据的潜在不可靠性对陪审团进行警告。

第 4.6 节规定了证明某些其他事项的程序。

第 4.1 节—证明标准

140 民事程序：证明标准

（1）在民事程序中，法院如果确信一方当事人的案件按照概率权衡已经得到证明，则必须认定该当事人的案件已经得到证明。

（2）法院在确定其是否已经达到确信时，应当虑及的事项包括但是不限于：

（a）诉因或者抗辩的性质；以及

（b）程序标的的性质；以及

(c) the gravity of the matters alleged.

141 Criminal proceedings: standard of proof

(1) In a criminal proceeding, the court is not to find the case of the prosecution proved unless it is satisfied that it has been proved beyond reasonable doubt.

(2) In a criminal proceeding, the court is to find the case of a defendant proved if it is satisfied that the case has been proved on the balance of probabilities.

142 Admissibility of evidence: standard of proof

(1) Except as otherwise provided by this Act, in any proceeding the court is to find that the facts necessary for deciding:

(a) a question whether evidence should be admitted or not admitted, whether in the exercise of a discretion or not; or

(b) any other question arising under this Act;

have been proved if it is satisfied that they have been proved on the balance of probabilities.

(2) In determining whether it is so satisfied, the matters that the court must take into account include:

(a) the importance of the evidence in the proceeding; and

(b) the gravity of the matters alleged in relation to the question.

Part 4.2—Judicial notice

143 Matters of law

(1) Proof is not required about the provisions and coming into operation (in whole or in part) of:

（c）所称事项的严重性。

141 刑事程序：证明标准

（1）在刑事程序中，法院不得认定检控方的案件已经得到证明，除非其确信对该案件的证明已经排除了合理怀疑。

（2）在刑事程序中，法院如果确信被告的案件按照概率权衡已经得到证明，则应当认定该被告的案件已经得到证明。

142 证据的可采性：证明标准

（1）除本法另有规定外，在任何程序中，如果法院确信根据概率权衡，为确定下列事项所必需的事实已经得到证明，则法院应当认定这些事实已经得到证明：

（a）证据是否应当被采纳的问题，无论法院是否在行使自由裁量权；或者

（b）起因于本法的任何其他问题。

（2）法院在确定其是否已经达到确信时，必须考虑的事项包括：

（a）证据在程序中的重要性；以及

（b）与上述问题有关的所称事项的严重性。

第 4.2 节—司法认知

143 法律事项

（1）下列法律以及是否（全部或者部分）生效无需证明：

(a) an Act, a State Act, an Act or Ordinance of a Territory or an Imperial Act in force in Australia; or

(b) a regulation, rule or by–law made, or purporting to be made, under such an Act or Ordinance; or

(c) a Proclamation or order of the Governor–General, the Governor of a State or the Administrator or Executive of a Territory made, or purporting to be made, under such an Act or Ordinance; or

(d) an instrument of a legislative character (for example, a rule of court) made, or purporting to be made, under such an Act or Ordinance, being an instrument that is required by or under a law to be published, or the making of which is required by or under a law to be notified, in any government or official gazette (by whatever name called).

(2) A judge may inform himself or herself about those matters in any way that the judge thinks fit.

(3) A reference in this section to an Act, being an Act of an Australian Parliament, includes a reference to a private Act passed by that Parliament.

Note: Section 5 extends the operation of this provision to proceedings in all Australian courts.

144 Matters of common knowledge

(1) Proof is not required about knowledge that is not reasonably open to question and is:

(a) common knowledge in the locality in which the proceeding is being held or generally; or

(b) capable of verification by reference to a document the authority of which cannot reasonably be questioned.

（a）澳大利亚现行有效的法律、州法律、领地的法律、法令或者皇室训令；或者

（b）根据或者载明根据上述法律、法令所制定的条例、规则或者附则；或者

（c）总督、州长或者领地行政长官根据或者载明根据上述法律或者法令发布的《公告》或者命令；

（d）根据或者载明根据上述法律或者法令所制定、为法律所要求或者根据法律应当在任何政府或者官方公报（不论名称如何）公布，或者其制定为法律所要求或者根据法律应当在任何政府或者官方公报（不论名称如何）予以通告的立法性文件（例如法院规则）。

（2）法官可以采取其认为适当的任何方式了解上述事项。

（3）本条所称法律，作为澳大利亚国会制定的法律，包括国会所通过的非公知法。

注释：第 5 条将本规定的运作扩展到了所有澳大利亚法院的程序。

144 常识事项

（1）不受合理质疑并且属于下列情况的知识无需证明：

（a）程序进行地的常识或者一般性常识；或者

（b）能够为其权威性不受合理质疑的文件所核实的知识。

(2) The judge may acquire knowledge of that kind in any way the judge thinks fit.

(3) The court (including, if there is a jury, the jury) is to take knowledge of that kind into account.

(4) The judge is to give a party such opportunity to make submissions, and to refer to relevant information, relating to the acquiring or taking into account of knowledge of that kind as is necessary to ensure that the party is not unfairly prejudiced.

145 Certain Crown certificates

This Part does not exclude the application of the principles and rules of the common law and of equity relating to the effect of a certificate given by or on behalf of the Crown with respect to a matter of international affairs.

Part 4.3—Facilitation of proof

Division 1—General

146 Evidence produced by processes, machines and other devices

(1) This section applies to a document or thing:

    (a) that is produced wholly or partly by a device or process; and

    (b) that is tendered by a party who asserts that, in producing the document or thing, the device or process has produced a particular outcome.

(2) If it is reasonably open to find that the device or process is one that, or is of a kind that, if properly used, ordinarily produces that outcome, it is presumed (unless evidence sufficient to raise doubt about the presumption is adduced)

（2）法官可以采取其认为适当的任何方式获得上述知识。

（3）法院（如果有陪审团的话，包括陪审团）应当考虑上述知识。

（4）为保证当事人免受不公平的损害，法官应当就获得或者考虑此类知识，赋予当事人提交或者查阅有关信息所必需的机会。

145 某些政府证明书

本节不排除适用与政府或者代表政府就国际事务事项作出的证明书效力有关的普通法和衡平法原则与规则。

第 4.3 节—证明的简化

第 1 目—一般规定

146 由工序、机器和其他设备生成的证据

（1）本条适用于下列书证或者物证：

（a）全部或者部分是由设备或者工序生成的；并且

（b）是由主张在该书证或者物证生成过程中，该设备或者工序生成了某具体结果的当事人提交的。

（2）如果可以合理地认定，该设备或者工序经适当使用通常会生成该结果，则应当推定在相关场合生成该

that, in producing the document or thing on the occasion in question, the device or process produced that outcome.

Note:

Example: It would not be necessary to call evidence to prove that a photocopier normally produced complete copies of documents and that it was working properly when it was used to photocopy a particular document.

147 Documents produced by processes, machines and other devices in the course of business

(1) This section applies to a document:

    (a) that is produced wholly or partly by a device or process; and

    (b) that is tendered by a party who asserts that, in producing the document, the device or process has produced a particular outcome.

(2) If:

    (a) the document is, or was at the time it was produced, part of the records of, or kept for the purposes of, a business (whether or not the business is still in existence); and

    (b) the device or process is or was at that time used for the purposes of the business;

it is presumed (unless evidence sufficient to raise doubt about the presumption is adduced) that, in producing the document on the occasion in question, the device or process produced that outcome.

(3) Subsection (2) does not apply to the contents of a document that was produced:

    (a) for the purpose of conducting, or for or in contemplation of or in connection with, an Australian

书证或者物证时，该设备或者工序产生了该结果，除非就该推定提出了足够的质疑证据。

注释：

示例：不需要传召证据来证明，复印机通常能生成文件的完整复制件，并且在使用该复印机复制具体文件时，其工作正常。

147 业务过程中由工序、机器和其他设备生成的书证

（1）本条适用于符合下列情况的书证：

（a）全部或者部分是由设备或者工序生成；并且

（b）由主张在该书证或者物证生成过程中，该设备或者工序生成了某具体结果的当事人所提交。

（2）如果存在下列情况，则应当推定在相关场合生成该文件时，设备或者工序生成了该结果，除非就该推定提出了足够的质疑证据：

（a）该书证是或者在其生成时是业务记录的一部分，或者是为业务目的而保管的记录的一部分，无论该业务是否依然存在；并且

（b）该设备或者工序用于或者在当时用于业务目的。

（3）（2）并不适用于在下列情况下生成的书证内容：

（a）为在或者准备在澳大利亚或者海外进行程序而生成的书证，或者其生成与澳大利亚或者

or overseas proceeding; or

(b) in connection with an investigation relating or leading to a criminal proceeding.

Note: Section 182 gives this section a wider application in relation to Commonwealth records and certain Commonwealth documents.

148 Evidence of certain acts of justices, lawyers and notaries public

It is presumed, unless the contrary is proved, that a document was attested or verified by, or signed or acknowledged before, a justice of the peace, Australian lawyer or notary public, if:

(a) an Australian law requires, authorises or permits it to be attested, verified, signed or acknowledged by a justice of the peace, an Australian lawyer or a notary public, as the case may be; and

(b) it purports to have been so attested, verified, signed or acknowledged.

149 Attestation of documents

It is not necessary to adduce the evidence of an attesting witness to a document (not being a testamentary document) to prove that the document was signed or attested as it purports to have been signed or attested.

Note: Section 182 gives this section a wider application in relation to Commonwealth records and certain Commonwealth documents.

150 Seals and signatures

(1) If the imprint of a seal appears on a document and purports to be the imprint of:

海外程序有关；或者

（b）其生成涉及与刑事程序相关的调查或者导致
刑事程序的调查。

注释：就联邦记录和某些联邦文件，第 182 条赋予了本条
更为广泛的适用。

148 太平绅士、律师和公证人的某些行为证据

在下列情况下，推定某书证得到了太平绅士、澳大利亚
律师或者公证人的见证或者核实，或者是在这些人员面
前签署或者公证的，有相反证明者除外：[1]

（a）澳大利亚法律要求、授权或者允许太平绅士、
澳大利亚律师或者公证人对该书证进行见证、
核实、签署或者公证，视情况而定；并且

（b）该书证载明已经得到了上述见证、核实、签
署或者公证。

149 书证的见证

无需提出某书证（非遗嘱性书证）的见证人之证言，来
证明该书证如其所载明的那样已经签署或者见证。

注释：就联邦记录和某些联邦文件，第 182 条赋予了本条
更为广泛的适用。

150 印章与签名

（1）如果书证盖有印章之印记，并载明为下列印章之印
记，则应推定该印记为该印章之印记，该书证已经
如其载明的那样经合法加盖印章，有相反证据证明
者除外：

Section 150

    (a) a Royal Great Seal; or

    (b) the Great Seal of Australia; or

    (c) another seal of the Commonwealth; or

    (d) a seal of a State, a Territory or a foreign country; or

    (e) the seal of a body (including a court or a tribunal), or a body corporate, established by a law of the Commonwealth, a Territory or a foreign country; or

    (f) the seal of a court or tribunal established by a law of a State;

it is presumed, unless the contrary is proved, that the imprint is the imprint of that seal, and the document was duly sealed as it purports to have been sealed.

Note: This subsection differs from subsection 150(1) of the NSW Act.

(2) If the imprint of a seal appears on a document and purports to be the imprint of the seal of an office holder, it is presumed, unless the contrary is proved, that:

    (a) the imprint is the imprint of that seal; and

    (b) the document was duly sealed by the office holder acting in his or her official capacity; and

    (c) the office holder held the relevant office when the document was sealed.

(3) If a document purports to have been signed by an office holder in his or her official capacity, it is presumed, unless the contrary is proved, that:

    (a) the document was signed by the office holder acting in that capacity; and

    (b) the office holder held the relevant office when the document was signed.

（a）王室玉玺；或者

（b）澳大利亚国玺；或者

（c）其他联邦印章；或者

（d）州、领地或者外国印章；或者

（e）根据联邦、领地或者外国法律设立的机构（包括法院或者裁判庭）或者法人的印章；或者

（f）根据州法律设立的法院或者裁判庭的印章。

注释：本款不同于《新南威尔士州证据法》之 150（1）的规定。

（2）如果书证盖有印章之印记，并载明为公职人员印章之印记，则应推定存在下列情况，有相反证明者除外：

（a）该印记为该印章之印记；并且

（b）该书证已经为该公职人员以其公职身份合法加盖该印章；并且

（c）在书证加盖印章时，该公职人员担任相关公职。

（3）如果书证载明为公职人员以其公职身份所签署，则应推定存在下列情况，有相反证明者除外：

（a）该书证为该公职人员以该身份所签署；并且

（b）在书证签署时，该公职人员担任相关公职。

(4) In this section:

office holder means:

(a) the Sovereign; or

(b) the Governor–General; or

(c) the Governor of a State; or

(d) the Administrator of a Territory; or

(e) a person holding any other office under an Australian law or a law of a foreign country.

(5) This section extends to documents sealed, and documents signed, before the commencement of this section.

> Note 1: Section 5 extends the application of this section to proceedings in all Australian courts.
>
> Note 2: *Australian law* is defined in the Dictionary.

151 Seals of bodies established under State law

(1) If the imprint of a seal appears on a document and purports to be the imprint of the seal of a body (other than a court or a tribunal), or a body corporate, established by Royal Charter or a law of a State, it is presumed, unless the contrary is proved, that:

(a) the imprint is the imprint of that seal; and

(b) the document was duly sealed as it purports to have been sealed.

(2) This section extends to documents sealed before the commencement of this section.

> Note: The NSW Act has no equivalent provision for section 151.

152 Documents produced from proper custody

If a document that is or purports to be more than 20 years old is produced from proper custody, it is presumed, unless

（4）在本条中：

公职人员是指：

（a）君主；或者

（b）总督；或者

（c）州长；或者

（d）领地行政长官；或者

（e）依据澳大利亚法律或者外国法律担任任何其他公职的人。

（5）本条扩展适用于本条实施之前已经加盖印章或者已经签署的书证。

注释 1：第 5 条将本规定的运作扩展到了所有澳大利亚法院的程序。

注释 2：**澳大利亚法律**的定义见《术语》。

151 根据州法律设立的机构的印章

（1）如果书证盖有印章之印记，并载明为根据皇家特许状或者州法设立的机构（法院或者裁判庭除外）或者法人印章之印记，则应推定存在下列情况，有相反证明者除外：

（a）该印记为该印章之印记；并且

（b）该书证已经如其所称经合法加盖该印章。

（2）本条扩展适用于本条实施前已经加盖印章的书证。

注释：《新南威尔士州证据法》没有与第 151 条相应的规定。

152 出自适当保管处所的书证

如果书证已经存在或者载明存在 20 年以上，并且出自适当的保管处所，则应推定存在下列情况，有相反证明者

the contrary is proved, that:

(a) the document is the document that it purports to be; and

(b) if it purports to have been executed or attested by a person—it was duly executed or attested by that person.

Note: Section 182 gives this section a wider application in relation to Commonwealth records and certain Commonwealth documents.

Division 2—Matters of official record

153 Gazettes and other official documents

(1) It is presumed, unless the contrary is proved, that a document purporting:

(a) to be any government or official gazette (by whatever name called) of the Commonwealth, a State, a Territory or a foreign country; or

(b) to have been printed by the Government Printer or by the government or official printer of a State or Territory; or

(c) to have been printed by authority of the government or administration of the Commonwealth, a State, a Territory or a foreign country;

is what it purports to be and was published on the day on which it purports to have been published.

(2) If:

(a) there is produced to a court:

(i) a copy of any government or official gazette (by whatever name called) of the Commonwealth, a State, a Territory or a foreign country; or

除外：

 （a）该书证为其所载明的书证；并且

 （b）如果该书证载明已经某人签署或者见证，则
   其已经该某人适当签署或者见证。

> 注释：就联邦记录和某些联邦文件，第 182 条赋予了本条
> 更为广泛的适用。

第 2 目—官方记录事项

153 公报和其他公文

（1）如果书证载明下列事项，则应推定该书证是其所载
明的书证，并且是在其载明的期日公布的，有相反
证明者除外：

 （a）为联邦、州、领地或者外国的任何政府或者
   官方公报，无论名称如何；或者

 （b）为政府印务局、州或者领地的政府或者官方
   印务机构所印制；或者

 （c）为联邦、州、领地或者外国的政府或者行政
   机构所印制。

（2）在下列情况下，则应推定有关作为是正当做出的，
如果做出该作为的期日已经在下述复制件或者书
证中载明，则该作为是在该期日做出的，有相反证
明者除外：

 （a）下列复制件或者书证被出示给法院：

   （i）联邦、州、领地或者外国的任何政府或者
     官方公报（无论名称如何）的复制件；或
     者

(ii) a document that purports to have been printed by the Government Printer or by the government or official printer of a State or Territory; or

(iii) a document that purports to have been printed by authority of the government or administration of the Commonwealth, a State, a Territory or a foreign country; and

(b) the doing of an act:

(i) by the Governor–General or by the Governor of a State or the Administrator of a Territory; or

(ii) by a person authorised or empowered to do the act by an Australian law or a law of a foreign country;

is notified or published in the copy or document;

it is presumed, unless the contrary is proved, that the act was duly done and, if the day on which the act was done appears in the copy or document, it was done on that day.

Note: Section 5 extends the operation of this provision to proceedings in all Australian courts.

154 Documents published by authority of Parliaments etc.

It is presumed, unless the contrary is proved, that a document purporting to have been printed by authority of an Australian Parliament, a House of an Australian Parliament, a committee of such a House or a committee of an Australian Parliament:

(a) is what it purports to be; and

(b) was published on the day on which it purports to have been published.

Note 2: Section 5 extends the application of this section to proceedings in all Australian courts.

（ii）载明为政府印务局、州或者领地的政府或者官方印务机构所印制的书证；或者

（iii）载明为联邦、州、领地或者外国的政府或者行政机构所印制的书证；并且

（b）下列人员的某作为在该复制件或者书证中得以通告或者公布：

（i）总督、州长或者领地的行政首长；或者

（ii）根据澳大利亚法律或者外国法律有权或者被授权做出该作为的人员。

注释：第 5 条将本规定的运作扩展适用于所有澳大利亚法院的程序。

154 议会等机构公布的文件

如果书证载明该书证是由澳大利亚议会、澳大利亚议会的某院、该院的委员会或者澳大利亚议会的某委员会的机构所印制，则应当推定存在下列情况，有相反证明者除外：

（a）该书证是其所载明的书证；并且

（b）该书证是在其载明的期日公布的。

注释 2：第 5 条将本规定的运作扩展适用于所有澳大利亚法院的程序。

155 Evidence of official records

(1) Evidence of a Commonwealth record or of a public record of a State or Territory may be adduced by producing a document that:

    (a) purports to be such a record and to be signed or sealed by:

        (i) a Minister, or a Minister of the State or Territory, as the case requires; or

        (ii) a person who might reasonably be supposed to have custody of the record; or

    (b) purports to be a copy of or extract from the record that is certified to be a true copy or extract by:

        (i) a Minister, or a Minister of the State or Territory, as the case requires; or

        (ii) a person who might reasonably be supposed to have custody of the record.

(2) If such a document is produced, it is presumed, unless evidence that is sufficient to raise doubt about the presumption is adduced, that:

    (a) the document is the record, copy or extract that it purports to be; and

    (b) the Minister, Minister of the State or Territory or person:

    (i) signed or sealed the record; or

    (ii) certified the copy or extract as a true copy or extract;

    as the case requires.

> Note 1:   Subsection 155(1) differs from subsection 155(1) of the NSW Act. The NSW provision refers to evidence of a public document of a State or Territory rather than

155 官方记录证据

（1）关于联邦记录或者州、领地的公共记录的证据可以通过出示下列书证而提出：

（a）载明为上述记录，并且是由下列人员签署或者加盖印章的：

（i）部长或者州、领地的部长，视情况而定；或者

（ii）可以合理地认为是保管上述记录的人员；或者

（b）载明是经下列人员核证为真实复制件或者摘录的上述记录的复制件或者摘录：

（i）部长或者州、领地的部长，视情况而定；或者

（ii）可以合理地认为是保管上述记录的人员；或者

（2）如果出示了上述书证，则应当推定存在下列情况，提出足够证据对该推定提出疑问者除外：

（a）该书证是其所载明的记录、复制件或者摘录；并且

（b）部长或者州、领地的部长或者人员，视情况而定：

（i）签署了该记录或者为其加盖了印章；或者

（ii）已核证该复制件或者摘录是真实的复制件或者摘录，视情况而定。

注释 1：155（1）不同于《新南威尔士州证据法》之 155（1）。新南威尔士州的规定所称是州或者领地的公共文

evidence of a public record of a State or Territory.

Note 2: Section 5 extends the application of this section to proceedings in all Australian courts.

155A Evidence of Commonwealth documents

(1) Evidence of a Commonwealth document may be adduced by producing a document that purports to be, or to be a copy of or extract from, the Commonwealth document that is certified to be the Commonwealth document, or to be a true copy or extract, as the case may be, by:

   (a) a Minister; or

   (b) a person who might reasonably be supposed to have custody of the Commonwealth document.

(2) If such a document is produced, it is presumed, unless evidence that is sufficient to raise doubt about the presumption is adduced, that:

   (a) the document is the Commonwealth document, or the copy of or extract from the Commonwealth document, that it purports to be; and

   (b) the Minister or person certified the document as being the Commonwealth document or a true copy or extract, as the case requires.

Note 1: The NSW Act has no equivalent provision for section 155A.

Note 2: Section 5 extends the application of this section to proceedings in all Australian courts.

156 Public documents

(1) A document that purports to be a copy of, or an extract from or summary of, a public document and to have been:

件证据，而不是州或者领地的公共记录证据。

注释2：第5条将本条的运作扩展适用于所有澳大利亚法院的程序。

155A 联邦文件证据

（1）联邦文件证据，可以通过出示载明其为经过下列人员核证为联邦文件或者联邦文件的真实复制件或者摘录的书证，或者其复制件或者摘录而提出，视情况而定：

（a）部长；或者

（b）可以合理地认为是保管该联邦文件的人员。

（2）如果出示了上述书证，则应当推定存在下列情况，提出足够证据对该推定提出疑问者除外：

（a）该书证是其载明的联邦文件，或者该联邦文件的复制件或者摘录；并且

（b）部长或者有关人员已核证该书证是联邦文件，或者联邦文件的复制件或者摘录，视情况而定。

注释1：《新南威尔士州证据法》没有与第155A条相应的规定。

注释2：第5条将本条的运作扩展适用于了所有澳大利亚法院的程序。

156 公共文件

（1）如果书证载明是公共文件的复制件、摘录或者概要，并且存在下列情况，则推定该书证是该公共文件的复制件、摘录或者概要，有相反证明者除外：

(a) sealed with the seal of a person who, or a body that, might reasonably be supposed to have the custody of the public document; or

(b) certified as such a copy, extract or summary by a person who might reasonably be supposed to have custody of the public document;

is presumed, unless the contrary is proved, to be a copy of the public document, or an extract from or summary of the public document.

(2) If an officer entrusted with the custody of a public document is required by a court to produce the public document, it is sufficient compliance with the requirement for the officer to produce a copy of, or extract from, the public document if it purports to be signed and certified by the officer as a true copy or extract.

(3) It is sufficient production of a copy or extract for the purposes of subsection (2) if the officer sends it by prepaid post, or causes it to be delivered, to:

(a) the proper officer of the court in which it is to be produced; or

(b) the person before whom it is to be produced.

(4) The court before which a copy or extract is produced under subsection (2) may direct the officer to produce the original public document.

Note: Section 182 gives this section a wider application in relation to Commonwealth records.

157 Public documents relating to court processes

Evidence of a public document that is a judgment, act or other process of an Australian court or a foreign

（a）已加盖经可以合理地认为保管该公共文件的
人员或者机构的印章；或者

（b）可以合理地认为是保管该公共文件的人员已
核证为上述复制件、摘录或者概要。

（2）如果法院要求受委托保管公共文件的官员出示
该公共文件，该官员向法院出示载明由该官员
签署并且核证为该公共文件的真实复制件或者
摘录的复制件或者摘录，即已充分遵循了法院
的要求。

（3）就（2）之目的而言，如果该官员通过预付邮费邮
局寄发，或者将其送交下列人员，即已足够出示了
该有关公共文件的复制件或者摘录：

（a）要求出示该公共文件的法院的适当官员；或
者

（b）要求出示该公共文件的人员。

（4）根据（2）要求出示公共文件的复制件或者摘录
的法院，可以指示该官员出示该公共文件的原
件。

注释：就联邦记录，第 182 条赋予了本条更为广泛的适用。

157 与法院文书有关的公共文件

如果公共文件是某澳大利亚法院或者外国法院作出的判
决、决定或者其他文书，或者存放于该某澳大利亚法院
或外国法院的文件，关于该公共文件的证据可以通过出
示载明其为该公共文件的复制件并具有下列情形的书证

court, or that is a document lodged with an Australian court or a foreign court, may be adduced by producing a document that purports to be a copy of the public document and that:

(a) is proved to be an examined copy; or

(b) purports to be sealed with the seal of that court; or

(c) purports to be signed by a judge, magistrate, registrar or other proper officer of that court.

Note: Section 5 extends the operation of this provision to proceedings in all Australian courts.

158 Evidence of certain public documents

(1) If:

(a) a public document, or a certified copy of a public document, of a State or Territory is admissible for a purpose in that State or Territory under the law of that State or Territory; and

(b) it purports to be sealed, or signed and sealed, or signed alone, as directed by the law of that State or Territory;

it is admissible in evidence to the same extent and for that purpose in all courts:

(c) without proof of:

(i) the seal or signature; or

(ii) the official character of the person appearing to have signed it; and

(d) without further proof in every case in which the original document could have been received in evidence.

(2) A public document of a State or Territory that is admissible in evidence for any purpose in that State or Territory under

而提出：

> （a）已经证明为经过核对的复制件；或者
>
> （b）载明已加盖该某法院之印章；或者
>
> （c）载明已经法官、治安法官、登记官或者该某法院的其他适当官员所签署。
>
> 注释：第 5 条将本规定的运作扩展适用于所有澳大利亚法院的程序。

158 关于特定公共文件的证据

（1）如果：

> （a）州或者领地的公共文件或者公共文件的核证复制件可以根据该州或者领地的法律在该州或者领地为某一目的而采纳；并且
>
> （b）载明根据州或者领地的法律已经盖章、签署并盖章或者仅经签署；

则其可以在下列情况下，为上述目的在所有法院同样采纳为证据：

> （c）无需证明：
>
> > （i）上述印章或者签字；或者
> >
> > （ii）签署该公共文件的人员的官方性质；以及
>
> （d）在原件本可以采纳为证据的每个案件中，无需进一步证明。

（2）如果州或者领地的公共文件，可以根据该州或者领地的法律，无需证明下列事项而在该州或者领地为任何目的而采纳，则其可以在无下列证明的情况下，为任何目的在所有法院同样采

the law of that State or Territory without proof of:

   (a) the seal or signature authenticating the document; or

   (b) the judicial or official character of the person appearing to have signed the document;

   is admissible in evidence to the same extent and for any purpose in all courts without such proof.

(3) This section only applies to documents that are public records of a State or Territory.

> Note 2:   Section 5 extends the operation of this provision to proceedings in all Australian courts.

159 Official statistics

A document that purports:

   (a) to be published by the Australian Statistician; and

   (b) to contain statistics or abstracts compiled and analysed by the Australian Statistician under the *Census and Statistics Act 1905*;

   is evidence that those statistics or abstracts were compiled and analysed by the Australian Statistician under that Act.

> Note: Section 5 extends the application of this section to proceedings in all Australian courts.

Division 3—Matters relating to post and communications

160 Postal articles

(1) It is presumed (unless evidence sufficient to raise doubt about the presumption is adduced) that a postal article sent by prepaid post addressed to a person at a specified address

纳为证据：

（a）验真该文件的印章或者签字；或者

（b）签署该书证的人员的司法或者官方性质。

（3）本条仅适用于作为州或者领地的公共记录的书
证。

> 注释 2：第 5 条将本规定的运作扩展适用于所有澳大利亚
> 法院的程序。

159 官方统计

载明下列事项的书证，是证明这些统计或者概要系由澳
大利亚统计局长根据下述法律所编纂和分析的证据：

（a）由澳大利亚统计局长公布；并且

（b）包含有澳大利亚统计局长根据《1905 年普
查和统计法》进行编纂和分析的统计或者
概要。

> 注释：第 5 条将本条的运作扩展适用于所有澳大利亚法院
> 的程序。

第 3 目—与邮政和通信有关的事项

160 邮品

（1）预付邮资寄给澳大利亚或者外部领地指定地址的
某人的邮品，推定于邮件寄发后第四个工作日寄
达指定地址，提出足够证据对该推定提出疑问者

in Australia or in an external Territory was received at that
address on the fourth working day after having been posted.

(2) This section does not apply if:

    (a) the proceeding relates to a contract; and

    (b) all the parties to the proceeding are parties to the
contract; and

    (c) subsection (1) is inconsistent with a term of the
contract.

(3) In this section:

working day means a day that is not:

    (a) a Saturday or a Sunday; or

    (b) a public holiday or a bank holiday in the place to which
the postal article was addressed.

Note: Section 182 gives this section a wider application in relation
to postal articles sent by a Commonwealth agency.

161 Electronic communications

(1) If a document purports to contain a record of an electronic
communication other than one referred to in section 162,
it is presumed (unless evidence sufficient to raise doubt
about the presumption is adduced) that the communication:

    (a) was sent or made in the form of electronic communication
that appears from the document to have been the form by
which it was sent or made; and

    (b) was sent or made by or on behalf of the person by or
on whose behalf it appears from the document to have
been sent or made; and

    (c) was sent or made on the day on which, at the time at
which and from the place from which it appears from
the document to have been sent or made; and

除外。[2]

（2）在下列情况下，本条并不适用：

（a）该程序与合同有关；并且

（b）程序所有当事人皆为合同当事人；并且

（c）（1）与合同条款之规定不一致。

（3）在本条中：

工作日是指并非下列期日之期日：

（a）星期六或者星期日；或者

（b）邮品寄达地的公共假日或者银行假日。

注释：就联邦机构寄发的邮品，第 182 条赋予了本条更为
广泛的适用。

161　电子通信

（1）如果书证载明包含有第 162 条所称的电子通信
之外的电子通信记录，则应当推定该通信存在
下列情形，提出足够证据对该推定提出疑问者
除外：

（a）已经采用书证所显示的方式发送或者制作；
并且

（b）是由已经发送或者制作的书证显示的人或者
其代表发送或者制作的；并且

（c）是在已经发送或者制作的书证显示的日期、
时间和地点发送或者制作的；并且

      (d) was received at the destination to which it appears from the document to have been sent; and

      (e) if it appears from the document that the sending of the communication concluded at a particular time⊖was received at that destination at that time.

  (2) A provision of subsection (1) does not apply if:

      (a) the proceeding relates to a contract; and

      (b) all the parties to the proceeding are parties to the contract; and

      (c) the provision is inconsistent with a term of the contract.

Note: Section 182 gives this section a wider application in relation to Commonwealth records.

162 Lettergrams and telegrams

  (1) If a document purports to contain a record of a message transmitted by means of a lettergram or telegram, it is presumed (unless evidence sufficient to raise doubt about the presumption is adduced) that the message was received by the person to whom it was addressed 24 hours after the message was delivered to a post office for transmission as a lettergram or telegram.

  (2) This section does not apply if:

      (a) the proceeding relates to a contract; and

      (b) all the parties to the proceeding are parties to the contract; and

      (c) subsection (1) is inconsistent with a term of the contract.

Note: Section 182 gives this section a wider application in relation to Commonwealth records.

（d）是在已经发送或者制作的书证显示的目的地

接收的；并且

（e）如果已经发送或者制作的书证是在具体时间

结束发送的，则它是在上述目的地的该时间

接收到的。

（2）在下列情况下，（1）并不适用：

（a）该程序与合同有关；并且

（b）程序所有当事人皆为合同当事人；并且

（c）该规定与合同条款之规定不一致。

注释：就联邦记录，第182条赋予了本条更为广泛的适用。

162 信件电报与电报

（1）如果书证载明包含有经信件电报和电报传输的讯息

记录，则应当推定该讯息在作为信件电报或者电报

交付邮局传输后 24 小时内为指定接收人所接收，

提出足够证据对该推定提出疑问者除外。

（2）在下列情况下，本条并不适用：

（a）该程序与合同有关；并且

（b）程序所有当事人皆为合同当事人；并且

（c）第（1）款与合同条款之规定不一致。

注释：就联邦记录，第182条赋予了本条更为广泛的适用。

163 Proof of letters having been sent by Commonwealth agencies

(1) A letter from a Commonwealth agency addressed to a person at a specified address is presumed (unless evidence sufficient to raise doubt about the presumption is adduced) to have been sent by prepaid post to that address on the fifth business day after the date (if any) that, because of its placement on the letter or otherwise, purports to be the date on which the letter was prepared.

(2) In this section:

business day means a day that is not:

(a) a Saturday or a Sunday; or

(b) a public holiday or bank holiday in the place in which the letter was prepared.

letter means any form of written communication that is directed to a particular person or address, and includes:

(a) any standard postal article within the meaning of the *Australian Postal Corporation Act 1989*; and

(b) any envelope, packet, parcel, container or wrapper containing such a communication; and

(c) any unenclosed written communication that is directed to a particular person or address.

Note 1: The NSW Act has no equivalent provision for section 163.

Note 2: Section 5 extends the operation of this section to proceedings in all Australian courts.

163 联邦机构寄发的信件之证明

（1）对于联邦机构寄给指定地址的某人的信件，则应推定在附加于信件上或者以其他方式载明的信件制作期日后已经由预付邮资邮局在第五个营业日寄达指定地址，提出足够证据对该推定提出疑问者除外。

（2）在本条中：

营业日是指并非下列期日之期日：

（a）星期六或者星期日；或者

（b）信件制作地的公共假日或者银行假日。

信件是指寄给具体人员或者地址的任何形式的书面通信，并且包括：

（a）《1989 年澳大利亚邮政公司法》所指的任何标准邮品；以及

（b）容纳上述通信的任何信封、包裹、邮包、容器或包装物；以及

（c）寄给具体人员或者地址的任何未封的书面通信。

> 注释 1：《新南威尔士州证据法》没有与第 163 条相应的规定。

> 注释 2：第 5 条将本条的运作扩展适用于了所有澳大利亚法院的程序。

Part 4.4—Corroboration

164 Corroboration requirements abolished

(1) It is not necessary that evidence on which a party relies be corroborated.

(2) Subsection (1) does not affect the operation of a rule of law that requires corroboration with respect to the offence of perjury or a similar or related offence.

(3) Despite any rule, whether of law or practice, to the contrary, but subject to the other provisions of this Act, if there is a jury, it is not necessary that the judge:

    (a) warn the jury that it is dangerous to act on uncorroborated evidence or give a warning to the same or similar effect; or

    (b) give a direction relating to the absence of corroboration.

Part 4.5—Warnings and information

165 Unreliable evidence

(1) This section applies to evidence of a kind that may be unreliable, including the following kinds of evidence:

    (a) evidence in relation to which Part 3.2 (hearsay evidence) or 3.4 (admissions) applies;

    (b) identification evidence;

    (c) evidence the reliability of which may be affected by age, ill health (whether physical or mental), injury or the like;

    (d) evidence given in a criminal proceeding by a witness,

第 4.4 节—补强

164 废除补强要求

(1)对当事人所依赖的证据进行补强并非必需。

(2)(1)不影响要求对伪证或者类似犯罪、相关犯罪进行补强的法律规则的运作。[3]

(3)即使法律规则或者法院程序规则有相反规定,但根据本法的其他规定,在有陪审团的情况下,则法官的下列行为并非必需:

    (a)警告陪审团说根据未经补强的证据而行动是危险的,或者作出具有同样或者类似效果的警告;或者

    (b)作出与补强阙如相关的指示。

第 4.5 节—警告与告知

165 不可靠的证据

(1)本条适用于可能不可靠的证据,包括下列证据在内:

    (a)第 3.2 节(传闻证据)或者第 3.4 节(自认)所适用的证据;

    (b)辨认证据;

    (c)可靠性可能会受到年龄、不良健康(无论是生理的还是精神的)、损伤等类似情形影响的证据;

    (d)可以合理认为与引起该程序的事件具有刑

being a witness who might reasonably be supposed to have been criminally concerned in the events giving rise to the proceeding;

(e) evidence given in a criminal proceeding by a witness who is a prison informer;

(f) oral evidence of questioning by an investigating official of a defendant that is questioning recorded in writing that has not been signed, or otherwise acknowledged in writing, by the defendant;

(g) in a proceeding against the estate of a deceased person —evidence adduced by or on behalf of a person seeking relief in the proceeding that is evidence about a matter about which the deceased person could have given evidence if he or she were alive.

(2) If there is a jury and a party so requests, the judge is to:

(a) warn the jury that the evidence may be unreliable; and

(b) inform the jury of matters that may cause it to be unreliable; and

(c) warn the jury of the need for caution in determining whether to accept the evidence and the weight to be given to it.

(3) The judge need not comply with subsection (2) if there are good reasons for not doing so.

(4) It is not necessary that a particular form of words be used in giving the warning or information.

(5) This section does not affect any other power of the judge to give a warning to, or to inform, the jury.

(6) Subsection (2) does not permit a judge to warn or inform a jury in proceedings before it in which a child gives evidence that the reliability of the child's evidence may

事关联性的证人，在刑事程序中所作的证言；

（e）作为监狱密告者在刑事程序中所作的证言；

（f）关于未经被告签名或者以其他书面形式承认的采用书面形式记录的调查人员对被告进行的询问的口头证据；

（g）在就死者的遗产提起的程序中，在该程序中寻求救济的人或者代表该某人的人就死者如果活着将可以作证之事项提出的证据。

（2）如果有陪审团且当事人提出如下要求，法官应当：

（a）警告陪审团该证据可能不可靠；并且

（b）告知陪审团可能导致该证据不可靠的事项；并且

（c）警告陪审团在决定是否采纳该证据以及赋予该证据的证明力时需要谨慎。

（3）如果有充分的理由不如此行为，法官不需要遵行（2）。

（4）法官在进行上述警告或者告知时，无需使用具体形式的语言。

（5）本条并不影响法官对陪审团进行警告或者告知的任何其他权力。

（6）在儿童作证的程序中，（2）并不允许法官对陪审团进行警告或者告知说儿童证言的可靠性可能会

be affected by the age of the child. Any such warning or information may be given only in accordance with subsections 165A(2) and (3).

165A Warnings in relation to children's evidence

(1) A judge in any proceeding in which evidence is given by a child before a jury must not do any of the following:

    (a) warn the jury, or suggest to the jury, that children as a class are unreliable witnesses;

    (b) warn the jury, or suggest to the jury, that the evidence of children as a class is inherently less credible or reliable, or requires more careful scrutiny, than the evidence of adults;

    (c) give a warning, or suggestion to the jury, about the unreliability of the particular child's evidence solely on account of the age of the child;

    (d) in the case of a criminal proceeding—give a general warning to the jury of the danger of convicting on the uncorroborated evidence of a witness who is a child.

(2) Subsection (1) does not prevent the judge, at the request of a party, from:

    (a) informing the jury that the evidence of the particular child may be unreliable and the reasons why it may be unreliable; and

    (b) warning or informing the jury of the need for caution in determining whether to accept the evidence of the particular child and the weight to be given to it;

if the party has satisfied the court that there are circumstances (other than solely the age of the child) particular to the child that affect the reliability of the child's evidence and that warrant the giving of a

受到其年龄的影响。仅可依照 165A（2）和（3）
进行上述警告或者告知。

165A 与儿童证言有关的警告

（1）在儿童在陪审团前作证的任何程序中，法官不得从
事任何下列活动：

（a）警告陪审团或者向陪审团暗示，儿童是一类
不可靠的证人；

（b）警告陪审团或者向陪审团暗示，儿童证言是一
类具有固有不可信性或者不可靠性的证言，或
者与成人证言相比，需要进行更为审慎的审查；

（c）仅依据儿童的年龄而就具体儿童证言的不可
靠性对陪审团进行警告或者暗示；

（d）在刑事程序中，就根据儿童证人未经补强的
证言而作出定罪裁决的危险，对陪审团作出
一般警告。

（2）如果当事人使法院确信，有具体儿童的情况（仅
仅是儿童的年龄要除外），影响了其证言的可靠性，
且这要求作出警告或者告知，则（1）并不禁止法
官根据一方当事人的请求，从事下列活动：

（a）告知陪审团，具体儿童的证言可能不可能以
及为什么可能不可靠的原因；以及

（b）警告或者告知陪审团，在决定是否接受具
体儿童的证言以及赋予其证明力时，需要

warning or the information.

(3) This section does not affect any other power of a judge to give a warning to, or to inform, the jury.

165B Delay in prosecution

(1) This section applies in a criminal proceeding in which there is a jury.

(2) If the court, on application by the defendant, is satisfied that the defendant has suffered a significant forensic disadvantage because of the consequences of delay, the court must inform the jury of the nature of that disadvantage and the need to take that disadvantage into account when considering the evidence.

(3) The judge need not comply with subsection (2) if there are good reasons for not doing so.

(4) It is not necessary that a particular form of words be used in informing the jury of the nature of the significant forensic disadvantage suffered and the need to take that disadvantage into account, but the judge must not in any way suggest to the jury that it would be dangerous or unsafe to convict the defendant solely because of the delay or the forensic disadvantage suffered because of the consequences of the delay.

(5) The judge must not warn or inform the jury about any forensic disadvantage the defendant may have suffered because of delay except in accordance with this section, but this section does not affect any other power of the judge to give any warning to, or to inform, the jury.

(6) For the purposes of this section:

(a) delay includes delay between the alleged offence and its being reported; and

(b) significant forensic disadvantage is not to be regarded

谨慎。

（3）本条并不影响法官对陪审团进行警告或者告知的任
何其他权力。

165B 检控迟延

（1）本条适用于有陪审团的刑事程序。

（2）如果根据被告的申请，法院确信被告因迟延的结
果而遭受了法证上的不利，法院必须告知陪审团
该不利的性质，以及在审酌证据时需要考虑该不
利。[4]

（3）如果有充分理由不如此行为，则法官不需要遵行
（2）。

（4）法院在告知陪审团该不利的性质，以及在审酌证据
时需要考虑该不利时，无需采用具体形式的言语，
但是法官不得仅因迟延或者迟延后果造成的法证
上的不利，以任何方式向陪审团暗示，判定被告有
罪是危险的或者不安全的。

（5）法官不得就被告因迟延可能遭受的法证上的不利警
告或者告知陪审团，依据本条者除外，但是本条并
不影响法官对陪审团进行警告或者告知的其他权
力。

（6）就本条目的而言：

（a）迟延包括所称犯罪与报案之间的迟延；以及

（b）仅仅存在迟延不能被视为能够证明存在严重

as being established by the mere existence of a delay.

Part 4.6—Ancillary provisions

Division 1—Requests to produce documents or call witnesses

> Note: Section 182 gives this Division a wider application in relation to Commonwealth records and certain Commonwealth documents.

166 Definition of request

In this Division:

request means a request that a party (the *requesting party*) makes to another party to do one or more of the following:

(a) to produce to the requesting party the whole or a part of a specified document or thing;

(b) to permit the requesting party, adequately and in an appropriate way, to examine, test or copy the whole or a part of a specified document or thing;

(c) to call as a witness a specified person believed to be concerned in production or maintenance of a specified document or thing;

(d) to call as a witness a specified person in whose possession or under whose control a specified document or thing is believed to be or to have been at any time;

(e) in relation to a document of the kind referred to in paragraph (b) or (c) of the definition of *document* in the Dictionary—to permit the requesting party, adequately and in an appropriate way, to examine and test the document and the way in which it was produced and has been kept;

的法证上的不利。

第 4.6 节—附带规定

第 1 目—出示书证或者传唤证人之请求

> 注释：就联邦记录和某些联邦文件，第 182 条赋予了本目
> 更为广泛的适用。

166 请求的定义

在本目中：

请求是指一方当事人（**请求方**）向另一方当事人提出的
从事下列某项或者多项行为的请求：

（a）向请求方出示指定的书证或者物证的全部或
者一部分；

（b）允许请求方充分地以适当的方式查验、测试
或者复制指定的书证或者物证的全部或者一
部分；

（c）传唤被认为与特定书证或者物品的制作或者
保管有关的特定人员作为证人；

（d）传唤被认为在任何时候持有、控制或者曾经
持有、控制特定书证或者物品的特定人员作
为证人；

（e）就《术语》中**书证**的定义的（b）或者（c）
所称书证而言，允许请求方充分地以适当的
方式查验或者测试该书证，以及生成或者保
管该书证的方式；

(f) in relation to evidence of a previous representation⊖ to call as a witness the person who made the previous representation;

(g) in relation to evidence that a person has been convicted of an offence, being evidence to which subsection 92(2) applies—to call as a witness a person who gave evidence in the proceeding in which the person was so convicted.

167 Requests may be made about certain matters

A party may make a reasonable request to another party for the purpose of determining a question that relates to:

(a) a previous representation; or

(b) evidence of a conviction of a person for an offence; or

(c) the authenticity, identity or admissibility of a document or thing.

168 Time limits for making certain requests

(1) If a party has given to another party written notice of its intention to adduce evidence of a previous representation, the other party may only make a request to the party relating to the representation if the request is made within 21 days after the notice was given.

(2) Despite subsection (1), the court may give the other party leave to make a request relating to the representation after the end of that 21 day period if it is satisfied that there is good reason to do so.

(3) If a party has given to another party written notice of its intention to adduce evidence of a person's conviction of an offence in order to prove a fact in issue, the other party may only make a request relating to evidence of the

（f）就先前表述证据而言，传唤作出该先前表述的人作为证人；

（g）就本法 92（2）所要适用的关于某人已经被定某罪的证据而言，传唤在该某人被定罪的程序中作证的人为证人。

167 可以就某些事项提出请求

为确定与下列事项有关的问题，一方当事人可以向另一方当事人提出合理请求：

（a）先前表述；或者

（b）关于某人因某罪而被定罪的证据；或者

（c）书证或者物证的真实性、同一性或者可采性。

168 提出某些请求的时限

（1）如果一方当事人已经就其提出先前表述证据之意图，向另一方当事人发出书面通知，其他当事人仅可以在上述通知发出之日起 21 日内，就该表述向该当事人提出请求。

（2）尽管有（1），如果法院确信存在合理理由，可以允许其他当事人在上述 21 日期间结束之后，就该表述提出请求。

（3）如果一方当事人已经就其提出关于某人因犯罪被定罪的证据以证明某争议事实之意图，向另一当事人发出书面通知，其他当事人仅可以在上述通

conviction if the request is made within 21 days after the notice is given.

(4) Despite subsection (3), the court may give the other party leave to make a request relating to evidence of the conviction after the end of that 21 day period if it is satisfied that there is good reason to do so.

(5) If a party has served on another party a copy of a document that it intends to tender in evidence, the other party may only make a request relating to the document if the request is made within 21 days after service of the copy.

(6) If the copy of the document served under subsection (5) is accompanied by, or has endorsed on it, a notice stating that the document is to be tendered to prove the contents of another document, the other party may only make a request relating to the other document if the request is made within 21 days after service of the copy.

(7) Despite subsections (5) and (6), the court may give the other party leave to make a request relating to the document, or other document, after the end of the 21 day period if it is satisfied that there is good reason to do so.

169 Failure or refusal to comply with requests

(1) If the party has, without reasonable cause, failed or refused to comply with a request, the court may, on application, make one or more of the following orders:

   (a) an order directing the party to comply with the request;

   (b) an order that the party produce a specified document or thing, or call as a witness a specified person, as mentioned in section 166;

   (c) an order that the evidence in relation to which the request was made is not to be admitted in evidence;

知发出之日起 21 日内，就该定罪证据向该当事人

提出请求。

（4）尽管有（3），如果法院确信存在合理理由，可以

允许其他当事人在上述 21 日期间结束之后，就该

定罪证据提出请求。

（5）如果一方当事人已向另一方当事人送达其准备提交

为证据的书证复制件，其他当事人仅可以在上述复

制件送达之日起 21 日内，就该书证提出请求。

（6）如果根据（5）送达的书证复制件同时附有或者背

书有表明该书证将提交法院以证明其他书证之内

容的通知，其他当事人仅可以在上述复制件送达之

日起 21 日内，就该其他书证提出请求。

（7）尽管有（5）和（6），如果法院确信存在合理理由，

可以允许其他当事人在上述 21 日期间结束之后，

就该书证或者其他书证提出请求。

169 未能或者拒绝遵行请求

（1）如果当事人没有合理理由，未能或者拒绝遵行某请

求，法院可以根据申请，作出下列一项或者多项命

令：

（a）责令该当事人遵行该请求的命令；

（b）如第 166 条规定的那样，责令当事人出示指

定的书证或者物证，或者传唤指定人作为证

人的命令；

（c）与请求有关的证据不得被采纳为证据的命

令；

    (d) such order with respect to adjournment or costs as is just.

(2) If the party had, within a reasonable time after receiving the request, informed the other party that it refuses to comply with the request, any application under subsection (1) by the other party must be made within a reasonable time after being so informed.

(3) The court may, on application, direct that evidence in relation to which a request was made is not to be admitted in evidence if an order made by it under paragraph (1)(a) or (b) is not complied with.

(4) Without limiting the circumstances that may constitute reasonable cause for a party to fail to comply with a request, it is reasonable cause to fail to comply with a request if:

    (a) the document or thing to be produced is not available to the party; or

    (b) the existence and contents of the document are not in issue in the proceeding in which evidence of the document is proposed to be adduced; or

    (c) the person to be called as a witness is not available.

(5) Without limiting the matters that the court may take into account in relation to the exercise of a power under subsection (1), it is to take into account:

    (a) the importance in the proceeding of the evidence in relation to which the request was made; and

    (b) whether there is likely to be a dispute about the matter to which the evidence relates; and

    (c) whether there is a reasonable doubt as to the authenticity or accuracy of the evidence that is, or the document the contents of which are, sought to be proved; and

（d）就延期审理或者费用作出的有充分根据的命令。

（2）如果当事人在收到上述请求的合理时间内就其拒绝遵行该请求通知了其他当事人，则该其他当事人根据（1）提出的任何申请必须在接到通知后的合理期间内提出。

（3）如果法院根据（1）（a）或者（b）作出的命令没有得到遵行，则法院可以根据申请，指示与该请求有关的证据不得被采纳为证据。

（4）构成当事人未能遵行某请求的合理理由之情形，包括但是不限于下列情形：

（a）当事人得不到需要出示的书证或者物品；或者

（b）在准备提出书证证据的程序中，就书证的存在或者内容不存在争议；或者

（c）被作为证人传唤的人不能到庭。

（5）法院在行使（1）规定的权力时，应当虑及的事项包括但是不限于：

（a）所请求的证据在程序中的重要性；并且

（b）与证据有关的事项是否可能存在争议；并且

（c）是否就试图证明的证据或者试图证明其内容的书证的真实性或者准确性存在合理疑问；并且

(d) whether there is a reasonable doubt as to the authenticity of the document or thing that is sought to be tendered; and

(e) if the request relates to evidence of a previous representation— whether there is a reasonable doubt as to the accuracy of the representation or of the evidence on which it was based; and

(f) in the case of a request referred to in paragraph (g) of the definition of *request* in section 166—whether another person is available to give evidence about the conviction or the facts that were in issue in the proceeding in which the conviction was obtained; and

(g) whether compliance with the request would involve undue expense or delay or would not be reasonably practicable; and

(h) the nature of the proceeding.

Note: Clause 5 of Part 2 of the Dictionary is about the availability of documents and things, and clause 4 of Part 2 of the Dictionary is about the availability of persons.

Division 2—Proof of certain matters by affidavits or written statements

Note: Section 182 gives this Division a wider application in relation to Commonwealth records and certain Commonwealth documents.

170 Evidence relating to certain matters

(1) Evidence of a fact that is, because of a provision of this Act referred to in the Table, to be proved in relation to a document or thing may be given by a person permitted under section 171 to give such evidence.

第 170 条

（d）是否就试图提交为证据的书证或者物证的真实性存在合理怀疑；并且

（e）在请求与先前表述证据有关的情况下，是否就该表述或者其所依据的证据的准确性存在合理怀疑；并且

（f）在第 166 条**请求**的定义中（g）所称请求情况下，其他人员是否可以到庭就定罪或者该定罪程序中的争议事实作证；并且

（g）遵循请求是否将带来不合理的成本或者迟延，或者不具有合理的可行性；并且

（h）程序的性质。

注释：《术语》第 2 部分第 5 条规定了书证和物证的可得性，《术语》第 2 部分第 4 条规定了人员的到庭问题。

第 2 目—通过宣誓陈述书或者书面陈述证明某些事项

注释：就联邦记录和某些联邦文件，第 182 条赋予了本目更为广泛的适用。

170 与某些事项有关的证据

（1）根据下表所列本法之规定，就书证或者物证而言，证明某事实的证据，可以由根据本法第 171 条所允许的人员提供。

TABLE

Provisions of this Act	Subject matter
Section 48	Proof of contents of documents
Sections 63, 64 and 65	Hearsay exceptions for *first-hand* hearsay
Section 69	Hearsay exception for business records
Section 70	Hearsay exception for tags, labels and other writing
Section 71	Hearsay exception for telecommunications
The provisions of Part 4.3	Facilitation of proof
Section 182	Commonwealth records

Note: The table differs from the table in subsection 170(1) of the NSW Act because that Act has no equivalent to section 182 of this Act.

(2) Evidence may be given by affidavit or, if the evidence relates to a public document, by a written statement.

171 Persons who may give such evidence

(1) Such evidence may be given by:

(a) a person who, at the relevant time or afterwards, had a position of responsibility in relation to making or keeping the document or thing; or

(b) except in the case of evidence of a fact that is to be proved in relation to a document or thing because of section 63, 64 or 65—an authorised person.

(2) Despite paragraph (1)(b), evidence must not be given under this section by an authorised person who, at the relevant time or afterwards, did not have a position of responsibility

表

本法规定	主题
第 48 条	书证内容的证明
第 63 条、第 64 条和第 65 条	**第一手**传闻的传闻例外
第 69 条	业务记录的传闻例外
第 70 条	标牌、标签和其他写字纸的传闻例外
第 71 条	通信的传闻例外
第 4.3 节之规定	证明的简化
第 182 条	联邦记录

注释：本表不同于《新南威尔士州证据法》170（1）的列表，这是因为该法没有与本法第 182 条相应的规定。

（2）该证据可以以宣誓陈述书的形式提供。如果该证据与公共文件有关，也可以以书面陈述形式提供。

171 可以提供上述证据的人

（1）上述证据可以由下列人员提供：

（a）在当时或者此后，居于负责制作或者保管书证或者物证之岗位的人员；或者

（b）除因第 63 条、第 64 条或者第 65 条就书证或者物证使用证据证明有关事实之情形外的被授权人员。

（2）尽管有（1）（b），在当时或者此后并不居于负有制作或者保管书证或者物证职责之岗位的人员，

in relation to making or keeping the document or thing unless it appears to the court that:

 (a) it is not reasonably practicable for the evidence to be given by a person who had, at the relevant time or afterwards, a position of responsibility in relation to making or keeping the document or thing; or

 (b) having regard to all the circumstances of the case, undue expense would be caused by calling such a person as a witness.

(3) In this section:

authorised person means:

 (a) if the evidence is given at a place outside Australia:

  (i) an Australian Diplomatic Officer, or an Australian Consular Officer, within the meaning of the *Consular Fees Act 1955*, exercising his or her function in that place; or

  (ii) an employee of the Commonwealth, authorised under paragraph 3(c) of the *Consular Fees Act 1955*, exercising his or her function in that place; or

  (iii) an employee of the Australian Trade Commission, authorised under paragraph 3(d) of the *Consular Fees Act 1955*, exercising his or her function in that place; or

 (b) an AFP employee (within the meaning of the *Australian Federal Police Act 1979*); or

 (c) a special member of the Australian Federal Police (within the meaning of the *Australian Federal Police Act 1979*); or

 (d) a person authorised by the Attorney–General for the purposes of this section.

不得根据本条提供证据，除非在法院看来：

（a）由在当时或者此后居于负有制作或者保管书
证或者物证职责之岗位的人员提供证据，不
具有合理的可行性；或者

（b）虑及案件所有情况，将上述人员传唤为证人，
将会造成不当耗费。

（3）在本条中：

被授权人员是指：

（a）在提供证据的地点在澳大利亚之外的情况
下：

（i）在当地履行职能的《1995 年领事费用法》
含义上的澳大利亚外交官员或者领事官
员；或者

（ii）在当地履行职能的根据《1995 年领事费
用法》3（c）授权的联邦雇员；或者

（iii）在当地履行职能的根据《1995 年领事
用法》3（d）授权的澳大利亚贸易委员会
的雇员；或者

（b）澳大利亚联邦警察机构雇员（含义见《1979
年澳大利亚联邦警察法》）；或者

（c）澳大利亚联邦警察机构的特别成员 （含义
见《1979 年澳大利亚联邦警察法》）；或
者[5]

（d）经司法部长为本条之目的授权的人。

> Note: Subsection 169(3) of the NSW Act differs from subsection (3).

172 Evidence based on knowledge, belief or information

(1) Despite Chapter 3, the evidence may include evidence based on the knowledge and belief of the person who gives it, or on information that that person has.

(2) An affidavit or statement that includes evidence based on knowledge, information or belief must set out the source of the knowledge or information or the basis of the belief.

173 Notification of other parties

(1) A copy of the affidavit or statement must be served on each party a reasonable time before the hearing of the proceeding.

(2) The party who tenders the affidavit or statement must, if another party so requests, call the deponent or person who made the statement to give evidence but need not otherwise do so.

Division 3—Foreign law

174 Evidence of foreign law

(1) Evidence of a statute, proclamation, treaty or act of state of a foreign country may be adduced in a proceeding by producing:

    (a) a book or pamphlet, containing the statute, proclamation, treaty or act of state, that purports to have been printed by the government or official printer of the country or by authority of the government or administration of the country; or

注释：《新南威尔士州证据法》169（3）不同于本条（3）。

172 基于知识、信念或者信息的证据

（1）尽管有第 3 章，证据可以包括基于有关人员的知识和信念的证据，或者基于该某人所拥有的信息的证据。

（2）包含基于知识、信息或者信念的证据的宣誓陈述书或者陈述，必须列明知识或者信息的来源，或者信念的根据。

173 对其他当事人的通知

（1）宣誓陈述书或者陈述的复制件必须在程序听证开始之前的合理时间内送达每个当事人。

（2）将宣誓陈述书或者陈述提交为证据的当事人，在其他当事人提出请求的情况下，必须传唤宣誓陈述人或者作出陈述的人员作证，但是不需采取其他方式从事上述活动。

第 3 目—外国法律

174 关于外国法律的证据

（1）在程序中，可以通过出示下列材料来提出关于外国制定法、公告、条约或者国家行为的证据：

（a）载明由外国政府、官方印务局或者外国政府或者行政机构印制的包含外国制定法、公告、条约或者国家行为的书籍或者印刷册；或者

(b) a book or other publication, containing the statute, proclamation, treaty or act of state, that appears to the court to be a reliable source of information; or

(c) a book or pamphlet that is or would be used in the courts of the country to inform the courts about, or to prove, the statute, proclamation, treaty or act of state; or

(d) a copy of the statute, proclamation, treaty or act of state that is proved to be an examined copy.

(2) A reference in this section to a statute of a foreign country includes a reference to a regulation or by–law of the country.

175 Evidence of law reports of foreign countries

(1) Evidence of the unwritten or common law of a foreign country may be adduced by producing a book containing reports of judgments of courts of the country if the book is or would be used in the courts of the country to inform the courts about the unwritten or common law of the country.

(2) Evidence of the interpretation of a statute of a foreign country may be adduced by producing a book containing reports of judgments of courts of the country if the book is or would be used in the courts of the country to inform the courts about the interpretation of the statute.

176 Questions of foreign law to be decided by judge

If, in a proceeding in which there is a jury, it is necessary to ascertain the law of another country which is applicable to the facts of the case, any question as to the effect of the evidence adduced with respect to that law is to be decided by the judge alone.

（b）在法院看来是可靠信息来源的包含有制定法、
公告、条约或者国家行为的书籍或者其他印
刷品；或者

（c）外国法院用于了解或者证明制定法、公告、
条约或者国家行为的书籍或者印刷册；或者

（d）证明为经过核对的制定法、公告、条约或者
国家行为的复制件。

（2）本条所称外国制定法，包括外国的条例或者细则。

175 关于外国法律汇编的证据

（1）关于外国不成文法或者普通法的证据，可以通过提
出该外国法院用于了解该国不成文法或者普通法
的包含有法院判例汇编的书籍来进行。

（2）关于对外国成文法的解释的证据，可以通过提出外
国法院用于了解该国成文法解释的包含有法院判
例汇编的书籍来进行。

176 外国法律问题由法官裁决

在有陪审团的程序中，如果有必要确认适用于本案事实
的外国法律，关于就该外国法律提出的证据之效力的任
何问题，仅由法官裁决。

Division 4—Procedures for proving other matters

177 Certificates of expert evidence

(1) Evidence of a person's opinion may be adduced by tendering a certificate (**expert certificate**) signed by the person that:

    (a) states the person's name and address; and

    (b) states that the person has specialised knowledge based on his or her training, study or experience, as specified in the certificate; and

    (c) sets out an opinion that the person holds and that is expressed to be wholly or substantially based on that knowledge.

(2) Subsection (1) does not apply unless the party seeking to tender the expert certificate has served on each other party:

    (a) a copy of the certificate; and

    (b) a written notice stating that the party proposes to tender the certificate as evidence of the opinion.

(3) Service must be effected not later than:

    (a) 21 days before the hearing; or

    (b) if, on application by the party before or after service, the court substitutes a different period—the beginning of that period.

(4) Service for the purposes of subsection (2) may be proved by affidavit.

(5) A party on whom the documents referred to in subsection (2) are served may, by written notice served on the party proposing to tender the expert certificate, require the party to call the person who signed the certificate to give evidence.

第 4 目—证明其他事项的程序

177 专家证据证明书

（1）可以通过提交某人签署的证明书（**专家证明书**），
来提出该某人的意见证据。该证明书应当：

（a）说明该某人的姓名和住址；以及

（b）说明该专家基于其训练、学习或者经验，拥
有证明书所列的有关专门知识；以及

（c）列明该某人所持意见，并表明该意见全部或
者主要基于该专门知识。

（2）（1）并不适用，除非寻求将专家证明书提交法院
的当事人，已经向其他各方当事人送达如下文件：

（a）该证明书的复制件；以及

（b）说明该当事人准备将该证明书提交为意见证
据的书面通知。

（3）上述文件之送达，必须不迟于：

（a）听审前 21 日；或者

（b）根据该当事人在上述文件送达前后提出的
申请，法院重新指定的不同期间的起始之
日。

（4）为（2）之目的进行的送达，可以通过宣誓陈述书
予以证明。

（5）（2）所称文件之被送达人，可以向准备提交专家
证明书的当事人送达书面通知，要求该当事人传唤
签署证明书的专家作证。

(6) The expert certificate is not admissible as evidence if such a requirement is made.

(7) The court may make such order with respect to costs as it considers just against a party who has, without reasonable cause, required a party to call a person to give evidence under this section.

178 Convictions, acquittals and other judicial proceedings

(1) This section applies to the following facts:

    (a) the conviction or acquittal before or by an applicable court of a person charged with an offence;

    (b) the sentencing of a person to any punishment or pecuniary penalty by an applicable court;

    (c) an order by an applicable court;

    (d) the pendency or existence at any time before an applicable court of a civil or criminal proceeding.

(2) Evidence of a fact to which this section applies may be given by a certificate signed by a judge, a magistrate or a registrar or other proper officer of the applicable court:

    (a) showing the fact, or purporting to contain particulars, of the record, indictment, conviction, acquittal, sentence, order or proceeding in question; and

    (b) stating the time and place of the conviction, acquittal, sentence, order or proceeding; and

    (c) stating the title of the applicable court.

(3) A certificate given under this section showing a conviction, acquittal, sentence or order is also evidence of the particular offence or matter in respect of which the conviction, acquittal, sentence or order was had, passed or made, if stated in the certificate.

（6）在提出上述要求的情况下，专家证明书不得被采纳
为证据。

（7）对于无合理理由而根据本条要求一方当事人传唤某
人作证的当事人，法院可以命令该当事人承担法院
认为正当的费用。[6]

178 定罪、无罪开释和其他司法程序

（1）本条适用于下列事实：

（a）审理被指控犯罪之人的相关法院作出的定罪
或者无罪开释；

（b）相关法院对某人科处的任何处罚或者罚金；

（c）相关法院作出的命令；

（d）民事或者刑事程序在任何时候在相关法院的
未决或者存在之状态。

（2）本条适用的关于某事实的证据，可以由相关法院的
法官、治安法官、登记官或者法院的其他适当官员
以其签署的下列证明书形式提供：

（a）说明有关记录、控诉、定罪、无罪开释、量刑、
命令或者程序的事实，或者载明包含有这些
事实的细节；以及

（b）说明定罪、无罪开释、量刑、命令或者程序
的时间和地点；以及

（c）说明相关法院的名称。

（3）根据本条作出的说明定罪、无罪开释、量刑或者命
令的证明书，也是关于在证明书中说明的曾通过或
者作出的定罪、无罪开释、量刑或者命令所涉及的
具体犯罪或者事项的证据。

(4) A certificate given under this section showing the pendency or existence of a proceeding is also evidence of the particular nature and occasion, or ground and cause, of the proceeding, if stated in the certificate.

(5) A certificate given under this section purporting to contain particulars of a record, indictment, conviction, acquittal, sentence, order or proceeding is also evidence of the matters stated in the certificate.

(6) In this section:

acquittal includes the dismissal of the charge in question by an applicable court.

applicable court means an Australian court or a foreign court.

Note: Section 91 excludes evidence of certain judgments and convictions.

179 Proof of identity of convicted persons—affidavits by members of State or Territory police forces

(1) This section applies if a member of a police force of a State or Territory:

    (a) makes an affidavit in the form prescribed by the regulations for the purposes of this section; and

    (b) states in the affidavit that he or she is a fingerprint expert for that police force.

(2) For the purpose of proving before a court the identity of a person alleged to have been convicted in that State or Territory of an offence, the affidavit is evidence in a proceeding that the person whose fingerprints are shown on a fingerprint card referred to in the affidavit and marked for identification:

    (a) is the person referred to in a certificate of conviction, or certified copy of conviction annexed to the affidavit, as

（4）根据本条作出的说明某程序的未决或者存在之状态
的证明书，也是该证明书中说明的程序的具体性
质、起因或者根据和理由的证据。

（5）根据本条作出的载明包含有记录、控诉、定罪、无
罪开释、量刑、命令或者程序的细节的证明书，也
是该证明书中所说明的事项的证据。

（6）在本条中：

无罪开释包括相关法院对有关指控的驳回。

相关法院是指澳大利亚法院或者外国法院。

注释：第 91 条排除了关于某些判决和定罪的证据。

179 被定罪者身份的证明——州或者领地警察机构成员所作的宣誓陈述书

（1）如果州或者领地警察机构的成员从事了下列活动，
则适用本条：

（a）为本条之目的，依照条例规定的形式制作了
宣誓陈述书；并且

（b）在宣誓陈述书中说明，该某人系该警察机构
的指纹专家。

（2）为在法院证明在该州或者领地已经因为犯罪被定罪
的某人之身份，在程序中该宣誓陈述书是关于其指
印出现在宣誓陈述书中所称并为辨认进行了标记
的指印卡上的人员有下列情况的证据：

（a）该某人是宣誓证明书所附的定罪证明书或者
经核证的定罪判决复制件所称的被定罪的人；

        having been convicted of an offence; and

    (b) was convicted of that offence; and

    (c) was convicted of any other offence of which he or she is stated in the affidavit to have been convicted.

(3) For the purposes of this section, if a Territory does not have its own police force, the police force performing the policing functions of the Territory is taken to be the police force of the Territory.

180 Proof of identity of convicted persons—affidavits by AFP employees or special members of the Australian Federal Police

(1) This section applies if an AFP employee (within the meaning of the *Australian Federal Police Act 1979*) or a special member of the Australian Federal Police (within the meaning of that Act):

    (a) makes an affidavit in the form prescribed by the regulations for the purposes of this section; and

    (b) states in the affidavit that he or she is a fingerprint expert for the Australian Federal Police.

(2) For the purpose of proving before a court the identity of a person alleged to have been convicted of an offence against a law of the Commonwealth, the affidavit is evidence in a proceeding that the person whose fingerprints are shown on a fingerprint card referred to in the affidavit and marked for identification:

    (a) is the person referred to in a certificate of conviction, or certified copy of conviction annexed to the affidavit, as having been convicted of an offence; and

    (b) was convicted of that offence; and

    (c) was convicted of any other offence of which he or she

以及

（b）该某人被判定构成该罪；以及

（c）该某人被判定构成宣誓陈述书中所说明的其他犯罪。

（3）就本条目的而言，如果一个领地并没有自己的警察机构，执行该领地警察职能的警察机构，视为该领地的警察机构。

180 被定罪者身份的证明——澳大利亚联邦警察机构雇员或者澳大利亚联邦警察机构特别成员的宣誓陈述书

（1）如果澳大利亚联邦警察机构雇员（含义见《1979年澳大利亚联邦警察法》）或者澳大利亚联邦警察机构特别成员（含义见该法）从事了下列活动，则适用本条：

（a）为本条之目的，依照条例规定的形式制作了宣誓陈述书；并且

（b）在宣誓陈述书中说明，该某人系澳大利亚联邦警察机构的指纹专家。

（2）为在法院证明因为违反联邦法律而被定罪的某人的身份，在程序中该宣誓陈述书是关于其指印出现在宣誓陈述书中所称并为辨认进行了标记的指印卡上的人员有下列情况的证据：

（a）该某人是宣誓证明书所附的定罪证明书或者经核证的定罪判决复制件所称的被定罪的人；以及

（b）该某人被判定构成该罪；以及

（c）该某人被判定构成宣誓陈述书中所说明的其

is stated in the affidavit to have been convicted.

181 Proof of service of statutory notifications, notices, orders and directions

(1) The service, giving or sending under an Australian law of a written notification, notice, order or direction may be proved by affidavit of the person who served, gave or sent it.

(2) A person who, for the purposes of a proceeding, makes an affidavit referred to in this section is not, because of making the affidavit, excused from attending for cross–examination if required to do so by a party to the proceeding.

他犯罪。

181 送达法定通告、通知、命令和指示的证明

（1）根据澳大利亚法律对书面通告、通知、命令或者指示的送达和送发，可以由送达人或者送发人以宣誓陈述书形式证明。

（2）为程序目的制作了本条所称宣誓陈述书的人员，在程序的一方当事人要求其出庭接受交叉询问的情况下，并不因已制作宣誓陈述书而可免于到庭接受交叉询问。

Chapter 5—Miscellaneous

182 Application of certain sections in relation to Commonwealth records, postal articles sent by Commonwealth agencies and certain Commonwealth documents

(1) Subject to this section, the provisions of this Act referred to in the following Table apply in relation to documents that:

(a) are, or form part of, Commonwealth records; or

(b) at the time they were produced were, or formed part of, Commonwealth records;

as if those sections applied to the extent provided for in section 5.

TABLE

Provisions of this Act	Subject matter
Sections 47, 48, 49 and 51	Documentary evidence
Section 69	Hearsay exception for business records
Subsection 70(1)	Hearsay exception for tags, labels and other writing
Section 71	Hearsay exception for electronic communications
Section 147	Documents produced by processes, machines etc. in the course of business
Section 149	Attestation of documents
Section 152	Documents produced from proper custody
Section 156	Public documents
Sections 161 and 162	Electronic communications, lettergrams and telegrams
Division 1 of Part 4.6	Requests to produce documents or call witnesses

第 5 章—其他规定

182 某些条文对联邦记录、联邦机构寄发的邮品和某些联邦文件的适用

（1）在遵守本条规定的情况下，下表所列本法之规定适用于下列书证时，适用第 5 条规定的范围：

（a）联邦记录或者联邦记录的一部分；或者

（b）生成时是联邦记录或者联邦记录的一部分。

表

本法规定	主题
第 47 条、第 48 条、第 49 条和第 51 条	书证
第 69 条	业务记录的传闻例外
70（1）	标牌、标签和其他写字纸的传闻例外
第 71 条	电子通信的传闻例外
第 147 条	业务过程中由工序、机器和其他设备等生成的文件
第 149 条	书证的见证
第 152 条	出自适当保管处所的书证
第 156 条	公共文件
第 161 条和第 162 条	电子通信、信件电报和电报
第 4.6 节第 1 目	出示书证或者传唤证人之请求

Section 182

TABLE

Provisions of this Act	Subject matter
Division 2 of Part 4.6	Proof of certain matters by affidavit or written statements
Section 183	Inferences about documents etc.

(2) For the purposes of subsection (1), section 69, subsection 70(1) and section 71 apply in relation to proceedings, other than proceedings in a federal court or (until the day fixed by Proclamation under subsection 4(6)) an ACT court, as if the references in those sections to the hearsay rule were references to any rule of law restricting the admissibility or use of hearsay evidence.

(3) Subsection (1) applies to subsection 70(1) only in relation to tags or labels that may reasonably be supposed to have been attached to objects in the course of carrying on an activity engaged in by a body, person or organisation referred to in the definition of *Commonwealth record* in the Dictionary.

(4) For the purposes of subsection (1) in relation to the application of subsection 70(1):

(a) the reference in subsection (1) to documents includes a reference to writing placed on objects; and

(b) the reference in subsection (3) to tags or labels attached to objects includes a reference to writing placed on objects.

(4A) Section 160 applies in relation to postal articles sent by a Commonwealth agency as if that section applied to the extent provided for in section 5.

(4B) Sections 47, 48, 49, 51, 147, 149 and 152, Divisions 1 and 2 of Part 4.6 and section 183 apply in relation to a

表

本法规定	主题
第 4.6 节第 2 目	通过宣誓陈述书或者书面陈述证明某些事项
第 183 条	关于书证等的推论

（2）就（1）之目的而言，第 69 条、第 70 条第 1 项和第 71 条适用于联邦法院或者（在根据 4（6）由《公告》确定的期日之前）澳大利亚首都领地法院之外的程序时，这些条款中所称传闻规则，是指限定传闻证据的可采性和用途的任何法律规则。

（3）（1）仅就可以合理地认为是由《术语》中关于**联邦记录**的定义所称的机构、人员或者组织在活动过程中置放于物品上的标牌或者标签适用于 70（1）。

（4）就（1）适用于 70（1）之目的而言：

（a）（1）所称书证，包括置放在物品上的写字纸；并且

（b）（3）所称附着或者置放在物品上的标牌或者标签包括置放在物品上的写字纸。

（4A）第 160 条适用于联邦机构寄发的邮品时，适用第 5 条规定的范围。

（4B）第 47 条、第 48 条、第 49 条、第 51 条、第 147 条、第 149 条、第 152 条、第 4.6 节第 1 目和第 2 目以及第 183 条，适用于下列联邦文件时，适用第 5 条

Commonwealth document that:

(a) is in the possession of a Commonwealth entity; or

(b) has been destroyed but was, immediately before its destruction, in the possession of a Commonwealth entity or someone else to whom it had been given by a Commonwealth entity for destruction;

as if the section or Division applied to the extent provided for in section 5.

(5) This section does not derogate from the operation of a law of a State or Territory that enables evidence of a matter referred to in this section to be given.

Note 1:   The NSW Act has no equivalent provision for section 182.

Note 2:   Section 5 extends the operation of this provision to proceedings in all Australian courts.

183 Inferences

If a question arises about the application of a provision of this Act in relation to a document or thing, the court may:

(a) examine the document or thing; and

(b) draw any reasonable inferences from it as well as from other matters from which inferences may properly be drawn.

Note: Section 182 gives this section a wider application in relation to Commonwealth records and certain Commonwealth documents.

184 Accused may admit matters and give consents

(1) In or before a criminal proceeding, a defendant may:

(a) admit matters of fact; and

(b) give any consent;

规定的范围：

(a) 为联邦实体所持有；或者

(b) 已经被销毁，但是在销毁之前，为联邦实体
所持有或者由联邦实体交由进行销毁的其他
人所持有。

(5) 本条并不克减州或者领地的使得本条所称事项的证
据得以提供的法律的运作。

> 注释 1：《新南威尔士州证据法》没有与第 182 条相对应
> 的规定。

> 注释 2：第 5 条将本规定扩展适用于所有澳大利亚法院的
> 程序。

183 推论

如果就本法规定对某书证或者物证的适用产生了疑问，
法院可以：

(a) 检视该书证或者物证；以及

(b) 既可以从中得出任何合理的推论，也可以从
其他可以据以进行适当推断的事项中作出任
何合理推论。

> 注释：就联邦记录和某些联邦文件，第 182 条赋予了本款
> 更为广泛的适用。

184 被指控者可以作出自认和同意

(1) 在刑事程序中或者刑事程序之前，被告可以像民事
程序中的当事人那样：

(a) 就事实事项进行自认，以及

(b) 作出任何同意。

that a party to a civil proceeding may make or give.

(2) A defendant's admission or consent is not effective for the purposes of subsection (1) unless:

(a) the defendant has been advised to do so by his or her Australian legal practitioner or legal counsel; or

(b) the court is satisfied that the defendant understands the consequences of making the admission or giving the consent.

185 Faith and credit to be given to documents properly authenticated

All public acts, records and judicial proceedings of a State or Territory that are proved or authenticated in accordance with this Act are to be given in every court, and in every public office in Australia, such faith and credit as they have by law or usage in the courts and public offices of that State or Territory.

Note: The NSW Act has no equivalent provision for section 185.

186 Swearing of affidavits before justices of the peace, notaries public and lawyers

(1) Affidavits for use in:

(a) an Australian court (other than a court of a Territory) in proceedings involving the exercise of federal jurisdiction; or

(b) a court of a Territory in proceedings involving the exercise of jurisdiction conferred by an Act of the Parliament;

may be sworn before any justice of the peace, notary public or Australian lawyer without the issue of any commission for taking affidavits.

(2) In this section:

proceedings includes proceedings that:

（2）就（1）之目的而言，被告的自认或者同意无效，除非：

（a）被告的澳大利亚法律执业者或者法律顾问建议其如此行事；或者

（b）法院确信被告理解作出自认或者同意的后果。

185 对经适当验真的书证的信赖

根据本法经过证明或者验真的州或者领地的所有公开法、记录和司法记录，应当在澳大利亚所有法院以及所有公共机构，得到如其依据法律或者惯例在该州或者领地的法院或者公共机构所享有的信赖。

注释：《新南威尔士州证据法》没有与第185条相对应的规定。

186 在太平绅士、公证人和律师面前就宣誓陈述书进行宣誓

（1）对于下列宣誓陈述书，可以在任何太平绅士、公证人和律师面前进行宣誓，无需签发任何主持该宣誓之委托：

（a）在澳大利亚法院（领地法院除外）涉及行使联邦司法管辖权的程序中使用的宣誓陈述书；或者

（b）在领地法院涉及行使议会制定的法律所赋予的司法管辖权的程序中使用的宣誓陈述书。

（2）在本条中：

程序包括下列程序：

       (a) relate to bail; or

       (b) are interlocutory proceedings or proceedings of a similar kind; or

       (c) are heard in chambers; or

       (d) relate to sentencing.

Note: The NSW Act has no equivalent provision for section 186.

187 Abolition of the privilege against self–incrimination for bodies corporate

(1) This section applies if, under a law of the Commonwealth or the Australian Capital Territory or in a proceeding in a federal court or an ACT court, a body corporate is required to:

       (a) answer a question or give information; or

       (b) produce a document or any other thing; or

       (c) do any other act whatever.

(2) The body corporate is not entitled to refuse or fail to comply with the requirement on the ground that answering the question, giving the information, producing the document or other thing or doing that other act, as the case may be, might tend to incriminate the body or make the body liable to a penalty.

188 Impounding documents

The court may direct that a document that has been tendered or produced before the court (whether or not it is admitted in evidence) is to be impounded and kept in the custody of an officer of the court or of another person for such period, and subject to such conditions, as the court thinks fit.

（a）与保释有关的程序；或者

（b）中间程序或者类似程序；或者

（c）在法官办公室听审的程序；或者

（d）与量刑有关的程序。

注释：《新南威尔士州证据法》没有与第 186 条相对应的规定。

187 废除法人的反对被迫自我归罪特免权

（1）根据联邦或者澳大利亚首都领地法律，或者在澳大利亚联邦法院或者首都地区法院进行的程序中，如果要求法人从事下列行为，则适用本条：

（a）回答问题或者提供信息；或者

（b）出示书证或者任何其他物证；或者

（c）从事任何其他行为。

（2）法人无权以有关回答问题、提供信息、出示书证或者其他物证或者从事其他行为（视情况而定）可能会使之负罪或者使之受到处罚为由，拒绝或者不遵行上述要求。[1]

188 扣管书证

法院可以指示扣管已经向法院提交或者出示的书证（不论其是否被采纳为证据），由法院官员或者他人在法院认为适当的期间内保管，并遵守法院认为适当的条件。[2]

189 The *voir dire*

(1) If the determination of a question whether:

(a) evidence should be admitted (whether in the exercise of a discretion or not); or

(b) evidence can be used against a person; or

(c) a witness is competent or compellable;

depends on the court finding that a particular fact exists, the question whether that fact exists is, for the purposes of this section, a preliminary question.

(2) If there is a jury, a preliminary question whether:

(a) particular evidence is evidence of an admission, or evidence to which section 138 applies; or

(b) evidence of an admission, or evidence to which section 138 applies, should be admitted;

is to be heard and determined in the jury's absence.

(3) In the hearing of a preliminary question about whether a defendant's admission should be admitted into evidence (whether in the exercise of a discretion or not) in a criminal proceeding, the issue of the admission's truth or untruth is to be disregarded unless the issue is introduced by the defendant.

(4) If there is a jury, the jury is not to be present at a hearing to decide any other preliminary question unless the court so orders.

(5) Without limiting the matters that the court may take into account in deciding whether to make such an order, it is to take into account:

(a) whether the evidence to be adduced in the course of that hearing is likely to be prejudicial to the defendant; and

189 预先审核

（1）如果对下列问题的决定取决于法院判定具体事实是
否存在，则就本条目的而言，该事实是否存在的问
题是一个预备性问题：

（a）证据是否应当被采纳（无论是否是行使自由
裁量权）；或者

（b）证据是否可被用于反对某人；或者

（c）证人是否具有作证能力或者可被强制作证。

（2）如果有陪审团，对下列预备性问题的听审和决定，
应在陪审团不在场的情况下进行：

（a）具体证据是否为自认证据，或者是第 138 条
所要适用的证据；或者

（b）自认证据，或者第 138 条所要适用的证据是
否应当被采纳。

（3）在关于被告的自认是否应当在刑事程序中被采纳为
证据（无论是否是行使自由裁量权）的预备性问题
听审中，对该自认真实与否的问题不予审理，除非
该问题是被告提出的。

（4）如果有陪审团，在关于任何其他预备性问题的听
审中，陪审团均不得在场，除非法院命令陪审团
在场。

（5）在决定是否作出上述命令时，法院应当虑及的事项
包括但是不限于：

（a）在该听审中提出的证据是否可能有损于被告；
以及

      (b) whether the evidence concerned will be adduced in the course of the hearing to decide the preliminary question; and

      (c) whether the evidence to be adduced in the course of that hearing would be admitted if adduced at another stage of the hearing (other than in another hearing to decide a preliminary question or, in a criminal proceeding, a hearing in relation to sentencing).

(6) Subsection 128(10) does not apply to a hearing to decide a preliminary question.

(7) In the application of Chapter 3 to a hearing to determine a preliminary question, the facts in issue are taken to include the fact to which the hearing relates.

(8) If a jury in a proceeding was not present at a hearing to determine a preliminary question, evidence is not to be adduced in the proceeding of evidence given by a witness at the hearing unless:

      (a) it is inconsistent with other evidence given by the witness in the proceeding; or

      (b) the witness has died.

190 Waiver of rules of evidence

(1) The court may, if the parties consent, by order dispense with the application of any one or more of the provisions of:

      (a) Division 3, 4 or 5 of Part 2.1; or

      (b) Part 2.2 or 2.3; or

      (c) Parts 3.2 to 3.8;

      in relation to particular evidence or generally.

Note: Matters related to evidence in child–related proceedings (within the meaning of section 69ZM of the Family Law Act

（b）有关证据是否将在确定预备性问题的听审中提出；以及

（c）如果在听审的其他阶段（确定预备性问题的另一听审或者刑事程序中关于量刑的听审除外）提出在确定预备性问题的听审中提出的证据，该证据是否会被采纳。

（6）128（10）并不适用于决定预备性问题的听审。

（7）在第 3 章适用于决定预备性问题的听审时，争议事实被视为包括与听审有关的事实。

（8）如果在某程序中，在确定预备性问题的听审时陪审团不在场，则在该程序中不得提出证人在该听审中作出的证言，除非：

（a）该证言与证人在该程序中提供的其他证言不一致；或者

（b）证人已经死亡。

190 证据规则的放弃

（1）如果诸当事人同意，法院可以作出命令，就具体证据或者一般性地免除适用下列章节的一项或者多项规定：

（a）第 2.1 节第 3 目、第 4 目或者第 5 目；或者

（b）第 2.2 节或者第 2.3 节；或者

（c）第 3.2 节至第 3.8 节。

注释：与儿童有关的程序（《1975 年家庭法法》第 69ZM

1975) are dealt with by that Act.

(2) In a criminal proceeding, a defendant's consent is not effective for the purposes of subsection (1) unless:

(a) the defendant has been advised to do so by his or her Australian legal practitioner or legal counsel; or

(b) the court is satisfied that the defendant understands the consequences of giving the consent.

(3) In a civil proceeding, the court may order that any one or more of the provisions mentioned in subsection (1) do not apply in relation to evidence if:

(a) the matter to which the evidence relates is not genuinely in dispute; or

(b) the application of those provisions would cause or involve unnecessary expense or delay.

(4) Without limiting the matters that the court may take into account in deciding whether to exercise the power conferred by subsection (3), it is to take into account:

(a) the importance of the evidence in the proceeding; and

(b) the nature of the cause of action or defence and the nature of the subject matter of the proceeding; and

(c) the probative value of the evidence; and

(d) the powers of the court (if any) to adjourn the hearing, to make another order or to give a direction in relation to the evidence.

191 Agreements as to facts

(1) In this section:

agreed fact means a fact that the parties to a proceeding have agreed is not, for the purposes of the proceeding, to be disputed.

第 191 条

条的意义）中的证据事项，由该法来处理。

（2）在刑事程序中，就（1）之目的而言，被告所作的同意无效，除非：

　（a）被告的澳大利亚法律执业者或者法律顾问建议其如此行为；或者

　（b）法院确信被告理解作出上述同意的后果。

（3）在民事程序中，在下列情况下，法院可以命令（1）所提及的一项或者多项规定并不适用于证据：

　（a）就与证据有关的事项并不存在真正的争议；或者

　（b）适用这些规定将导致或者牵涉不必要的费用或者迟延。

（4）法院在决定是否行使（3）所赋予的权力时，应当虑及的事项包括但是不限于：

　（a）证据在程序中的重要性；以及

　（b）诉因或者抗辩的性质，以及程序标的的性质；以及

　（c）证据的证明价值；以及

　（d）法院决定延期听审、就证据作出其他命令或者指示之权力（如果有的话）。

191 关于事实的协议

（1）在本条中：

协议事实是指程序的当事人已经达成协议，不需要为程序目的进行争辩的事实。

(2) In a proceeding:

    (a) evidence is not required to prove the existence of an agreed fact; and

    (b) evidence may not be adduced to contradict or qualify an agreed fact;

    unless the court gives leave.

(3) Subsection (2) does not apply unless the agreed fact:

    (a) is stated in an agreement in writing signed by the parties or by Australian legal practitioners, legal counsel or prosecutors representing the parties and adduced in evidence in the proceeding; or

    (b) with the leave of the court, is stated by a party before the court with the agreement of all other parties.

192 Leave, permission or direction may be given on terms

(1) If, because of this Act, a court may give any leave, permission or direction, the leave, permission or direction may be given on such terms as the court thinks fit.

(2) Without limiting the matters that the court may take into account in deciding whether to give the leave, permission or direction, it is to take into account:

    (a) the extent to which to do so would be likely to add unduly to, or to shorten, the length of the hearing; and

    (b) the extent to which to do so would be unfair to a party or to a witness; and

    (c) the importance of the evidence in relation to which the leave, permission or direction is sought; and

    (d) the nature of the proceeding; and

    (e) the power (if any) of the court to adjourn the hearing or to make another order or to give a direction in relation

（2）在程序中，除非为法院所许可：

（a）无需提出证据证明协议事实的存在；并且

（b）不得提出证据反驳或者限定协议事实。

（3）（2）并不适用，除非：

（a）协议事实已在当事人或者代理当事人的澳大利亚法律执业者、法律顾问或者公诉人签署的书面协议中列明，并在程序中已作为证据提出；或者

（b）经法院许可，协议事实由一方当事人向法院陈述，并得到了所有其他当事人的同意。

192 按照条件作出许可、允许或者指示

（1）如果根据本法，法院可以作出许可、准许或者指示，则法院可依照其认为适当的条件作出许可、准许或者指示。

（2）法院在决定是否作出许可、准许或者指示时，应当虑及的因素包括但是不限于：

（a）法院作出许可、准许或者指示将在何种程度上不合理地增加或者缩短听审时间；以及

（b）法院作出许可、准许或者指示将在何种程度上对一方当事人或者证人不公平；以及

（c）与寻求许可、准许或者指示有关的证据的重要性；以及

（d）程序的性质；以及

（e）法院决定延期听审、就该证据作出其他命令

to the evidence.

192A Advance rulings and findings

Where a question arises in any proceedings, being a question about:

(a) the admissibility or use of evidence proposed to be adduced; or

(b) the operation of a provision of this Act or another law in relation to evidence proposed to be adduced; or

(c) the giving of leave, permission or direction under section 192;

the court may, if it considers it to be appropriate to do so, give a ruling or make a finding in relation to the question before the evidence is adduced in the proceedings.

193 Additional powers

(1) The powers of a court in relation to:

(a) the discovery or inspection of documents; and

(b) ordering disclosure and exchange of evidence, intended evidence, documents and reports;

extend to enabling the court to make such orders as the court thinks fit (including orders about methods of inspection, adjournments and costs) to ensure that the parties to a proceeding can adequately, and in an appropriate manner, inspect documents of the kind referred to in paragraph (b) or (c) of the definition of *document* in the Dictionary.

(2) The power of a person or body to make rules of court extends to making rules, not inconsistent with this Act or the regulations, prescribing matters:

或者指示的权力（如果有的话）。

192A 预先裁决和认定

如果在任何程序中就下列事项出现疑问，法院在认为适当的情况下，可以在程序中提出证据之前，就该问题作出裁决或者认定：

（a）准备提出的证据的可采性或者用途；或者

（b）就准备提出的证据，本法或者其他法律之规定的适用；或者

（c）根据第 192 条作出许可、准许或者指示。

193 额外权力

（1）法院就下列事项的权力，扩展至使法院能够在认为适当时作出有关命令（包括关于证据的查阅方法、延期审理以及费用的命令），以保证程序当事人能够以足够且适当的方式查阅《术语》中关于**书证**定义的（b）或者（c）所称之书证：

（a）书证的案情先悉或者查阅；以及

（b）命令披露和交换证据、意图使用的证据、书证和报告。

（2）某人或者机构制定法院规则之权力，扩展至使其能够制定与本法或者条例不相抵触的规则，来规定如下事项：

(a) required or permitted by this Act to be prescribed; or

(b) necessary or convenient to be prescribed for carrying out or giving effect to this Act.

(3) Without limiting subsection (2), rules made under that subsection may provide for the discovery, exchange, inspection or disclosure of intended evidence, documents and reports of persons intended to be called by a party to give evidence in a proceeding.

(4) Without limiting subsection (2), rules made under that subsection may provide for the exclusion of evidence, or for its admission on specified terms, if the rules are not complied with.

194 Witnesses failing to attend proceedings

*   *   *   *   *

Note: The NSW Act includes a provision about the consequences of a witness failing to appear when called in any civil or criminal proceedings.

195 Prohibited question not to be published

(1) A person must not, without the express permission of a court, print or publish:

(a) any question that the court has disallowed under section 41; or

(b) any question that the court has disallowed because any answer that is likely to be given to the question would contravene the credibility rule; or

(c) any question in respect of which the court has refused to give leave under Part 3.7.

Penalty: 60 penalty units.

（a）本法要求或者准许加以规定的事项；或者

（b）为实施本法或者使本法生效而有必要或者为便利起见而规定的事项。

（3）在不限制（2）的前提下，根据该款制定的规则可以规定对当事人拟传唤出庭作证的证人意图使用的证据、书证和报告的案情先悉、交换、查阅或者披露。

（4）在不限制（2）的前提下，根据该款制定的规则可以规定没有遵行这些规则情况下，证据的排除或者基于特定条件的采纳问题。

194 证人未能出席程序

   *   *   *   *   *

注释：《新南威尔士州证据法》包括了一个关于证人在刑事或者民事程序中经传唤未能出席之后果的规定。

195 被禁止的问题不得公布

（1）未经法院明确准许，不得刊行或者公布：

（a）法院根据第 41 条不允许的任何询问；或者

（b）由于对该询问的可能回答将与可信性规则相抵触，因而法院不允许的问题；或者

（c）法院根据第 3.7 节拒绝许可的任何询问。

处罚：60 罚金单位。

Section 197

    (2) Subsection (1) is an offence of strict liability.

> Note 1: For strict liability, see section 6.1 of the Criminal Code.
>
> Note 2: Subsection 195(2) does not appear in the NSW Act, because section 6.1 of the Criminal Code (which deals with strict liability) applies only to this Act.

196 Proceedings for offences

    *   *   *   *   *

> Note: The NSW Act includes a provision about procedure for dealing with offences against the Act or regulations.

197 Regulations

The Governor–General may make regulations, not inconsistent with this Act, prescribing matters:

  (a) required or permitted by this Act to be prescribed; or

  (b) necessary or convenient to be prescribed for carrying out or giving effect to this Act.

（2）（1）是一种严格责任犯罪。

> 注释1：严格责任参见《刑法典》第6.1条。

> 注释2：《新南威尔士州证据法》并无195（2），因为《刑法典》第6.1条（对严格责任的规定）仅适用于本法。

196 处理犯罪的程序

*　　　*　　　*　　　*　　　*

> 注释：《新南威尔士州证据法》有一条款规定了处理违反该法或者条例的犯罪的程序。

197 条例

总督有权制定与本法不相抵触的条例，规定下列事项：

（a）本法要求规定或者允许规定的事项；或者

（b）为施行本法或者使本法生效有必要规定或者为便利起见而规定的事项。

Schedule—Oaths and Affirmations

Subsections 21(4) and 22(2)

Oaths by witnesses

I swear (or the person taking the oath may promise) by Almighty God (or the person may name a god recognised by his or her religion) that the evidence I shall give will be the truth, the whole truth and nothing but the truth.

Oaths by interpreters

I swear (or the person taking the oath may promise) by Almighty God (or the person may name a god recognised by his or her religion) that I will well and truly interpret the evidence that will be given and do all other matters and things that are required of me in this case to the best of my ability.

Affirmations by witnesses

I solemnly and sincerely declare and affirm that the evidence I shall give will be the truth, the whole truth and nothing but the truth.

Affirmations by interpreters

I solemnly and sincerely declare and affirm that I will well and truly interpret the evidence that will be given and do all other matters and things that are required of me in this case to the best of my ability.

附录—宣誓与郑重声明

21（4）和 22（2）

证人的宣誓

我向全能的上帝（该某人可以呼其宗教认可的神明之名）发誓（宣誓的人可以承诺），我所作证言将是事实，全部是事实，除了事实之外别无其他。

传译人员的宣誓

我向全能的上帝（该某人可以呼其宗教认可的神明之名）发誓（宣誓的人可以承诺），我将恰当、如实地传译证人所作证言，尽我全力做好要求我在本案中所做的任何其他事项。

证人的郑重声明

我郑重、真诚地宣布和确认，我所作证言将是事实，全部是事实，除了事实之外别无其他。

传译人员的郑重声明

我郑重、真诚地宣布和确认，我将恰当、如实地传译证人所作证言，尽我全力做好要求我在本案中所做的任何其他事项。

Dictionary

Section 3

Part 1—Definitions

ACT court means the Supreme Court of the Australian Capital Territory or any other court of the Australian Capital Territory, and includes a person or body that, in performing a function or exercising a power under a law of the Australian Capital Territory, is required to apply the laws of evidence.

Note: The NSW Act does not include this definition.

admission means a previous representation that is:

(a) made by a person who is or becomes a party to a proceeding (including a defendant in a criminal proceeding); and

(b) adverse to the person's interest in the outcome of the proceeding.

asserted fact is defined in section 59.

associated defendant, in relation to a defendant in a criminal proceeding, means a person against whom a prosecution has been instituted, but not yet completed or terminated, for:

(a) an offence that arose in relation to the same events as those in relation to which the offence for which the defendant is being prosecuted arose; or

(b) an offence that relates to or is connected with the offence for which the defendant is being prosecuted.

Australia includes the external Territories.

术　语

第3条

第1部分　定义

澳大利亚首都领地法院是指澳大利亚首都领地最高法院或者任何其他澳大利亚首都领地法院，并包括根据澳大利亚首都领地法律履行职能或者行使权力时需要适用证据法的人员或者机构。

> 注释：《新南威尔士州证据法》并不包括这一定义。

自认是指如下先前表述：

　　（a）该先前表述是程序的一方当事人（包括刑事程序中的被告）作出的；并且

　　（b）就程序的结果而言，该先前表述对该某人的利益不利。

主张的事实的定义见第59条。

关联被告，就刑事程序中的被告而言，是指因下列犯罪已经被检控，但是该检控还没有完成或者终结的人员：

　　（a）引起被告正在被检控的犯罪的同一事件所引起的犯罪；或者

　　（b）与被告正在被检控的犯罪有关或者联系在一起的犯罪。

澳大利亚包括外部领地。

Part 1—Definitions

Australian court means:

(a) the High Court; or

(b) a court exercising federal jurisdiction; or

(c) a court of a State or Territory; or

(d) a judge, justice or arbitrator under an Australian law; or

(e) a person or body authorised by an Australian law, or by consent of parties, to hear, receive and examine evidence; or

(f) a person or body that, in exercising a function under an Australian law, is required to apply the laws of evidence.

Australian law means a law of the Commonwealth, a State or a Territory.

Note: See clause 9 of Part 2 of the Dictionary for the meaning of law.

Australian lawyer means a person who is admitted to the legal profession by a Supreme Court of a State or Territory under a law of a State or Territory specified in the regulations.

Australian legal practitioner means an Australian lawyer who holds a practising certificate under a law of a State or Territory specified in the regulations.

Australian or overseas proceeding means a proceeding (however described) in an Australian court or a foreign court.

Australian Parliament means the Parliament, a Parliament of a State or a Legislative Assembly of a Territory.

Australian practising certificate means a practising certificate granted under a law of a State or Territory specified in the regulations.

Australian–registered foreign lawyer means a person who

澳大利亚法院是指：

    （a）最高法院；或者

    （b）行使联邦司法管辖权的法院；或者

    （c）州或者领地法院；或者

    （d）澳大利亚法律规定的法官或者仲裁员；或者

    （e）经澳大利亚法律授权或者当事人同意，听取、接收和查验证据的人员或者机构；或者

    （f）根据澳大利亚法律履行职能时需要适用证据法的人员或者机构。

澳大利亚法律是指澳大利亚联邦、州或者领地的法律。

注释：参见《术语》第 2 部分第 9 条关于法律的含义的规定。

澳大利亚律师是指为州或者领地最高法院根据条例中规定的州或者领地的法律接纳入法律职业的人员。

澳大利亚法律执业者是指根据条例中规定的州或者领地的法律持有执业证书的澳大利亚律师。

澳大利亚或者海外程序是指澳大利亚法院或者外国法院内的程序，无论如何描述。

澳大利亚议会是指议会、州议会或者领地的立法会。

澳大利亚执业证书是指根据条例中规定的州或者领地的法律颁发的执业证书。

澳大利亚注册的外国律师是指根据条例中规定的州或者

is registered as a foreign lawyer under a law of a State or Territory specified in the regulations.

Australian Statistician means the Australian Statistician referred to in subsection 5(2) of the *Australian Bureau of Statistics Act 1975*, and includes any person to whom the powers of the Australian Statistician under section 12 of the *Census and Statistics Act 1905* have been delegated.

business is defined in clause 1 of Part 2 of this Dictionary.

case of a party means the facts in issue in respect of which the party bears the legal burden of proof.

child means a child of any age and includes the meaning given in subclause 10(1) of Part 2 of this Dictionary.

civil penalty is defined in clause 3 of Part 2 of this Dictionary.

civil proceeding means a proceeding other than a criminal proceeding.

client is defined in section 117.

coincidence evidence means evidence of a kind referred to in subsection 98(1) that a party seeks to have adduced for the purpose referred to in that subsection.

coincidence rule means subsection 98(1).

Commonwealth agency means:

(a) an Agency within the meaning of the *Public Service Act 1999*; or

(b) a House of the Parliament; or

(c) a person or body holding office, or exercising power, under or because of the Constitution or a law of the Commonwealth; or

(d) a body or organisation, whether incorporated or unincorporated, established for a public purpose:

领地的法律注册为外国律师的人员。

澳大利亚统计局长是指《1975 年澳大利亚统计局法》5（2）所规定的澳大利亚统计局长，也包括根据《1905 年普查和统计法》第 12 条被授予澳大利亚统计局长权力的人员。

业务的定义见本《术语》第 2 部分第 1 条。

当事人的**案件**是指当事人承担法律上的证明负担的争议事实。

儿童是指任何年龄的儿童，包括本《术语》第 2 部分 10（1）规定的含义。

民事处罚的定义见本《术语》第 2 部分第 3 条。

民事程序是指刑事程序以外的程序。

委托人的定义见第 117 条。

巧合证据是指 98（1）所称的当事人为该款规定之目的试图提出的证据。

巧合规则的含义见 98（1）。

联邦机构是指：

  （a）《1999 年公共服务法》所指机构；或者

  （b）议会的议院；或者

  （c）根据或者基于《宪法》或者联邦法律担任公职或者行使权力的人员或者机构；或者

  （d）由下列法律或者人员为公共目的所设立的机构或者组织，不论其是否已经成为公司法人：

      (i)   by or under a law of the Commonwealth or of a Territory (other than the Australian Capital Territory, the Northern Territory or Norfolk Island); or

    (ii)   by the Governor–General; or

   (iii)   by a Minister.

Commonwealth document means:

  (a) a document in the nature of a form, application, claim or return, or any document of a similar kind, that has, in accordance with a Commonwealth law, or in connection with the provision of money or any other benefit or advantage by the Commonwealth, been filed or lodged with a Commonwealth entity or given or sent (including sent by a form of electronic transmission) to a Commonwealth entity; and

  (b) any of the following documents:

      (i)   a report of the passengers or crew on a ship or aircraft that has been communicated to Customs under section 64ACA or 64ACB of the *Customs Act 1901*;

    (ia)   a report relating to the passengers or crew on an aircraft or ship that has been communicated to the Department administered by the Minister who administers the *Migration Act 1958* under Division 12B of Part 2 of that Act;

    (ii)   a ship's inward cargo adjustment report delivered to an officer under subregulation 46(3) of the Customs Regulations;

   (iii)   an entry made under the *Customs Act 1901* or *Excise Act 1901* in relation to goods;

（ⅰ）联邦或者领地（澳大利亚首都领地、北领
地或者诺福克岛除外）法律；或者

（ⅱ）总督；或者

（ⅲ）部长。

联邦文件是指：

（a）根据联邦法律，或者与联邦提供金钱或者其
他利益、便利有关的，由联邦实体存档或者
保管的或者向该实体发送的（包括电子传输
形式）报表、申请、主张或者申报性质的文
件或者类似文件；以及

（b）下列任何文件：

（ⅰ）根据《1901 年海关法》第 64ACA 条或者
第 64ACB 条，轮船或者飞行器的乘客或
者乘务人员向澳大利亚海关总署进行通报
的报告；

（ia）就轮船或者飞行器的乘客或者乘务人员已
经向根据《1958 年移民法》第 2 章第 12B
节实施该法的部长所署理的部进行通报的
报告；

（ⅱ）根据《海关条例》46（3）向官员呈送的
轮船进港货物调节报告；

（ⅲ）根据《1901 年海关法》或者《1901 年税收法》
就货物制作的目录；

(iv) a form or statement given to a Collector under regulation 41 of the Customs Regulations;

(v) a passenger card given to an officer under subregulation 3.01(3) of the Migration Regulations;

(vi) a report referred to in section 46 of the Ozone Protection and Synthetic Greenhouse Gas Management Act 1989 that has been given under that section to the Minister administering that Act;

(vii) any other document prescribed by the regulations for the purposes of this paragraph.

Commonwealth entity means:

(a) an Agency within the meaning of the *Public Service Act 1999*; or

(b) the Parliament, a House of the Parliament, a committee of a House of the Parliament or a committee of the Parliament; or

(c) a person or body other than a Legislative Assembly holding office, or exercising power, under or because of the Constitution or a law of the Commonwealth; or

(d) a body or organisation other than a Legislative Assembly, whether incorporated or unincorporated, established for a public purpose:

(i) by or under a law of the Commonwealth or of a Territory (other than the Australian Capital Territory, the Northern Territory or Norfolk Island); or

(ii) by the Governor–General; or

(iii) by a Minister; or

(e) any other body or organisation that is a Commonwealth owned body corporate.

（iv）根据《海关条例》第 41 条向关长提交的报表或者声明；

（v）根据《移民条例》3.01（3）向官员提交的乘客卡；

（vi）《1989 年臭氧层保护与合成温室气体管理法》第 46 条所指的根据该条已向实施该法的部长提交的报告；

（vii）为本款目的由条例规定的任何其他文件。

联邦实体是指：

（a）《1999 年公共服务法》所指机构；或者

（b）澳大利亚议会、澳大利亚议会的议院、该议院的委员会或者澳大利亚议会的委员会；以及

（c）根据或者基于《宪法》或者联邦法律担任公职或者行使权力的人员或者机构，立法会除外；或者

（d）由下列法律或者人员为公共目的所设立的机构或者组织，不论其是否已经成为公司法人，立法会除外：

（i）联邦或者领地（澳大利亚首都领地、北领地或者诺福克岛除外）法律；或者

（ii）总督；或者

（iii）部长；或者

（e）任何其他作为联邦所有的法人的机构或者组织。

Commonwealth owned body corporate means a body corporate that, were the Commonwealth a body corporate, would, for the purposes of the *Corporations Act 2001*, be:

(a) a wholly–owned subsidiary of the Commonwealth; or

(b) a wholly–owned subsidiary of another body corporate that is, under this definition, a Commonwealth owned body corporate because of the application of paragraph (a) (including the application of that paragraph together with another application or other applications of this paragraph).

Commonwealth record means a record made by:

(a) an Agency within the meaning of the *Public Service Act 1999*; or

(b) the Parliament, a House of the Parliament, a committee of a House of the Parliament or a committee of the Parliament; or

(c) a person or body other than a Legislative Assembly holding office, or exercising power, under or because of the Constitution or a law of the Commonwealth; or

(d) a body or organisation other than a Legislative Assembly, whether incorporated or unincorporated, established for a public purpose:

(i) by or under a law of the Commonwealth or of a Territory (other than the Australian Capital Territory, the Northern Territory or Norfolk Island); or

(ii) by the Governor–General; or

联邦所有的法人是指在联邦是一个法人的情况下，就《2001 年公司法》目的而言，属于下列情况的法人：

(a) 联邦的全资下属机构；或者

(b) 根据本定义，因适用（a）而是联邦所有的法人的另一法人的全资下属机构（包括与该款的另一适用或者本款的其他适用一起适用该款）。

联邦记录是指由下列人员、机构或者组织制作并保管的记录，但是并不包括根据或者基于《宪法》或者联邦法律担任公职或者行使权力的人员或者机构制作的与其担任公职或者行使权力无关的记录：

(a)《1999 年公共服务法》所指机构；或者

(b) 澳大利亚议会、澳大利亚议会的议院、该议院的委员会或者澳大利亚议会的委员会；以及

(c) 根据或者基于《宪法》或者联邦法律担任公职或者行使权力的人员或者机构，立法会除外；或者

(d) 由下列法律或者人员为公共目的所设立的机构或者组织，不论其是否已经成为公司法人，立法会除外：

(i) 联邦或者领地（澳大利亚首都领地、北领地或者诺福克岛除外）法律；或者

(ii) 总督；或者

(iii) by a Minister; or

(e) any other body or organisation that is a Commonwealth owned body corporate;

and kept or maintained by a person, body or organisation of a kind referred to in paragraph (a), (b), (c), (d) or (e), but does not include a record made by a person or body holding office, or exercising power, under or because of the Constitution or a law of the Commonwealth if the record was not made in connection with holding the office concerned, or exercising the power concerned.

confidential communication is defined in section 117.

confidential document is defined in section 117.

Note: The NSW Act includes a definition of court.

credibility of a person who has made a representation that has been admitted in evidence means the credibility of the representation, and includes the person's ability to observe or remember facts and events about which the person made the representation.

credibility of a witness means the credibility of any part or all of the evidence of the witness, and includes the witness's ability to observe or remember facts and events about which the witness has given, is giving or is to give evidence.

credibility evidence is defined in section 101A.

credibility rule means section 102.

criminal proceeding means a prosecution for an offence and includes:

(a) a proceeding for the committal of a person for trial or sentence for an offence; and

(b) a proceeding relating to bail;

but does not include a prosecution for an offence that is a prescribed taxation offence within the meaning of Part III

（iii）部长；或者

（e）任何其他作为联邦所有的法人的机构或者组织。

秘密交流的定义见第 117 条。

秘密文件的定义见第 117 条。

注释：《新南威尔士州证据法》包含关于法院的定义。

作出了已经被采纳为证据的表述之人的**可信性**，是指该表述的可信性，并且包括该某人观察和记忆有关表述事实和事件的能力。

证人的**可信性**是指证人证言的部分或者全部可信性，并且包括证人观察和记忆已经作证、正在作证或者将要作证的事实和事件的能力。

可信性证据的定义见第 101A 条。

可信性规则的含义见第 102 条。

刑事程序是指对犯罪的检控，并且包括：

（a）因犯罪将某人交付审判或者量刑的程序；以及

（b）与保释有关的程序；

但是不包括对《1953 年税收管理法》第三部分所指规定

of the *Taxation Administration Act 1953*.

cross–examination is defined in subclause 2(2) of Part 2 of this Dictionary.

cross–examiner means a party who is cross–examining a witness.

de facto partner is defined in clause 11 of Part 2 of this Dictionary.

document means any record of information, and includes:

(a) anything on which there is writing; or

(b) anything on which there are marks, figures, symbols or perforations having a meaning for persons qualified to interpret them; or

(c) anything from which sounds, images or writings can be reproduced with or without the aid of anything else; or

(d) a map, plan, drawing or photograph.

Note: See also clause 8 of Part 2 of this Dictionary on the meaning of document.

electronic communication has the same meaning as it has in the *Electronic Transactions Act 1999*.

examination in chief is defined in subclause 2(1) of Part 2 of this Dictionary.

exercise of a function includes performance of a duty.

fax, in relation to a document, means a copy of the document that has been reproduced by facsimile telegraphy.

federal court means:

(a) the High Court; or

(b) any other court created by the Parliament (other than the Supreme Court of a Territory);

and includes a person or body (other than a court or

的税收犯罪的检控。

交叉询问的定义见本《术语》第 2 部分 2（2）。

交叉询问者是指正在对证人进行交叉询问的当事人。

事实配偶的定义见本《术语》第 2 部分第 11 条。

书证 / 文件是指对信息的任何记录，并且包括：

（a）载有写迹的任何物品；或者

（b）载有对于有解释资格的人员而言具有意义的标记、数字、符号或者穿孔的任何物品；或者

（c）借助或者无需借助任何物品可以重现的声音、形象或者写迹；或者

（d）地图、设计图、图画或者照片。

注释：还请参见本《术语》第 2 部分第 8 条关于书证的含义的规定。

电子通信的含义同《1999 年电子交易法》之规定。

主询问的定义见本《术语》第 2 部分 2（1）。

行使职能，包括履行职责。

传真，就书证而言，是指经由传真电报所复制的书证复制件。

联邦法院是指下列法院，并且包括在根据联邦法律履行职能或者行使权力时需要适用证据法的人员或者机构，州或者领地的法院或者治安法官除外：

（a）最高法院；或者

magistrate of a State or Territory) that, in performing a function or exercising a power under a law of the Commonwealth, is required to apply the laws of evidence.

Note: The NSW Act does not include this definition.

foreign court means any court (including any person or body authorised to take or receive evidence, whether on behalf of a court or otherwise and whether or not the person or body is empowered to require the answering of questions or the production of documents) of a foreign country or a part of such a country.

function includes power, authority or duty.

government or official gazette includes the *Gazette*.

Note 1: The definition of *government or official gazette* differs from the definition of the same expression in the NSW Act.

Note 2: The NSW Act includes definitions of *Governor of a State* and *Governor–General*. Those terms are not defined in this Act because they are defined in sections 16A and 16B of the Acts Interpretation Act 1901.

hearsay rule means subsection 59(1).

identification evidence means evidence that is:

(a) an assertion by a person to the effect that a defendant was, or resembles (visually, aurally or otherwise) a person who was, present at or near a place where:

(i) the offence for which the defendant is being prosecuted was committed; or

(ii) an act connected to that offence was done;

at or about the time at which the offence was committed or the act was done, being an assertion that is based wholly or partly on what the person making

（b）议会设立的任何其他法院，领地最高法院除
　　　外。

　　　注释：《新南威尔士州证据法》并不包含该定义。

外国法院是指外国或者该国的一部分的任何法院，包括经授权提取证据或者接收证据的任何人员或者机构，无论其代表法院还是其他机构，无论该某人员或者机构是否被授权要求对提问作出回答或者要求出示书证。

职能包括权力、职权或者职责。

政府或者官方公报包括《公报》。

　　　注释1：政府或者官方公报的定义与《新南威尔士州证据法》
　　　　　　　中的同一表述不同。

　　　注释2：《新南威尔士州证据法》包含有州长和总督的定义。
　　　　　　　这些术语在本法中没有作出界定，这是因为《1901
　　　　　　　年法律解释法》第 16A 条和第 16B 条对此作出了界
　　　　　　　定。

传闻规则的含义见 59（1）。

辨认证据是指关于下列主张的证据：

（a）某人完全或者部分根据其在犯罪和行为发生
　　　的地点和时间所见、所听或者以其他方式进
　　　行的感知作出的，被告是或者像（在视觉、
　　　听觉或者其他方面）在犯罪和行为发生时出
　　　现在下列地点或者在该地点附近的人员的主
　　　张：

（i）被告正在被检控的犯罪的实施地；或者

the assertion saw, heard or otherwise perceived at that place and time; or

(b) a report (whether oral or in writing) of such an assertion.

investigating official means:

(a) a police officer (other than a police officer who is engaged in covert investigations under the orders of a superior); or

(b) a person appointed by or under an Australian law (other than a person who is engaged in covert investigations under the orders of a superior) whose functions include functions in respect of the prevention or investigation of offences.

joint sitting means:

(a) in relation to the Parliament—a joint sitting of the members of the Senate and of the House of Representatives convened by the Governor–General under section 57 of the Constitution or convened under any Act; or

(b) in relation to a bicameral legislature of a State—a joint sitting of both Houses of the legislature convened under a law of the State.

judge, in relation to a proceeding, means the judge, magistrate or other person before whom the proceeding is being held.

law is defined in clause 9 of Part 2 of this Dictionary.

leading question means a question asked of a witness that:

(a) directly or indirectly suggests a particular answer to the question; or

(b) assumes the existence of a fact the existence of which is in dispute in the proceeding and as to the existence of which the witness has not given evidence before the

第 1 部分　定义

（ⅱ）与该犯罪有关的行为的发生地；或者

（b）关于上述主张的报告，无论口头还是书面形式。

调查人员是指：

（a）警察，根据上级命令进行秘密调查的警察除外；或者

（b）根据澳大利亚法律任命，其职能包括预防或者调查犯罪职能的人员，根据上级命令进行秘密调查的警察除外。

联席会议：

（a）就议会而言，是指总督根据《宪法》第 57 条或者任何其他法律之规定召集的参议院和众议院议员的联席会议；或者

（b）就州的两院制立法机关而言，是指根据州法召集的立法机构两院的联席会议。

法官，就某程序而言，是指主持该程序的法官、治安法官或者其他人员。

法律的定义见本《术语》第 2 部分第 9 条。

诱导性问题是指向证人提出的下列问题：

（a）直接或者间接暗示了具体答案的问题；或者

（b）假设某事实的存在，而在程序中就该事实存在争议，并且在向该证人提出该问题之前证

question is asked.

legal counsel means an Australian lawyer employed in or by a government agency or other body who by law is exempted from holding an Australian practising certificate, or who does not require an Australian practising certificate, to engage in legal practice in the course of that employment.

Note: Examples of legal counsel are in–house counsel and government solicitors.

Legislative Assembly means any present or former Legislative Assembly of a Territory, and includes the Australian Capital Territory House of Assembly.

offence means an offence against or arising under an Australian law.

opinion rule means section 76.

overseas–registered foreign lawyer means a natural person who is properly registered to engage in legal practice in a foreign country by an entity in the country having the function, conferred by the law of the country, of registering persons to engage in legal practice in the country.

parent includes the meaning given in subclause 10(2) of Part 2 of this Dictionary.

picture identification evidence is defined in section 115.

police officer means:

(a) a member or special member of the Australian Federal Police; or

(b) a member of the police force of a State or Territory.

postal article has the same meaning as in the Australian Postal Corporation Act 1989.

previous representation means a representation made otherwise than in the course of giving evidence in the proceeding in which evidence of the representation is

人还没有就该事实是否存在作证的问题。

法律顾问是指政府机关或者其他机构所雇佣，依法免于持有澳大利亚执业证书或者并不要求持有澳大利亚执业证书，在该雇佣过程中从事法律执业活动的澳大利亚律师。

> 注释：法律顾问的例子包括内部顾问和政府沙律师。

立法会是指领地的任何现行或者前立法会，并且包括澳大利亚首都领地立法院。

犯罪是指违反或者起因于澳大利亚法律所构成的犯罪。

意见规则的含义见第 76 条。

海外注册外国律师，是指在外国由经该国法律赋权，具有对该国从事法律执业的活动的人员履行注册职能的实体之适当登记，在该国从事法律执业活动的自然人。

父母包括《术语》第 2 部分 10（2）所指含义。

图片辨认证据的定义见第 115 条。

警察是指：

　　（a）澳大利亚联邦警察机构的成员或者特别成员；

　　　　或者

　　（b）州或者领地警察机构的成员。

邮品的含义同《1989 年澳大利亚邮政公司法》之规定。

先前表述是指在寻求将某表述提出作为证据的程序中的作证过程之外所作的表述。

sought to be adduced.

prior consistent statement of a witness means a previous representation that is consistent with evidence given by the witness.

prior inconsistent statement of a witness means a previous representation that is inconsistent with evidence given by the witness.

probative value of evidence means the extent to which the evidence could rationally affect the assessment of the probability of the existence of a fact in issue.

prosecutor means a person who institutes or is responsible for the conduct of a prosecution.

public document means a document that:

    (a) forms part of the records of the Crown in any of its capacities; or

    (b) forms part of the records of the government of a foreign country; or

    (c) forms part of the records of a person or body holding office or exercising a function under or because of the Constitution, an Australian law or a law of a foreign country; or

    (d) is being kept by or on behalf of the Crown, such a government or such a person or body;

and includes the records of the proceedings of, and papers presented to:

    (e) an Australian Parliament, a House of an Australian Parliament, a committee of such a House or a committee of an Australian Parliament; and

    (f) a legislature of a foreign country, including a House or committee (however described) of such a legislature.

证人的**先前一致陈述**是指与该证人所作证言一致的先前表述。

证人的**先前不一致陈述**是指与该证人所作证言不一致的先前表述。

证据的**证明价值**是指证据可以对争议事实存在可能性进行的评估产生理性影响的程度。

公诉人是指提起或者负责进行检控的人。

公共文件是指：

　　（a）构成政府记录的一部分的文件；或者

　　（b）构成外国政府记录的一部分的文件；或者

　　（c）构成根据或者基于《宪法》、澳大利亚法律或者外国法律担任公职或者行使职能的人员或者机构的记录的一部分的文件；或者

　　（d）代表政府、上述政府、上述人员或者机构所保管的文件。

公共文件还包括下列机构的程序记录和向其提交的文件：

　　（e）澳大利亚议会、澳大利亚议会的议院、该议院的委员会或者澳大利亚议会的委员会；以及

　　（f）　外国立法机构，包括该立法机构的议院或者委员会（不论如何表述）。

re–examination is defined in subclauses 2(3) and (4) of Part 2 of this Dictionary.

registered, in relation to legal practice in a foreign country, means having all necessary licences, approvals, admissions, certificates or other forms of authorisation (including practising certificates) required by or under legislation for engaging in legal practice in that country.

representation includes:

(a) an express or implied representation (whether oral or in writing); or

(b) a representation to be inferred from conduct; or

(c) a representation not intended by its maker to be communicated to or seen by another person; or

(d) a representation that for any reason is not communicated.

seal includes a stamp.

tendency evidence means evidence of a kind referred to in subsection 97(1) that a party seeks to have adduced for the purpose referred to in that subsection.

tendency rule means subsection 97(1).

traditional laws and customs of an Aboriginal or Torres Strait Islander group (including a kinship group) includes any of the traditions, customary laws, customs, observances, practices, knowledge and beliefs of the group.

visual identification evidence is defined in section 114.

witness includes the meaning given in clause 7 of Part 2 of this Dictionary.

再询问的定义见《术语解释》第 2 部分 2（3）和（4）。

注册（的），就外国的法律执业活动而言，是指具有立法所要求的为在该国从事法律执业活动而必需的所有执照、批准、许可、证明书或者其他形式的授权（包括执业证书）。

表述包括：

> （a）明示或者默示的表述（无论是口头的还是书面的）；或者
>
> （b）从行为中推论出的表述；或者
>
> （c）进行表述的人员作出的并不准备与他人进行交流或者为他人所见的表述；或者
>
> （d）基于任何理由没有进行交流的表述。

印章包括图章。

倾向证据是指 97（1）所称的当事人提出旨在实现该条款所称目的证据。

倾向规则的含义见 97（1）。

土著民和 Torres 海峡岛民群体（包括相似群体）的**传统法律与习俗**，包括该群体的任何传统、习惯法、习俗、惯例、例行做法、知识和信仰。

视像辨认证据的定义见第 114 条。

证人包括本《术语》第 2 部分第 7 条规定的含义。

Part 2—Other Expressions

1 References to businesses

(1) A reference in this Act to a ***business*** includes a reference to the following:

(a) a profession, calling, occupation, trade or undertaking;

(b) an activity engaged in or carried on by the Crown in any of its capacities;

(c) an activity engaged in or carried on by the government of a foreign country;

(d) an activity engaged in or carried on by a person holding office or exercising power under or because of the Constitution, an Australian law or a law of a foreign country, being an activity engaged in or carried on in the performance of the functions of the office or in the exercise of the power (otherwise than in a private capacity);

(e) the proceedings of an Australian Parliament, a House of an Australian Parliament, a committee of such a House or a committee of an Australian Parliament;

(f) the proceedings of a legislature of a foreign country, including a House or committee (however described) of such a legislature.

(2) A reference in this Act to a business also includes a reference to:

(a) a business that is not engaged in or carried on for profit; or

(b) a business engaged in or carried on outside Australia.

第 2 部分 其他措辞

1 所称业务

（1）本法所称**业务**包括以下：

（a）专业、职业、行业、商业或者事业；

（b）政府所从事或者进行的活动；

（c）外国政府从事或者进行的活动；

（d）根据或者基于《宪法》、澳大利亚法律或者
外国法律担任公职或者行使权力的人员，从
事或者进行的履行职能或者行使权力的活动，
以个人名义从事或进行的活动除外；

（e）澳大利亚议会、澳大利亚议会的议院、该议
院的委员会或者澳大利亚议会的委员会进行
的程序；

（f）外国立法机构，包括该立法机构的议院或者
委员会（不论如何表述）进行的程序。

（2）本法所称业务还包括：

（a）非为营利目的所从事或者进行的业务；或者

（b）在澳大利亚境外从事或者进行的业务。

Part 2—Other Expressions

2 References to examination in chief, cross–examination and re–examination

(1) A reference in this Act to *examination in chief* of a witness is a reference to the questioning of a witness by the party who called the witness to give evidence, not being questioning that is re–examination.

(2) A reference in this Act to *cross–examination* of a witness is a reference to the questioning of a witness by a party other than the party who called the witness to give evidence.

(3) A reference in this Act to *re–examination* of a witness is a reference to the questioning of a witness by the party who called the witness to give evidence, being questioning (other than further examination in chief with the leave of the court) conducted after the cross–examination of the witness by another party.

(4) If a party has recalled a witness who has already given evidence, a reference in this Act to re–examination of a witness does not include a reference to the questioning of the witness by that party before the witness is questioned by another party.

3 References to civil penalties

For the purposes of this Act, a person is taken to be liable to a civil penalty if, in an Australian or overseas proceeding (other than a criminal proceeding), the person would be liable to a penalty arising under an Australian law or a law of a foreign country.

4 Unavailability of persons

(1) For the purposes of this Act, a person is taken not to be available to give evidence about a fact if:

2 所称主询问、交叉询问和再询问

(1) 本法所称对证人的**主询问**，是指由传唤证人作证的当事人对该证人的询问，不包括再询问时对证人的询问。

(2) 本法所称对证人的**交叉询问**，是指由传唤证人作证的当事人之外的当事人对该证人的询问。

(3) 本法所称对证人的**再询问**，是指传唤证人作证的当事人在对方当事人对证人进行了交叉询问之后对证人进行的询问，而不是指经法院许可进行的进一步主询问。

(4) 如果当事人又传唤了已经作证的证人，本法所称对证人的再询问，并不包括证人在被其他当事人询问之前由该当事人进行的询问。

3 所称民事处罚

就本法目的而言，如果在澳大利亚或者海外程序（刑事程序除外）中某人要对起因于澳大利亚法律或者外国法律的处罚承担责任，则视为该某人要对民事处罚承担责任。

4 有关人员不能到庭

(1) 就本法目的而言，在下列情况下，视为某人不能到庭就某事实作证：

    (a) the person is dead; or

    (b) the person is, for any reason other than the application of section 16 (Competence and compellability: judges and jurors), not competent to give the evidence about the fact; or

    (c) it would be unlawful for the person to give evidence about the fact; or

    (d) a provision of this Act prohibits the evidence being given; or

    (e) all reasonable steps have been taken, by the party seeking to prove the person is not available, to find the person or to secure his or her attendance, but without success; or

    (f) all reasonable steps have been taken, by the party seeking to prove the person is not available, to compel the person to give the evidence, but without success.

(2) In all other cases the person is taken to be available to give evidence about the fact.

5 Unavailability of documents and things

For the purposes of this Act, a document or thing is taken not to be available to a party if and only if:

    (a) it cannot be found after reasonable inquiry and search by the party; or

    (b) it was destroyed by the party, or by a person on behalf of the party, otherwise than in bad faith, or was destroyed by another person; or

    (c) it would be impractical to produce the document or thing during the course of the proceeding; or

    (d) production of the document or thing during the course

（a）该某人已经死亡；或者

（b）该某人因适用第 16 条（证人能力与强制作证：法官和陪审员）之外的任何其他原因，不具备就该事实作证的能力；或者

（c）该某人就该事实作证不合法；或者

（d）本法某规定禁止作证；或者

（e）寻求证明该某人不能到庭的当事人，为找到该某人或者促使其出庭，已经采取了所有的合理措施，但是没有成功；或者

（f）寻求证明该某人不能到庭的当事人，为强制该某人作证，已经采取了所有的合理措施，但是没有成功。

（2）在所有其他情况下，视为该某人能够到庭就事实作证。

5 书证与物证的不可得

就本法目的而言，当且仅当下列情况下，书证和物证视为不可得：

（a）当事人进行了合理的查询和搜索后不能找到；或者

（b）为当事人或者代表当事人的人非恶意所毁损，或者为他人所毁损；或者

（c）在程序中出示有关书证或者物证不可行；或者

（d）在程序中出示有关书证或者物证会导致某人

of the proceeding could render a person liable to conviction for an offence; or

(e) it is not in the possession or under the control of the party and:

(i) it cannot be obtained by any judicial procedure of the court; or

(ii) it is in the possession or under the control of another party to the proceeding concerned who knows or might reasonably be expected to know that evidence of the contents of the document, or evidence of the thing, is likely to be relevant in the proceeding; or

(iii) it was in the possession or under the control of such a party at a time when that party knew or might reasonably be expected to have known that such evidence was likely to be relevant in the proceeding.

6 Representations in documents

For the purposes of this Act, a representation contained in a document is taken to have been made by a person if:

(a) the document was written, made or otherwise produced by the person;

(b) the representation was recognised by the person as his or her representation by signing, initialling or otherwise marking the document.

7 Witnesses

(1) A reference in this Act to a witness includes a reference to a party giving evidence.

(2) A reference in this Act to a witness who has been called by a party to give evidence includes a reference to the party

因某犯罪而被定罪；或者

（e）不为当事人占有或者控制，并且：

（i）不能通过法院的任何程序所获得；或者

（ii）为有关诉讼程序中知道或者可以合理地期待其知道该书证内容或者物证可能与该程序有关的另一方当事人占有或者控制；或者

（iii）当事人知道或者可能合理地期待其知道该书证内容或者物证可能与该程序有关时，该书证或者物证为上述当事人所占有或者控制。

6 书证中的表述

就本法目的而言， 在下列情况下，书证中包含的表述视为为某人所作：

（a）该书证为该某人所书写、制作或者以其他方式生成；

（b）该某人通过签名、缩写签名或者其他在书证上作记号的方式认可该表述为其表述。

7 证人

（1）本法所称证人包括作证的当事人。

（2）本法所称被一方当事人传唤作证的证人，包括作证的当事人。

giving evidence.

(3) A reference in this clause to a party includes a defendant in a criminal proceeding.

8 References to documents

A reference in this Act to a document includes a reference to:

(a) any part of the document; or

(b) any copy, reproduction or duplicate of the document or of any part of the document; or

(c) any part of such a copy, reproduction or duplicate.

8A References to offices etc.

In this Act:

(a) a reference to a person appointed or holding office under or because of an Australian law or a law of the Commonwealth includes a reference to an APS employee; and

(b) in that context, a reference to an office is a reference to the position occupied by the APS employee concerned.

9 References to laws

(1) A reference in this Act to a law of the Commonwealth, a State, a Territory or a foreign country is a reference to a law (whether written or unwritten) of or in force in that place.

(2) A reference in this Act to an Australian law is a reference to an Australian law (whether written or unwritten) of or in force in Australia.

10 References to children and parents

(1) A reference in this Act to a child of a person includes a

（3）本条所称当事人包括刑事程序中的被告。

8　所称书证

本法所称书证，包括：

（a）书证的任何一部分；或者

（b）书证或者书证的任何一部分的复制件、复制品或者复本；或者

（c）上述复制件、复制品或者复本的任何一部分。

8A　所称公职等

在本法中，

（a）所称根据或者基于澳大利亚法律或者联邦法律被任命或者担任公职的人员，包括澳大利亚公共服务委员会的雇员；并且

（b）在该语境下，所称公职，是指有关澳大利亚公共服务委员会雇员所居的岗位。

9　所称法律

（1）本法所称联邦、州、领地或者外国法律，是指该地方之法律或者在该地方有效之法律，无论是成文法还是非成文法。

（2）本法所称澳大利亚法律，是指澳大利亚之法律或者在澳大利亚有效之法律，无论是成文法还是非成文法。

10　所称子女与父母

（1）本法所称某人的子女，包括：

reference to:

(a) an adopted child or ex–nuptial child of the person; or

(b) a child living with the person as if the child were a member of the person's family.

(2) A reference in this Act to a parent of a person includes a reference to:

(a) an adoptive parent of the person; or

(b) if the person is an ex–nuptial child—the person's natural father; or

(c) the person with whom a child is living as if the child were a member of the person's family.

11 References to de facto partners

(1) A reference in this Act to a de facto partner of a person is a reference to a person who is in a de facto relationship with the person.

(2) A person is in a de facto relationship with another person if the two persons have a relationship as a couple and are not legally married.

(3) In determining whether two persons are in a de facto relationship, all the circumstances of the relationship are to be taken into account, including such of the following matters as are relevant in the circumstances of the particular case:

(a) the duration of the relationship;

(b) the nature and extent of their common residence;

(c) the degree of financial dependence or interdependence, and any arrangements for financial support, between them;

(d) the ownership, use and acquisition of their property;

（a）该某人收养的子女或者非婚生子女；或者

（b）与该某人共同生活，如同该某人之家庭成员
　　的儿童。

（2）本法所称某人的父母，包括：

（a）该某人的养父母；或者

（b）在该某人为非婚生子女的情况下，该某人的
　　自然生父；或者

（c）儿童与之共同生活，如同其家庭成员的人
　　员。

11　所称事实配偶

（1）本法所称事实配偶，是指与某人有事实关系的
　　人。

（2）如果两个人未行法律上的结婚则有了夫妻关系，则
　　一个人与另一个就是有事实关系。

（3）在确定两个人是否有事实关系时，该关系的所有情
　　况都应当虑及，包括在具体案件情况中相关的下列
　　事项：

（a）该关系的持续时间；

（b）其共同居所的性质和范围；

（c）经济依赖或者相互依赖程度，以及他们之间
　　的经济资助安排；

（d）其财产的所有权、使用权和收益权；

Part 2—Other Expressions

   (e) the degree of mutual commitment to a shared life;

   (f) the care and support of children;

   (g) the reputation and public aspects of the relationship.

(4) No particular finding in relation to any circumstance is to be regarded as necessary in deciding whether two persons have a relationship as a couple.

(5) For the purposes of subclause (3), the following matters are irrelevant:

   (a) whether the persons are different sexes or the same sex;

   (b) whether either of the persons is legally married to someone else or in another de facto relationship.

第 2 部分　其他措辞

　　　（e）对共同生活的相互忠诚程度；

　　　（f）对子女的关照和抚养；

　　　（g）该关系的声望和公众看法。

（4）在确定两个人是否存在夫妻关系时，对任何情况的
　　　具体认定并非必需。

（5）　就（3）之目的而言，下列事项不相关：

　　　（a）有关人员是异性还是同性；

　　　（b）二者之一是否同他人存在合法婚姻或者另一
　　　　　事实关系。

Notes to the Evidence Act 1995

Note 1

The *Evidence Act 1995* as shown in this compilation comprises Act No. 2, 1995 amended as indicated in the Tables below.

For application, saving or transitional provisions made by the *Corporations (Repeals, Consequentials and Transitionals) Act 2001, see* Act No. 55, 2001.

For all other relevant information pertaining to application, saving or transitional provisions *see* Table A.

Table of Acts

Act	Number and year	Date of Assent	Date of commencement	Application, saving or transitional provisions
Evidence Act 1995	2, 1995	23 Feb 1995	Ss. 4–197 and Schedule: 18 Apr 1995 Remainder: Royal Assent	
Family Law Reform (Consequential Amendments) Act 1995	140, 1995	12 Dec 1995	Schedule 2: 26 Dec 1995 (a)	—
Statute Law Revision Act 1996	43, 1996	25 Oct 1996	Schedule 2 (item 54): (b)	—
Law and Justice Legislation Amendment Act 1997	34, 1997	17 Apr 1997	Schedule 6: Royal Assent (c)	—
Law and Justice Legislation Amendment Act 1999	125, 1999	13 Oct 1999	Schedule 6: Royal Assent (d)	—

对《1995 年证据法》的注释

注释 1

本汇编中的《1995 年证据法》包括下表所列对 1995 年第 2 号法律的修正。

关于《2001 年公司（取消、相应修正和过渡）法》所作的适用、保留或者过渡性规定，参见 2001 年第 55 号法律。

与适用、保留或者过渡性规定有关的所有其他信息，参见表 A。

法律列表

法律名称	编号与年度	御准日期	施行日期	适用、保留或者过渡性规定
《1995 年证据法》	2, 1995	1995 年 2 月 23 日	第 4 条至第 197 条和附录：1995 年 4 月 18 日 其他：御准之日	
《1995 年家庭法律改革（相应修正）法》	140, 1995	1995 年 12 月 12 日	附录 2：1995 年 12 月 26 日（a）	—
《1996 年制定法法律修订法》	43, 1996	1996 年 10 月 25 日	附录 2（第 54 项）：（b）	—
《1997 年法律与正义立法修正法》	34, 1997	1997 年 4 月 17 日	附录 6：御准之日（c）	—
《1999 年法律与正义立法修正法》	125, 1999	1999 年 10 月 13 日	附录 6：御准之日（d）	—

Act	Number and year	Date of Assent	Date of commencement	Application, saving or transitional provisions
Public Employment (Consequential and Transitional) Amendment Act 1999	146, 1999	11 Nov 1999	Schedule 1 (items 434–437): 5 Dec 1999 (see Gazette 1999, No. S584) (e)	—
Corporate Law Economic Reform Program Act 1999	156, 1999	24 Nov 1999	Schedule 12 (items 1, 24): 24 Nov 2000 (f)	—
Australian Federal Police Legislation Amendment Act 2000	9, 2000	7 Mar 2000	2 July 2000 (see Gazette 2000, No. S328)	Sch. 3 (items 20, 25, 34, 35)
Law and Justice Legislation Amendment (Application of Criminal Code) Act 2001	24, 2001	6 Apr 2001	S. 4(1), (2) and Schedule 25: (g)	S. 4(1) and (2)
Corporations (Repeals, Consequentials and Transitionals) Act 2001	55, 2001	28 June 2001	Ss. 4–14 and Schedule 3 (items 174, 175): 15 July 2001 (see Gazette 2001, No. S285) (h)	Ss. 4–14 [see Note 1]
Border Security Legislation Amendment Act 2002	64, 2002	5 July 2002	Schedule 6 (items 16–18): 5 Jan 2003	—
Ozone Protection and Synthetic Greenhouse Gas Legislation Amendment Act 2003	126, 2003	5 Dec 2003	5 Dec 2003	—
Law and Justice Legislation Amendment Act 2004	62, 2004	26 May 2004	Schedule 1 (item 17): 27 May 2004	—

法律名称	编号与年度	御准日期	施行日期	适用、保留或者过渡性规定
《1999 年公共雇佣（相应修正和过渡）修正法》	146, 1999	1999 年 11 月 11 日	附录 1（第 434 项至第 437 项）：1999 年 12 月 5 日（参见《公报》1999, No. S584）（e）	—
《1999 年公司法律经济改革项目法》	156, 1999	1999 年 11 月 24 日	附录 12（第 1 项、第 24 项）：2000 年 11 月 24 日（f）	—
《2000 年澳大利亚联邦警察立法修正法》	9, 2000	2000 年 3 月 7 日	2000 年 7 月 2 日（参见《公报》2000, No. S328）	附录 3（第 20 项、第 25 项、第 34 项、第 35 项）
《2001 年法律与正义立法修正 < 刑法典 > 的适用法》	24, 2001	2001 年 4 月 6 日	4（1）、（2）和附录 25：（g）	4（1）和（2）
《2001 年公司（取消、相应修正和过渡）法》	55, 2001	2001 年 6 月 28 日	第 4 条至第 14 条和附录 3（第 174 项、第 175 项）：2001 年 7 月 15 日（参见《公报》2001, No. S285）（h）	第 4 条至第 14 条[参见注释 1]
《2002 年边界安全立法修正法》	64, 2002	2002 年 7 月 5 日	附录 6（第 16 项至第 18 项）：2003 年 1 月 5 日	—
《2003 年臭氧保护与合成温室气体立法修正法》	126, 2003	2003 年 12 月 5 日	2003 年 12 月 5 日	—
《2004 年法律与正义立法修正法》	62, 2004	2004 年 5 月 26 日	附录 1（第 17 项）：2004 年 5 月 27 日	—

Act	Number and year	Date of Assent	Date of commencement	Application, saving or transitional provisions
Statute Law Revision Act 2005	100, 2005	6 July 2005	Schedule 1 (item 14): Royal Assent	—
Family Law Amendment (Shared Parental Responsibility) Act 2006	46, 2006	22 May 2006	Schedule 3 (items 1, 8): 1 July 2006	Sch. 3 (item 8)
Evidence Amendment (Journalists' Privilege) Act 2007	116, 2007	28 June 2007	Schedule 1 (items 1, 2): 26 July 2007	—
Evidence Amendment Act 2008	135, 2008	4 Dec 2008	Schedule 1 (items 1–99) and Schedule 2 (items 1–13): 1 Jan 2009	Sch. 1 (items 95–99) and Sch. 2 (item 13)
Customs Legislation Amendment (Name Change) Act 2009	33, 2009	22 May 2009	Schedule 2 (item 30): 23 May 2009	—
Disability Discrimination and Other Human Rights Legislation Amendment Act 2009	70, 2009	8 July 2009	Schedule 3 (item 32): 5 Aug 2009	—
Statute Law Revision Act 2010	8, 2010	1 Mar 2010	Schedule 1 (item 26): Royal Assent	—
Evidence Amendment (Journalists' Privilege) Act 2011	21, 2011	12 Apr 2011	Schedule 1 (items 1–3): 13 Apr 2011	—
Acts Interpretation Amendment Act 2011	46, 2011	27 June 2011	Schedule 2 (item 566) and Schedule 3 (items 10, 11): 27 Dec 2011	Sch. 3 (items 10, 11)

法律名称	编号与年度	御准日期	施行日期	适用、保留或者过渡性规定
《2005 年制定法法律修订法》	100, 2005	2005 年 7 月 6 日	附录 1（第 14 项）：御准之日	—
《2006 年家庭法律修正（共同承担父母责任）法》	46, 2006	2006 年 5 月 22 日	附录 3（第 1 项、第 8 项）：2006 年 7 月 1 日	附录 3（第 8 项）
《2007 年证据修正（记者特免权）法》	116, 2007	2007 年 6 月 28 日	附录 1（第 1 项、第 2 项）：2007 年 7 月 26 日	—
《2008 年证据修正法》	135, 2008	2008 年 12 月 4 日	附录 1（第 1 项至第 99 项）和附录 2（第 1 项至第 13 项）：2009 年 1 月 1 日	附录 1（第 95 项至第 99 项）和附录 2（第 13 项）
《2009 年关税立法修正（名称改变）法》	33, 2009	2009 年 5 月 22 日	附录 2（第 30 项）：2009 年 5 月 23 日	—
《2009 年残障歧视和其他人权立法修正法》	70, 2009	2009 年 7 月 8 日	附录 3（第 32 项）：2009 年 8 月 5 日	—
《2010 年制定法法律修订法》	8, 2010	2010 年 3 月 1 日	附录 1（第 26 项）：御准之日	—
《2011 年证据修正（记者特免权）法》	21, 2011	2011 年 4 月 12 日	附录 1（第 1 项至第 3 项）：2011 年 4 月 13 日	—
《2011 年法律解释修正法》	46, 2011	2011 年 6 月 27 日	附录 2（第 566 项）和附录 3（第 10 项、第 11 项）：2011 年 12 月 27 日	附录 3（第 10 项、第 11 项）

Act	Number and year	Date of Assent	Date of commencement	Application, saving or transitional provisions
Clean Energy (Consequential Amendments) Act 2011	132, 2011	18 Nov 2011	Schedule 1 (item 260A): [see Note 2]	—

(a) The *Evidence Act 1995* was amended by Schedule 2 only of the *Family Law Reform (Consequential Amendments) Act 1995*, subsection 2(5) of which provides as follows:

> (5) Schedule 2 commences 14 days after the day on which this Act receives the Royal Assent.

(b) The *Evidence Act 1995* was amended by Schedule 2 (item 54) only of the *Statute Law Revision Act 1996*, subsection 2(2) of which provides as follows:

> (2) Each item in Schedule 2 commences or is taken to have commenced (as the case requires) at the time specified in the note at the end of the item.

Item 54 is taken to have commenced immediately after the commencement of section 130 of the *Evidence Act 1995*.

Section 130 commenced on 18 April 1995.

(c) The *Evidence Act 1995* was amended by Schedule 6 only of the Law and *Justice Legislation Amendment Act 1997*, subsection 2(1) of which provides as follows:

> (1) Subject to this section, this Act commences on the day on which it receives the Royal Assent.

(d) The *Evidence Act 1995* was amended by Schedule 6 only of the *Law and Justice Legislation Amendment Act 1999*, subsection 2(1) of which provides as follows:

> (1) Subject to this section, this Act commences on the day on which it

法律名称	编号与年度	御准日期	施行日期	适用、保留或者过渡性规定
《2011 年清洁能源（相应修正）法》	132, 2011	2011 年 11 月 18 日	附录 1（第 260A 项）：[参见注释 2]	—

（a）《1995 年证据法》为《1995 年家庭法律改革（相应修正）法》附录 2 所修正，该法 2（5）规定如下：

（5）附录 2 自本法取得御准之日后第 14 日开始施行。

（b）《1995 年证据法》为《1996 年制定法法律修订法》附录 2（第 54 项）所修正，该法 2（2）规定如下：

（2）附录 2 的每项自该项末尾的注释指定的时间施行或者视为自该时间施行（视情况而定）。

第 54 项视为《1995 年证据法》第 130 条施行后立即施行。

第 130 条自 1995 年 4 月 18 日起施行。

（c）《1995 年证据法》为《1997 年法律与正义立法修正法》附录 6 所修正，该法 2（1）规定如下：

（1）在遵守本条的情况下，本法自取得御准之日起施行。

（d）《1995 年证据法》为《1999 年法律与正义立法修正法》附录 6 所修正，该法 2（1）规定如下：

（1）在遵守本条的情况下，本法自取得御准之日起施行。

receives the Royal Assent.

(e) The *Evidence Act 1995* was amended by Schedule 1 (items 434 – 437) only of the *Public Employment (Consequential and Transitional) Amendment Act 1999*, subsections 2(1) and (2) of which provide as follows:

(1) In this Act, commencing time means the time when the *Public Service Act 1999* commences.

(2) Subject to this section, this Act commences at the commencing time.

(f) The *Evidence Act 1995* was amended by Schedule 12 (items 1 and 24) only of the *Corporate Law Economic Reform Program Act 1999*, subsection 2(4) of which provides as follows:

(4) If an item in Schedule 11 or 12 does not commence under subsection (2) within the period of 12 months beginning on the day on which this Act receives the Royal Assent, it commences on the first day after the end of that period.

(g) The *Evidence Act 1995* was amended by Schedule 25 only of the *Law and Justice Legislation Amendment (Application of Criminal Code) Act 2001*, subsection 2(1)(a) of which provides as follows:

(1) Subject to this section, this Act commences at the later of the following times:

(a) immediately after the commencement of item 15 of Schedule 1 to the *Criminal Code Amendment (Theft, Fraud, Bribery and Related Offences) Act 2000*;

Item 15 commenced on 24 May 2001.

(h) The *Evidence Act 1995* was amended by Schedule 3 (items 174 and 175) only of the *Corporations (Repeals, Consequentials and Transitionals) Act 2001*, subsection 2(3) of which provides as follows:

(3) Subject to subsections (4) to (10), Schedule 3 commences, or is taken to have commenced, at the same time as the *Corporations Act 2001*.

（e）《1995 年证据法》为《1999 年公共雇佣（相应和过渡）修正法》附录 1（第 434 项至第 437 项）所修正，该法 2（1）和（2）规定如下：

（1）在本法中，施行时间是指《1999 年公共服务法》施行的时间。

（2）在遵守本条的情况下，本法自施行时间起施行。

（f）《1995 年证据法》为《1999 年公司法律经济改革项目法》附录 12（第 1 项和第 24 项）所修正，该法 2（4）规定如下：

（4）如果根据（2），附录 11 或者 12 中的某项并没有在本法取得御准之日起 12 个月内施行，则其在该期间结束后的第 1 日起施行。

（g）《1995 年证据法》为《2001 年法律与正义立法修正（〈刑法典〉的适用）法》附录 25 所修正，该法 2（1）（a）规定如下：

（1）在遵守本条的情况下，本法自下列时间较迟之日起生效：

（a）在《2000 年刑法典（盗窃、欺诈、贿赂和相关犯罪）法》附录 1 第 15 项施行后；

第 15 项自 2001 年 5 月 24 日起施行。

（h）《1995 年证据法》为《2001 年公司（取消、相应修正和过渡）法》附录 3（第 174 项和第 175 项）所修正，该法 2（3）规定如下：

（3）在遵守（4）至（10）的情况下，附录 3 与《2001 年公司法》同时施行，或者视为与之同时施行。

Table of Amendments

ad. = added or inserted   am. = amended   rep. = repealed   rs. = repealed and substituted

Provision affected	How affected
Chapter 1	
Introductory Note	am. No. 100, 2005
Part 1.1	
S. 3	am. No. 46, 2011
Part 1.2	
S. 4	am. No. 140, 1995; No. 135, 2008
Note 4 to s. 4(1)	ad. No. 135, 2008
Note to s. 4(6)	am. No. 140, 1995
S. 5	am. No. 125, 1999; No. 135, 2008
S. 8	am. No. 156, 1999; No. 55, 2001
S. 8A	ad. No. 24, 2001
Chapter 2	
Part 2.1	
Division 1	
S. 13	rs. No. 135, 2008
S. 14	am. No. 135, 2008
Ss. 18, 19	am. No. 135, 2008
S. 20	am. No. 34, 1997; No. 135, 2008
Division 2	
S. 21	am. No. 135, 2008
S. 25	rep. No. 135, 2008
Division 3	
S. 29	am. No. 135, 2008
S. 33	am. No. 135, 2008
Division 4	
S. 37	am. No. 135, 2008
Division 5	
S. 41	rs. No. 135, 2008
S. 43	am. No. 34, 1997
Part 2.2	

修正表

ad. = 增添或者插入　　am. = 修正　　rep. = 取消　　rs. = 取消并取代

被修正的规定	修正情况
第 1 章	
引言性注释	am. No. 100, 2005
第 1.1 节	
第 3 条	am. No. 46, 2011
第 1.2 节	
第 4 条	am. No. 140, 1995; No. 135, 2008
对 4（1）的注释 4	ad. No. 135, 2008
对 4（6）的注释	am. No. 140, 1995
第 5 条	am. No. 125, 1999; No. 135, 2008
第 8 条	am. No. 156, 1999; No. 55, 2001
第 8A 条	ad. No. 24, 2001
第 2 章	
第 2.1 节	
第 1 目	
第 13 条	rs. No. 135, 2008
第 14 条	am. No. 135, 2008
第 18 条、第 19 条	am. No. 135, 2008
第 20 条	am. No. 34, 1997; No. 135, 2008
第 2 目	
第 21 条	am. No. 135, 2008
第 25 条	rep. No. 135, 2008
第 3 目	
第 29 条	am. No. 135, 2008
第 33 条	am. No. 135, 2008
第 4 目	
第 37 条	am. No. 135, 2008
第 5 目	
第 41 条	rs. No. 135, 2008
第 43 条	am. No. 34, 1997
第 2.2 节	

Provision affected	How affected
Note to s. 47	ad. No. 125, 1999
S. 48	am. No. 125, 1999
Note to s. 48	
Renumbered Note 1	No. 125, 1999
Note 2 to s. 48	ad. No. 125, 1999
Note to s. 49	ad. No. 125, 1999
S. 50	am. No. 125, 1999; No. 135, 2008
Note to s. 51	am. No. 125, 1999
Chapter 3	
Introductory Note	am. No. 135, 2008
Part 3.2	
Division 1	
S. 59	am. No. 125, 1999; No. 135, 2008
Note to s. 59(3)	am. No. 135, 2008
Ss. 60, 61	am. No. 135, 2008
Note to s. 61(2)	am. No. 135, 2008
Division 2	
Heading to s. 62	rs. No. 135, 2008
S. 62	am. No. 135, 2008
S. 63	am. No. 125, 1999
Ss. 64, 65	am. No. 125, 1999; No. 135, 2008
S. 66	am. No. 135, 2008
S. 66A	ad. No. 135, 2008
Note to s. 68(4)	ad. No. 34, 1997
Division 3	
Note 1 to s. 70(2)	am. No. 34, 1997
Ss. 71, 72	rs. No. 135, 2008
Part 3.3	
S. 76	am. No. 125, 1999
Note to s. 76	am. No. 135, 2008
S. 78A	ad. No. 135, 2008
S. 79	am. No. 135, 2008

被修正的规定	修正情况
对 47 条的注释	ad. No. 125, 1999
第 48 条	am. No. 125, 1999
对 48 条的注释	
重新编号的注释 1	No. 125, 1999
对第 48 条的注释 2	ad. No. 125, 1999
对第 49 条的注释	ad. No. 125, 1999
第 50 条	am. No. 125, 1999; No. 135, 2008
对第 51 条的注释	am. No. 125, 1999
第 3 章	
引言性注释	am. No. 135, 2008
第 3.2 节	
第 1 目	
第 59 条	am. No. 125, 1999; No. 135, 2008
对 59（3）的注释	am. No. 135, 2008
第 60 条、第 61 条	am. No. 135, 2008
对 61（2）的注释	am. No. 135, 2008
第 2 目	
第 62 条的标题	rs. No. 135, 2008
第 62 条	am. No. 135, 2008
第 63 条	am. No. 125, 1999
第 64 条、第 65 条	am. No. 125, 1999; No. 135, 2008
第 66 条	am. No. 135, 2008
第 66A 条	ad. No. 135, 2008
对 68（4）的注释	ad. No. 34, 1997
第 3 目	
对 70（2）的注释 1	am. No. 34, 1997
第 71 条、第 72 条	rs. No. 135, 2008
第 3.3 节	
第 76 条	am. No. 125, 1999
对第 76 条的注释	am. No. 135, 2008
第 78A 条	ad. No. 135, 2008
第 79 条	am. No. 135, 2008

Provision affected	How affected
Part 3.4	
S. 82	am. No. 125, 1999
Note to s. 82	ad. No. 135, 2008
S. 85	am. No. 135, 2008
S. 89	am. No. 135, 2008
Part 3.6	
S. 97	am. No. 135, 2008
S. 98	rs. No. 135, 2008
Part 3.7	
Division 1	
Div. 1 of Part 3.7	ad. No. 135, 2008
S. 101A	ad. No. 135, 2008
Division 2	
Heading to Div. 2 of Part 3.7	ad. No. 135, 2008
S. 102	rs. No. 135, 2008
Note to s. 102	
Renumbered Note 1	No. 34, 1997
Note 1 to s. 102	am. No. 34, 1997
	rs. No. 135, 2008
Note 2 to s. 102	ad. No. 34, 1997
	rs. No. 135, 2008
Ss. 103, 104	am. No. 135, 2008
S. 105	rep. No. 135, 2008
S. 106	rs. No. 135, 2008
S. 107	rep. No. 34, 1997
S. 108	am. No. 34, 1997; No. 135, 2008
Division 3	
Heading to Div. 3 of Part 3.7	ad. No. 135, 2008
S. 108A	ad. No. 34, 1997
	am. No. 135, 2008
S. 108B	ad. No. 135, 2008
Division 4	

被修正的规定	修正情况
第 3.4 节	
第 82 条	am. No. 125, 1999
对第 82 条的注释	ad. No. 135, 2008
第 85 条	am. No. 135, 2008
第 89 条	am. No. 135, 2008
第 3.6 节	
第 97 条	am. No. 135, 2008
第 98 条	rs. No. 135, 2008
第 3.7 节	
第 1 目	
第 3.7 节第 1 目	ad. No. 135, 2008
第 101A 条	ad. No. 135, 2008
第 2 目	
第 3.7 节第 2 目的标题.........	ad. No. 135, 2008
第 102 条	rs. No. 135, 2008
对第 102 条的注释	
重新编号后的注释 1.............	No. 34, 1997
对第 102 条的注释 1	am. No. 34, 1997
	rs. No. 135, 2008
对第 102 条的注释 2	ad. No. 34, 1997
	rs. No. 135, 2008
第 103 条、第 104 条	am. No. 135, 2008
第 105 条	rep. No. 135, 2008
第 106 条	rs. No. 135, 2008
第 107 条	rep. No. 34, 1997
第 108 条	am. No. 34, 1997; No. 135, 2008
第 3 目	
第 3.7 节第 3 目的标题.........	ad. No. 135, 2008
第 108A 条	ad. No. 34, 1997
	am. No. 135, 2008
第 108B 条	ad. No. 135, 2008
第 4 目	

Provision affected	How affected
Div. 4 of Part 3.7	ad. No. 135, 2008
S. 108C	ad. No. 135, 2008
Part 3.8	
S. 110	am. No. 135, 2008
S. 112	am. No. 135, 2008
Part 3.9	
S. 114	am. No. 135, 2008
Part 3.10	
Division 1	
Ss. 117, 118	am. No. 135, 2008
S. 120	am. No. 34, 1997
S. 122	rs. No. 135, 2008
Division 1A	
Div. 1A of Part 3.10	ad. No. 116, 2007
	rs. No. 21, 2011
Ss. 126A–126F	ad. No. 116, 2007
	rep. No. 21, 2011
Ss. 126G, 126H.............................	ad. No. 21, 2011
Division 2	
S. 128	am. No. 34, 1997
	rs. No. 135, 2008
Note to s. 128(7)	ad. No. 34, 1997
	rs. No. 135, 2008
S. 128A...	ad. No. 135, 2008
Division 3	
S. 130	am. No. 43, 1996
Division 4	
S. 131A...	ad. No. 116, 2007
	am. No. 21, 2011
S. 131B...	ad. No. 21, 2011
Part 3.11	
Heading to Part 3.11	rs. No. 135, 2008

被修正的规定	修正情况
第 3.7 节第 4 目	ad. No. 135, 2008
第 108C 条	ad. No. 135, 2008
第 3.8 节	
第 110 条...............................	am. No. 135, 2008
第 112 条...............................	am. No. 135, 2008
第 3.9 节	
第 114 条...............................	am. No. 135, 2008
第 3.10 节	
第 1 目	
第 117 条、第 118 条............	am. No. 135, 2008
第 120 条...............................	am. No. 34, 1997
第 122 条	rs. No. 135, 2008
第 1A 目	
第 3.10 节第 1A 目	ad. No. 116, 2007
	rs. No. 21, 2011
第 126A 条至第 126F 条	ad. No. 116, 2007
	rep. No. 21, 2011
第 126G 条、第 126H 条	ad. No. 21, 2011
第 2 目	
第 128 条...............................	am. No. 34, 1997
	rs. No. 135, 2008
对 128（7）的注释	ad. No. 34, 1997
	rs. No. 135, 2008
第 128A 条	ad. No. 135, 2008
第 3 目	
第 130 条	am. No. 43, 1996
第 4 目	
第 131A 条	ad. No. 116, 2007
	am. No. 21, 2011
第 131B 条	ad. No. 21, 2011
第 3.11 节	
第 3.11 节的标题	rs. No. 135, 2008

Provision affected	How affected
Note to s. 138(3)	am. No. 70, 2009
S. 139	am. No. 135, 2008
Chapter 4	
Part 4.3	
Division 1	
Note to s. 147	am. No. 125, 1999
S. 148	am. No. 135, 2008
Note to s. 149	am. No. 125, 1999
Note to s. 152	am. No. 125, 1999
Division 2	
Note to s. 154	rep. No. 34, 1997
Note 1 to s. 155	rs. No. 34, 1997
S. 155A	ad. No. 125, 1999
Note 1 to s. 158	rep. No. 34, 1997
Division 3	
Note to s. 160	am. No. 125, 1999
S. 161	rs. No. 135, 2008
S. 163	am. No. 125, 1999
Part 4.5	
Heading to Part 4.5	rs. No. 135, 2008
S. 165	am. No. 135, 2008
Ss. 165A, 165B	ad. No. 135, 2008
Part 4.6	
Division 1	
Note to heading to Div. 1 .... of Part 4.6	am. No. 125, 1999
Division 2	
Note to heading to Div. 2 .... of Part 4.6	am. No. 125, 1999
Note to s. 170(1)	ad. No. 34, 1997
S. 171	am. No. 9, 2000; No. 62, 2004
Division 4	

被修正的规定	修正情况
对 138（3）的注释	am. No. 70, 2009
第 139 条	am. No. 135, 2008

第 4 章

第 4.3 节

第 1 目

对第 147 条的注释	am. No. 125, 1999
第 148 条	am. No. 135, 2008
对第 149 条的注释	am. No. 125, 1999
对第 152 条的注释	am. No. 125, 1999

第 2 目

对 154 条的注释	rep. No. 34, 1997
对 155 条的注释 1	rs. No. 34, 1997
第 155A 条	ad. No. 125, 1999
对第 158 条的注释 1	rep. No. 34, 1997

第 3 目

对第 160 条的注释	am. No. 125, 1999
第 161 条	rs. No. 135, 2008
第 163 条	am. No. 125, 1999

第 4.5 节

第 4.5 节的标题	rs. No. 135, 2008
第 165 条	am. No. 135, 2008
第 165A 条、第 165B 条	ad. No. 135, 2008

第 4.6 节

第 1 目

对第 4.6 节第 1 目标题的注释	am. No. 125, 1999

第 2 目

对第 4.6 节第 2 目标题的注释	am. No. 125, 1999
对 170（1）的注释	ad. No. 34, 1997
第 171 条	am. No. 9, 2000; No. 62, 2004

第 4 目

Provision affected	How affected
Heading to s. 180	am. No. 9, 2000
S. 180	am. No. 9, 2000
Chapter 5	
Heading to s. 182	am. No. 125, 1999
S. 182	am. No. 125, 1999; No. 135, 2008
Note to s. 183	am. No. 125, 1999
S. 184	am. No. 135, 2008
S. 186	am. No. 135, 2008
S. 189	am. No. 8, 2010
S. 190	am. No. 135, 2008
Note to s. 190(1)	ad. No. 46, 2006
S. 191	am. No. 135, 2008
S. 192A	ad. No. 135, 2008
S. 195	am. No. 24, 2001
Dictionary	
Dictionary	am. No. 34, 1997; Nos. 125 and 146, 1999; No. 9, 2000; No. 55, 2001; No. 64, 2002; No. 126, 2003; No. 135, 2008; No. 33, 2009

被修正的规定	修正情况
第 180 条标题	am. No. 9, 2000
第 180 条	am. No. 9, 2000
第 5 章	
第 182 条标题	am. No. 125, 1999
第 182 条	am. No. 125, 1999; No. 135, 2008
对第 183 的注释	am. No. 125, 1999
第 184 条	am. No. 135, 2008
第 186 条	am. No. 135, 2008
第 189 条	am. No. 8, 2010
第 190 条	am. No. 135, 2008
对 190（1）的注释	ad. No. 46, 2006
第 191 条	am. No. 135, 2008
第 192A 条	ad. No. 135, 2008
第 195 条	am. No. 24, 2001
术语	
术语	am. No. 34, 1997; Nos. 125 and 146, 1999; No. 9, 2000; No. 55, 2001; No. 64, 2002; No. 126, 2003; No. 135, 2008; No. 33, 2009

Note 2

Clean Energy (Consequential Amendments) Act 2011 (No. 132, 2011)

The following amendment commences on 1 July 2012:

Schedule 1

260A   Part 1 of the Dictionary (subparagraph (b)(vi) of the definition
of Commonwealth document)

After "section 46", insert "or 46A".

As at 21 March 2012 the amendment is not incorporated in this compilation.

注释 2

《2011年清洁能源（相应修正）法》（No. 132, 2011）

下列修正自2012年7月1日起施行。

附录 1

260A 《术语》第1部分（联邦文件的定义的（b）（vi））

在"第46条"后，插入"或者第46A条"。

截至2012年3月21日，本修正尚未纳入本汇编中。

Table A

Application, saving or transitional provisions
Australian Federal Police Legislation Amendment Act 2000 (No. 9, 2000)

Schedule 3

20 Definition

In this Part:
commencing time means the time when this Part commences.

25 Amendments of the *Evidence Act 1995*

Evidence given by police officers

(1)   Section 33 of the *Evidence Act 1995* as in force at and after the commencing time applies as if a reference in that section to a police officer included a reference to a person who was a member or special member of the Australian Federal Police at any time before the commencing time.

Exclusion of records of oral questioning

(2)   Section 86 of the *Evidence Act 1995* as in force at and after the commencing time applies as if a reference in that section to an investigating official included a reference to a person who was a member or special member of the Australian Federal Police at any time before the commencing time.

Exclusion of evidence of identification by pictures

(3)   Section 115 of the *Evidence Act 1995* as in force at and after the commencing time applies as if a reference in that section to a police officer included a reference to a person who was a member or special member of the Australian Federal Police at any time before the commencing time.

表 A

适用、保留或者过渡性规定

《2000 年澳大利亚联邦警察立法修正法》（No. 9, 2000）

附录 3

20 定义

在本节中：

施行时间是指本节施行的时间。

25 对《1995 年证据法》的修正

警察所作证言

（1）   本节施行时和施行后有效的《1995 年证据法》第 33 条所适用的警察，包括在该施行时间前的任何时间曾是澳大利亚联邦警察机构的成员或者特别成员的人。

口头询问记录的排除

（2）   本节施行时和施行后有效的《1995 年证据法》第 86 条所适用的调查人员，包括在该施行时间前的任何时间曾是澳大利亚联邦警察机构的成员或者特别成员的人。

图片辨认证据的排除

（3）   本节施行时和施行后有效的《1995 年证据法》第 115 条所适用的警察，包括在该施行时间前的任何时间曾是澳大利亚联邦警察机构的成员或者特别成员的人。

Proof of certain matters

(4)   Section 171 of the *Evidence Act 1995* as in force at and after the commencing time applies as if a reference in that section to an authorised person included a reference to a person who was:

   (a)   a member of the Australian Federal Police at or above the rank of sergeant; or

   (c)   a staff member of the Australian Federal Police whose salary was at least equal to that of a sergeant in the Australian Federal Police;

at any time before the commencing time.

Fingerprint affidavits

(5).   Section 180 of the *Evidence Act 1995* as in force at and after the commencing time applies to an affidavit made under that section at any time before the commencing time in the same way as it does to an affidavit made under that section at or after the commencing time.

34   Warrants or writs etc. may continue to be executed

If, immediately before the commencing time, any warrant, writ, order, permission or other instrument (the ***authority***) issued under a law of the Commonwealth, a State or a Territory could be executed by a person who was at that time a member, staff member or special member of the Australian Federal Police, the authority continues to be able to be executed at and after the commencing time by the person in his or her capacity as:

   (a)   the Commissioner of the Australian Federal Police; or

   (b)   a Deputy Commissioner of the Australian Federal Police; or

   (c)   an AFP employee; or

   (d)   a special member of the Australian Federal Police;

某些事项的证明

（4） 本节施行时和施行后有效的《1995 年证据法》第 171 条所适用的被授权人员，包括在该施行时间前的任何时间曾是下列人员的人员：

（a） 曾是澳大利亚联邦警察机构警长或者警长以上警衔的成员；或者

（c） 澳大利亚联邦警察机构中，其薪水至少相当于澳大利亚联邦警察机构中警长之薪水的职员。

指印宣誓陈述书

（5） 本节施行时和施行后有效的《1995 年证据法》第 180 条，像适用于施行时或者施行后根据该条制作的宣誓陈述书一样，适用于施行之前的任何时间根据该条制作的宣誓陈述书。

34 令状或者饬令等可以继续执行

如果在施行前，根据联邦、州或者领地的法律签发的任何令状、饬令、命令、许可或者其他文书（**依据**）可以为当时是澳大利亚联邦警察机构的职员或者特别成员的人所执行，在施行时或者施行后，该依据能够继续为下列人员（均在施行时和施行后有效的《1979 年澳大利亚联邦警察法》的含义内）所执行：

（a）澳大利亚联邦警察机构行政长官；或者

（b）澳大利亚联邦警察机构副职行政长官；或者

（c）澳大利亚联邦警察机构雇员；或者

（d）澳大利亚联邦警察机构特别成员。

(all within the meaning of the *Australian Federal Police Act 1979* as in force at and after the commencing time).

Note: A person who is a member or staff member of the Australian Federal Police immediately before the commencing time is taken to be engaged as an AFP employee. Similarly, a person who is a special member of the Australian Federal Police immediately before the commencing time is taken to be appointed as a special member. See item 2 of this Schedule.

35 Regulations dealing with matters of a transitional or saving nature

(1) The Governor–General may make regulations, not inconsistent with any other provision of this Schedule, prescribing matters of a transitional or saving nature in relation to the amendments made by Schedule 1 or 2.

(2) Regulations made under this item within one year after the commencement of this item may commence on a day earlier than the day on which they are made, but not earlier than the commencement of this item.

Law and Justice Legislation Amendment (Application of Criminal Code) Act 2001 (No. 24, 2001)

4 Application of amendments

(1) Subject to subsection (3), each amendment made by this Act applies to acts and omissions that take place after the amendment commences.

(2) For the purposes of this section, if an act or omission is alleged to have taken place between 2 dates, one before and one on or after the day on which a particular amendment commences, the act or omission is alleged to have taken place before the amendment commences.

注释：在施行前是澳大利亚联邦警察机构的成员或者职员的人，视为
受聘的澳大利亚联邦警察机构雇员。与此类似，在施行前是澳
大利亚联邦警察机构的特别成员的人，视为被任命的特别成员。
参见本附录第 2 项。

35 关于过渡或者保留事项的条例

（1）总督可以制定不与本《附录》任何其他规定不一致的条例，就《附
录》1 或者 2 作出的修正，规定过渡或者保留事项。

（2）在本项施行后 1 年内根据本项制定的条例，可以在早于其制定
之日的期日施行，但是不得早于本项的施行期日。

————————

《2001 年法律与正义立法修正（〈刑法典〉之适用）法》（No. 24, 2001）

4 修正的适用

（1）在遵守（3）的情况下，本法所作的每个修正适用于修
正施行后发生的作为和不作为。

（2）就本条目的而言，如果所称某作为或者不作为发生在两
个期日之间，一个期日在具体的修正施行之前，另一个
期日为特定的修正施行之日或者之后，则应称该某作为
或者不作为发生在该修正施行之前。

————————

Family Law Amendment (Shared Parental Responsibility) Act 2006
    (No. 46, 2006)

Schedule 3

8 Application of amendments

The amendments made by Part 1 of this Schedule apply:

(a) to proceedings commenced by an application filed on or after 1 July 2006; and

(b) to proceedings commenced by an application filed before 1 July 2006, if the parties to the proceedings consent and the court grants leave.

Evidence Amendment Act 2008 (No. 135, 2008)

Schedule 1

95 Proceedings already begun

(1) Subject to this Part, the amendments made by this Schedule do not apply in relation to proceedings the hearing of which began before the commencement of this Schedule.

(2) The *Evidence Act 1995*, as in force immediately before that commencement, continues to apply in relation to proceedings the hearing of which began before that commencement.

96 Admissions

(1) The amendment made by this Schedule to section 85 of the *Evidence Act 1995* does not apply in relation to admissions made before the commencement of this Schedule.

(2) That section, as in force immediately before that commencement, continues to apply in relation to admissions made before that commencement.

《2006 年家庭法律修正（共同承担父母责任）法》（No. 46, 2006）

附录 3

8 修正的适用

本《附录》第 1 部分所作修正适用于：

（a）因在 2006 年 7 月 1 日或者此后提交申请而开始的程序；以及

（b）在程序当事人同意，并且法院作出许可的情况下，因在 2006 年 7 月 1 日之前提交申请而开始的程序。

———————

《2008 年证据修正法》（No. 135, 2008）

附录 1

95 已经开始的程序

（1）在遵守本节的情况下，本《附录》作出的修正并不适用于在本《附录》施行前已经开始的听审程序。

（2）该修正施行前有效的《1995 年证据法》，继续适用于在该修正施行前已经开始的听审程序。

96 自认

（1）本《附录》对《1995 年证据法》第 85 条所作修正，并不适用于在本《附录》施行前所作的自认。

（2）在本《附录》施行前有效的上述条文，继续适用于在该施行前所作的自认。

97 Failure or refusal to answer questions etc.

(1)   The amendment made by this Schedule to section 89 of the *Evidence Act 1995* does not apply in relation to any failure or refusal, before the commencement of this Schedule:

(a) to answer one or more questions; or

(b) to respond to a representation.

(2)   That section, as in force immediately before that commencement, continues to apply in relation to any such failure or refusal before that commencement.

98 Prior operation of notice provisions

If, before the commencement of this Schedule, a notice in writing of a kind referred to in section 97 or 98 of the *Evidence Act 1995* is given:

(a) in the circumstances provided for in that section; and

(b) in accordance with such requirements (if any) as would apply to the giving of the notice under that section after that commencement;

the notice is taken to have been given under that section as in force after that commencement.

99 Disclosure orders

Section 128A of the *Evidence Act 1995* as inserted by this Schedule does not apply in relation to any disclosure order made before the commencement of this Schedule.

Schedule 2

13 Application of amendments

The amendments made by this Schedule do not apply in relation to proceedings the hearing of which began before the commencement of this item.

---

97 未能或者拒绝回答询问等

（1）　　本《附录》对《1995 年证据法》第 89 条所作修正，并不
　　　　适用于在本《附录》施行前的下列行为：

　　　　　　（a）未能或者拒绝回答询问；或者

　　　　　　（b）未能或者拒绝对某表述作出回应。

（2）　　在本《附录》施行前有效的上述条文，继续适用于在该施
　　　　行前的上述未能或者拒绝回答、回应行为。

98 通知规定的先前运作

　　　　在本《附录》施行之前，如果《1995 年证据法》第 97
　　　　条或者第 98 条所称的书面通知是在下列情况下作出的，
　　　　则视为在本《附录》施行后根据该条作出的有效通知：

　　　　　　（a）在该条规定的情况下作出的；以及

　　　　　　（b）在本《附录》施行后根据该条适用于该通知的要
　　　　　　　求（如果有的话）作出的。

99 披露命令

　　　　本《附录》插入的《1995 年证据法》第 128A 条，并不
　　　　适用于在本《附录》施行前所作出的披露命令。

附录 2

13 修正的适用

　　　　本《附录》作出的修正并不适用于在本项施行前已经开
　　　　始的听审程序。

———

Acts Interpretation Amendment Act 2011 (No. 46, 2011)

Schedule 3

10 Saving—appointments

The amendments made by Schedule 2 do not affect the validity of an appointment that was made under an Act before the commencement of this item and that was in force immediately before that commencement.

11 Transitional regulations

The Governor–General may make regulations prescribing matters of a transitional nature (including prescribing any saving or application provisions) relating to the amendments and repeals made by Schedules 1 and 2.

《2011 年法律解释修正法》（No. 46, 2011）

附录 3

10 保留—任命

《附录》2 所作修正，并不影响根据本项施行前的法律所作的任命的有效性，以及在本项施行前有效的任命的有效性。

11 过渡性条例

总督可以制定条例，规定与《附录》1 和 2 所作修正和取消有关的过渡性事项（包括规定任何保留或者适用规定）。

译者注释

第 1 章　初步事项

【1】《元照英美法词典》"royal assent"条译为"御准",拉丁文为"regius assensus",指君主对议会两院通过的法案予以认可,从而使该法案成为议会法律 [Act of Parliament]。澳大利亚《1901 年法律解释法》(the Acts Interpretation Act 1901)第 5 条第 (1A) 款规定,1928 年 1 月 1 日后由总督代表英王给予《御准》的每部法律(改变《宪法》的法律除外),应当在该法律得到《御准》之日后的第 28 天生效,除非该法有相反意旨。

【2】澳大利亚《1901 年法律解释法》第 3 条对施行(commencement)的含义进行了规定:"(1) 在每部法律 [Act] 中,该法律或者法律规定的施行,是指该法律或者法律规定开始生效 [comes into operation]。(2) 如果法律或者根据法律的授权制定或者发布的任何文件 [instrument](包括任何规则、条例 [regulations] 或者附例 [by-laws] 明确规定在特定日期生效(无论使用的表述是'生效' [come into operation] 还是'施行' [commence]),则其应当在前一日届满后立即生效。"根据《1995 年证据法》第 2 条第(2)款的规定,本节和该法最后的《术语》于 1995 年 2 月 23 日起施行。其他规定于 1995 年 4 月 18 日起施行。

【3】澳大利亚《1901 年法律解释法》第 17 条规定,《公告》是指总督发布的在《公报》[the Gazette] 公布或者在根据《2003 年立

法文件法》[the Legislative Instruments Act 2003] 设立的《联邦立法文件登记系统》[the Federal Register of Legislative Instruments] 录入的《公告》。

【4】"Interlocutory proceedings" 译为 "中间程序"。《元照英美法词典》将 "interlocutory" 解释为 "中间的；临时的；暂时的；非最后的；在诉讼程序中进行的"，"通常指在诉讼过程中对与案件有关的某些事项或法律点作出的决定，而非对整个案件作出最终的处理"。澳大利亚法律改革委员会称 "Interlocutory proceedings" 是指 "非终局性、通常处理在案件审判准备中发生的程序性问题的程序，但是也包括未决案件审判中的禁令程序"。[1]

【5】根据《1995 年证据法》4(2)，只有在法院指示适用证据法，或者指示就特定事项适用证据法的情况下，才在量刑程序中适用证据法。在量刑程序中适用证据规则通常是不适当的，因为这会带来不必要的迟延和复杂。如果与量刑有关的每个事实都要正式证明，这会将量刑程序变成对抗制程序，则量刑程序就会因为成本的增加和拖延而迟滞，对于量刑而言有用的某些信息就会被排除。在 *Weininger v The Queen* 案件中，澳大利亚最高法院审查了《犯罪法》第 16A 条。该条要求法院在量刑中要考虑一系列 "相关且为法院所知" （they are relevant and known to the court）的指定事项。最高法院认为，"为法院所知" 一语不同于 "为证据所证明"，这意味着对此不应当解释为存在着这样的要求，即对在量刑听证中提出的事项要进行正式的证明和采纳。制定这一条的背景是，在量刑听证中长期确立的程序是，量刑法官所用的材料并没有得到可采证据的证明。[2] 澳大利亚最高法院同意维多利亚州上诉法院在 *R v Storey* 案件中的意见，

1　See ALRC 38, para 143, n 33.

2　*Weininger v The Queen* (2003) 212 CLR 629, [21].

即这对于避免就量刑引入"过多的繁枝细节"是很重要的。[3]

本条为被告规定了重要的保障措施，即在出于正义的利益而认为适当，或者在争议事实的证明对于量刑至关重要的情况下，法院必须指示适用证据法。参见 4(3) 和 4(4)。

【6】《1903 年司法法》第 79 条规定，每个州或者领地的法律，包括程序法和证据法，对该州或者领地行使联邦管辖权的法院都有约束力，宪法或者联邦法律另有规定者除外。《1903 年司法法》第 80 条规定，如果联邦法律并不适用，或者它们的规定不足以实施，或者不足以提供救济或者处罚，在适用并且不与宪法或者联邦法律不一致的情况下，为宪法或者行使管辖权的法院所在的州或者领地的有效法律所限定的普通法，规制所有行使联邦管辖权的法院所管辖的民事和刑事事项。根据《1995 年证据法》第 8 条的规定，《1995 年证据法》的适用优于《1903 年司法法》第 68 条、第 79 条、第 80 条和第 80A 条之规定，但是在这些普通法与《1995 年证据法》不一致的情况下，这些普通法继续有效。这意味着州或者领地法院行使联邦管辖权时，要适用州或者领地的法律，而不是《1995 年证据法》。

【7】这些法律中包含有关于反对被迫自我归罪特权的特别规定。《2001 年公司法》第 1316A 条规定，在公司法刑事程序中，法人（body corporate）无权以回答、信息、提交账簿或者其他物品等可能导致该法人入罪或者受到处罚而拒绝或者未能遵行回答问题、提供信息、出示账簿或者其他物品、从事其他行为等要求。《2001 年澳大利亚证券和投资委员会法》第 68 条也规定，不能以类似原因而拒绝或者未能提供信息、签署记录或者出示账簿。根据 8(3)，即使与《1995 年证据法》不一致，这些联邦法律也继续有效。

3　Ibid, [24]; *R v Storey* [1998] 1 VR 359, 372.

【8】"议会特免权"（parliamentary privilege）指的是澳大利亚联邦议会的权力和特免权（或者豁免）[the powers and privileges (or immunities)]。与议会特免权有关的法律直接源自澳大利亚联邦宪法第49条。[4] 该条规定，参议院和众议院以及各院议员和委员会的权力、特免权与豁免，由议会宣告；在未有宣告之前，应享有联邦成立时联合王国下议院及其议员和委员会的权力、特免权与豁免。这一规定将联合王国在 1901 年时关于议会特免权的法律纳入了澳大利亚宪法。关于议会特免权的法律经法院和《1987 年议会特免权法》（the Parliamentary Privileges Act 1987）得到了进一步的阐明。根据《1987年议会特免权法》第 16 条，在任何法院或者裁判庭程序中，就议会议程中的真相、动机、意图或者善意进行询问，提交证据，以就这些议程进行推论或者得出结论等，都是非法的。

【9】法官控制程序运行的权力长期以来就得到了确立，本条进一步强化了法官的这一权力。根据 10(1)，法院控制程序运行的权力不受本法影响，该法另有明文规定或者必要的意图者除外。由于每个法官都有权力或者义务来采取措施，保证审判的公平性，因此 10(2) 特别规定法院针对程序中的滥用程序行为的权力不受影响。延期审理是控制滥用程序行为的主要手段。

第 2 章—提出证据

【1】根据《1995 年证据法》13(1)，证人能力的一般标准是，

4　在历史上，该特免权源于 1688 年英国《权利法案》第 9 条。该条规定，"国会内之言论、辩论或议事之自由，不应在国会以外之任何法院或任何地方，受到弹劾或者询问"。(That the Freedome of Speech and Debates or Proceedings in Parlyament ought not to be impeached or questioned in any Court or Place out of Parlyament.)

该人无能力理解就该事实提出的问题；或者该人无能力就关于该事实的提问作出可被理解的回答，且该无能力无法克服。在 2008 年修正之前，该条规定的证人能力标准是证人能够对提问作出"合理的答复"。这一规定要求证人对问题的回答具有信息性、相关性和清晰性。[5] 新的标准则降低了要求。回答即使没有提供什么信息，对提问没有什么合理的相关性，也可能被认为"可被理解"。这一修改借鉴了英国《1999 年少年司法与刑事证据法》第 53 条之规定。

根据 13(1)，在证人缺乏能力状态可以克服的情况下，证人具有作证能力。第 30 条和第 31 条分别规定了证人不通晓英语、属聋、哑证人情况下如何克服该缺乏能力状态的例子。

【2】《1995 年证据法》13(4) 和 (5) 旨在允许儿童证人或者有智力障碍的人在无理解其在作证时有义务作出真实证言之能力的情况下作证。根据本法，非宣誓证言仍然是证据，与其他证据无二。

【3】根据《1995 年证据法》13(6)，应当推定一个人并不因为该条而无作证能力，有相反证明者除外。因此，相反证明之负担，由主张证人无作证能力的当事人承担。根据 142(1)，该当事人应当依照"概率权衡"证明这一点。

【4】根据《1995 年证据法》13(7)，已经由证人作出的证言，并不仅仅因为证人在作证完成之前死亡或者不再具有作证能力而不具有可采性。尽管如此，法院可以根据第 135 条或者第 137 条之规定行使自由裁量权来排除该证据，例如对方当事人没有对该证人进行交叉询问的重要机会的情况下。

【5】《1995 年证据法》17(2) 规定，被告没有作为检控方的证人作证之能力。17(3) 规定，不得强制关联被告作证来支持或者反对

5　See Australia Law Reform Commission, ALRC 26, vol 1, paras 239, 242.

刑事程序中的被告，除非该关联被告正在与被告分开审理。因此，关联被告有作证能力，但是不得被任何一方所强制作证，除非该关联被告得到了分别审理。

【6】《1995年证据法》对"可诉罪"并没有进行界定。根据《1914年犯罪法》第4G条的规定，违反联邦法律，可处12个月以上监禁之处罚的犯罪，是可诉罪，除非有相反意旨。

【7】法官所作的评论不同于法官对陪审团作出的指示或者警告。审判法官可以进行评论，但是不得就如何使用被告的沉默对陪审团进行指示。"因为它是评论，陪审团可以忽视它，且应当告知他们可以忽视它。相反，警告陪审团不得就该事实得出不可容许的结论，是法官的指示，陪审团需要遵行。"[6]

"评论"一词在《1995年证据法》中没有得到界定。新南威尔士州刑事上诉法院在 *R v Villar; R v Zugecic*[7] 案件中，采用了统一证据法之前的判例中使用的方法，即对被告未能作证的评论，是指直接或者间接表明被告本可以作证，但是没有作证的陈述。提及被告本可以作证，通常也暗含着被告没有作证，但是提及被告没有作证，并不必然意味着被告本可以作证。

【8】根据本条规定，在可诉罪刑事程序中，不同主体所作评论的法律地位是不同的。公诉人不能作出任何评论；法官可以作出评论，但是该评论不得暗示被告之所以未能作证是因为被告犯有有关罪行或者被告相信其有罪，除非该评论是程序中的其他被告作出的；其他共同被告可以作出任何评论；在共同被告作出有关评论的情况下，法官还可以就该评论作出评论。

【9】根据传统的普通法的一般规则，当事人自行传召证据。

6　*Azzopardi v R* (2000) 179 ALR 349.

7　[2004] NSWCCA 302 at [119].

《1995 年证据法》第 26 条并没有明确规定法院传唤证人的权力。但是考虑到第 11 条赋予法院的控制程序的一般权力，法院似乎在适当情况下可以传唤证人。在刑事程序中，判例认为只有在极端例外的情况下，法院才得传唤证人；[8]民事程序中也采用了类似的方法。

【10】《1995 年证据法》第 27 条并没有规定法官对证人进行的询问。根据普通法，当事人对证人进行询问是一般规则，法官仅为消除明显的含混才得询问。[9]同样，本条也没有规定陪审团成员对证人进行的询问。但是，法官可以运用法院控制程序的一般权力来允许这种询问。现行普通法的立场是，这种做法是不可取的，[10]如果得到允许的，也应当通过法官来询问。[11]

【11】《1995 年证据法》第 30 条并未就为保证公平审判而需要提供传译人员的其他情况作出规定。这些情况依据普通法来处理。

【12】《1995 年证据法》第 32 条使用了"唤醒记忆"（reviving memory）一词，而不是普通法上的"刷新记忆"（refreshing memory）一词。澳大利亚法律改革委员会认为，前者更准确地描述了实际发生的过程，即刺激现存的记忆，而不是形成新的记忆。[12]

本条仅仅规定了使用文件来唤醒记忆的事项，使用物品来唤醒记忆的问题，则由法官根据第 26 条规定的一般权力来加以规制。

【13】《1995 年证据法》第 32 条规定，经法院许可，证人在作证过程中，可以使用文件来试图唤醒其关于某事实或者意见的记忆。

8　See *R v Apostilides* (1984) 154 CLR 563 at 575.

9　*R v Olasiuk* (1973) 6 SASR 255.

10　See *Lo Presti v The Queen* (1994) 68 ALJR 477.

11　See *R v Pathare* [1981]1 NSWLR 124 (CCA); R v Lo Presti [1992] 1 VR 696 (CCA).

12　See Australia Law Reform Commission, ALRC 26, vol 1, para 614.

但是证人在庭上刷新记忆时，不是必须要使用其记忆清新时所制作的文件。这一规定具有更大的灵活性。根据 32(2)，证人对有关事件是否"记忆清新"，仅仅是法院要虑及的一个因素。而在普通法上，则要求所制作的文件具有同时性，即必须是证人在记忆清新时制作的。"同时性"如果按照字面意思解释的话，则意味着与有关事件同时发生，对此严格适用会排除本可使用的证据。此外，普通法上要求该用于刷新记忆的文件应当是证人制作或者采认的文件。而这在《1995 年证据法》中也不再是一个绝对的法律要求，而仅仅是法院在决定是否准许时所要考虑的因素。在 *R v Cassar; R v Sleiman*[13] 案件中，法官允许警察使用了一个并没有为 32(2)(b) 所规定的文件来刷新记忆，因为该文件所包含的信息及其制作环境使得其具有可靠性，并且它所包含的信息与证人在记忆清新时所记录的文件所包含的信息基本上是一致的，只不过后者丢失了。从这一案例可窥第 32 条与普通法的差异之一斑。

法院在作出许可决定时，不仅应当考虑 32(2) 之规定，还应当虑及 192(2) 所规定之事项。

【14】《1995 年证据法》第 33 条之规定源于《1900 年犯罪法》第 418 条。根据本条规定，警察在通过宣读以前由其制作的书面陈述或者以该陈述为引导，来为检控方提供主问证据之前，并不需要说明其已经穷尽其记忆或者为唤醒记忆而需要参阅其制作的书面陈述。

【15】《1995 年证据法》第 36 条废除了 *Walker v Walker*[14] 案件所确立的规则，即针对正式的传唤而出示、查阅文件的行为，在出示文件者坚持的情况下，将导致传唤者提交该文件。

---

13 （No 28) [1999] NSWSC 651.

14 （1937) 57 CLR 630.

【16】本条没有规定提出诱导性问题的后果。这是有意而为的。澳大利亚法律改革委员会说，"在不允许或者未授权情况下提出诱导性问题的后果没有规定。就像当前一样，当事人可以提出异议，要求法院命令不得提出该问题。如果对该问题作出了回答，则这种提问形式将影响回答的证明力"。[15]

【17】《1995年证据法》第38条规定，在当事人自己的证人作出了不利证言的情况下，允许当事人对该证人进行交叉询问，而不需要首先认定该证人是敌意证人。而在普通法上，当事人在对自己的证人进行交叉询问之前，该证人必须首先被法院宣布为敌意证人。《1995年证据法》对"不利（unfavourable）"一词并没有进行界定，但显而易见的是，与普通法上的"敌意（hostile）"相比，这一术语设定了更低的要求。澳大利亚法律改革委员会建议废止与"敌意"证人有关的法律，因为在证人仅仅作出不利证言的情况下，无法认定其敌意，因而无法对其证言进行检验。[16] 因此，《1995年证据法》第38条之规定降低了对不利证人进行交叉询问的门槛，更有利于导出事实真相。

【18】对抗制的一个基本原则是，在审判中被告方采取辩护行动之前，检控方应当全面、公平地将其案件呈现在事实审判者面前。因此，在交叉询问者已经终结其案件，需要再启其案件来提出先前不一致陈述的情况下，适用43(3)。

【19】《1995年证据法》47(2)规定，"有关书证的复制件，包括虽非有关书证的精密复制件，但在所有相关方面等同于有关书证的文件"。这一界定，有利于保证未能复制原件的不相关细节（例如原件的颜色）的书证不被排除。

---

15 See Australia Law Reform Commission, ALRC 26, vol 1, para 619.

16 See Australia Law Reform Commission, ALRC 26, vol 1, paras 294, 295, 625.

【20】《1995 年证据法》第 2.2 节规定，废除普通法证明书证内容的"原件"规则，[17] 而代之以更为灵活的做法，即可以使用 48(1)规定的"某一种或者多种方法来就有关书证的内容提出证据"。这一修改的目的是简化证明书证内容的规则，并虑及现代信息存储媒介和复制技术的特点。澳大利亚法律改革委员会认为，普通法上的原件或者最佳证据规则"复杂、缺乏灵活性，并且会带来高成本"。尽管要求提出原件会减少争论，但是该规则缺乏灵活性，会"大大增加诉讼成本"。"这些评论特别适用于现代书证和复制技术。对（这些）法律的批评支持进行改革"。[18]

【21】澳大利亚法律改革委员会认为，用复写纸复写形成的文件不能适用 48(1)(b)，因为这种方法涉及人的因素，没有内在的可靠性保证。[19]

【22】本条借鉴了美国《联邦证据规则》1006 的规定。[20]

第 3 章—证据的可采性

【1】《1995 年证据法》第 57 条使用了"暂定相关性"的概念，而没有使用"附条件相关性"这一概念。澳大利亚法律改革委员会认为，"附条件"一词有这样的含义，即先决条件必须要实现，如

17　参见《1995 年证据法》第 51 条。

18　澳大利亚法律改革委员会，同注 20 引文，第 648 段。

19　See Australia Law Reform Commission, ALRC 26, vol 1, para 651, n9.

20　美国《联邦证据规则》1006 规定："证据提出者可以使用概要、图表或者计算，证明不便于在法院加以审查的卷帙浩繁的书写品、录制品或者影像的内容。证据提出者必须将原件或者副本准备就绪，以供其他当事人在合理的时间和地点加以审查或者复制。法院可以命令证据提出者将它们在法院上出示。"

果使用了该术语，人们可能认为在采纳证据之前必须举行预先审核（*voir dire*）。[21]

【2】《1995年证据法》57(1)遵循了美国《联邦证据规则》的模式，规定真实性（验真）问题是相关性问题的一部分，而不是可采性的独立条件。在未能进行适当验真或者辨认的情况下，可能会依据第55条之规定将书证或者物证排除。

【3】《1995年证据法》57(2)规定，"如果关于某人的行为的证据的相关性取决于法院作出这样的认定，即该人与一个或者多个其他人曾具有共同目的，或者曾为促进该共同目的而行动，则无论其是非法共谋还是出于其他目的，法院可以使用该证据本身来确定是否存在共同目的。"换言之，如果某人的行为的相关性取决于是否存在共同目的，则法院可以使用该行为本身来确定是否存在该目的。最终要由陪审团来确定该共同目的是否已经被证实。

【4】《1995年证据法》第58条规定了书证和物证的自我验真程序，即法院可以为自我验真之目的而检视书证或者物证，以就该证据的真实性或者同一性得出合理推论，从而解决就其相关性产生的疑问。这一规定认识到在法院出示的大多数书证和物证事实上都是真实的，按照普通法来要求当事人证明其真实性将代价高昂。该条的意图是，为了确定书证或者物证的可采性，其初像真实性（其相关性取决于该真实性）可以在根据该证据本身得出的合理推论的帮助下来确定。证据的最终真实性问题，将由事实审判者确定。

【5】《1995年证据法》59(1)规定，传闻规则仅适用于"人"（person）所作的表述。因此，动物的行为、单纯机器所产生的信息不适用传闻规则。

21　See Australia Law Reform Commission, ALRC 26, vol 1, para 646.

【6】《1995 年证据法》60(1) 规定："如果先前表述证据之所以被采纳，是因为其就证明主张的事实之外之目的具有相关性，则该先前表述证据不适用传闻规则。"换言之，如果传闻可以为非传闻目的所采纳，则该证据也可以作为所主张事项的证据而被采纳。而根据普通法，如果先前表述证据因非传闻目的而被采纳，则该证据仅能用于该目的，而不能用于证明所主张事项的真实性，除非其属于某个传闻例外。澳大利亚法律改革委员会认为，"根据现行法律，为非传闻目的而可采的传闻证据不被排除，但是法院不得将其用作证明所陈述事实的证据。这是在进行不现实的区分。这个问题可以这样解决，即将传闻规则界定为防止采纳这样的传闻证据，即其在理性上仅仅是影响法院对所意图主张的事实的评估时才具有相关性。这将产生这样的效果，即为非传闻目的而具有相关性的证据（例如证明先前一致陈述或者不一致陈述，或者证明专家意见的基础的证据），也将作为关于所陈述事实的证据而可采。"[22]

【7】在 *Lee v The Queen*[23] 案件中，从警察引出的证言说，检控方传唤的证人 C 曾告诉他们，被告 L 曾向他作出自白。根据传闻规则的例外（第 81 条），关于该所称自白的证据是不可采的，因为关于该自白的证据不是第一手证据。然而，关于 C 对警察作出的表述证据与 C 的可信性有关，因为该表述与其庭上证言不一致（他否认了 L 曾向他作出自白）。据此，该表述被采纳，作为 L 实施了其被指控的犯罪的证据，交给了陪审团。澳大利亚最高法院判定，第 60 条仅适用于 C 所作的表述，而不是 L 所作的表述。因此，审判法官应当就 C 作出的 L 曾经自白的表述之有限使用，对陪审团作出清晰指示。要么就依据第 137 条排除该证据。60(3) 的规定体现了该判决的立场。

22　Australia Law Reform Commission, ALRC 26, vol 1, para 685.
23　(1998) 195 CLR 594.

【8】《1995 年证据法》61(1) 之规定，是为了保证该法关于证人能力的规定也适用于庭外陈述。换言之，在作出表述时，表述者必须就所主张的事实有作证能力。根据 61(3)，应当推定某人在作出表述时就所主张的事实有作证能力，除非证明相反。

【9】《1995 年证据法》61(2) 规定，本条的作证能力要求不适用于关于感觉、心态等的即时表述。因此，婴幼儿的哭声可以用来证明婴幼儿感到了疼痛，尽管他们不具有作证能力。

【10】《1995 年证据法》第 62 条就第一手传闻和其他更为遥远的传闻进行了区分，62(1) 规定，第一手传闻，"是指对所主张的事实有亲身知识的人所作的先前表述"。澳大利亚法律改革委员会认为，就事件发生时或者之后不久所作的陈述与更迟时间所作的陈述之间，应当进行区分。事件发生时或者之后不久所作的陈述可能是最不乏可靠性的描述。[24]

【11】《1995 年证据法》第 63 条规定，在民事程序中，在作出先前表述的人不能到庭就所主张的事实作证的情况下，传闻规则并不排除口头或者书面形式的第一手传闻。这一规定的目的在于保证当事人可以使用其能够得到的最好的证据。

【12】《1995 年证据法》64(2) 规定，在民事程序中，如果作出先前表述的人能够到庭就所主张的事实作证，在传唤该人作证将导致不合理的费用或者迟延，或者不具合理可行性等特定情况下，传闻规则并不排除口头或者书面形式的第一手传闻。

【13】《1995 年证据法》64(3) 规定，在民事程序中，如果作出表述之人已经或者将由法院传唤作证，则传闻规则并不排除口头或者书面形式的第一手传闻。这是考虑到这些人能够到庭就有关表述

24　Australia Law Reform Commission, ALRC 26, vol 1, para 678.

作证而作出的规定。

【14】《1995 年证据法》64(4) 规定，在对作出表述之人的主询问结束之前，不得提交包含适用 64(3) 的表述的书证，除非法院做出许可。这吸收了英国《1968 年民事证据法》的相关规定。这避免了证人在主询问中将其先前表述提交为证据，而不再口头作证的情况。

【15】《1995 年证据法》64(2) 规定了传闻例外的四种情况。这四种情况下都有一定程度的"可信性保证"。需要注意的是，这些传闻证据都是口头传闻证据，与此相比，65(8) 规定的辩护方可以提出的传闻证据，既可以是口头证据，也可以是书面证据。因此，该条对检控方提出的传闻证据的可采性问题要求更为严格。

【16】《1995 年证据法》65(3)—(6) 规定，在证人不能到庭的情况下，如果在澳大利亚或者海外程序中被告符合下列情形，则传闻规则不适用于在上述程序中作证时作出的先前表述证据：(a) 该被告就该表述对作出该表述的人进行了交叉询问；或者 (b) 该被告有合理的机会就该表述对作出该表述的人进行交叉询问。

【17】与检控方提出第一手传闻的权利相比，《1995 年证据法》65(8) 为辩护方提供了更大的空间，允许辩护方使用第三方作出的先前表述。但是，一旦被告的这种传闻证据被采纳，则检控方有权根据 65(9) 作出与此相应的反击。

【18】《1995 年证据法》66(3) 创设了 66(2) 的例外，即在该传闻证据是检控方提出，并不涉及人员、地点和物品的身份，并且提出该证据的目的是为了言明作出该表述的人将能够在澳大利亚或者海外程序中作出的证言的情况下，则仍然要使用传闻规则。

【19】《1995 年证据法》69(2) 规定了业务记录的传闻例外，这一例外既适用于第一手传闻，也适用于更遥远的传闻。

【20】这一规定的目的是为中间程序的操作提供便利。在中间

程序情况下，时间很短，常常很难提出直接、可采的证据。在提出某证据的当事人也提出了关于其来源的证据的情况下，传闻规则并不适用于该证据，有利于避免严格的传闻规则妨害实体正义的实现。

【21】《1995年证据法》79(2)是2008年新增加的内容。在司法实践中关于儿童的成长和行为的意见证据与法律程序的诸多事项有关，而在许多案件中，法院表现出不愿意采纳这种类型证据的倾向。针对这种情况，这一修改进一步强调了这种类型的专家意见证据术语意见证据规则的例外。

【22】《1995年证据法》81(1)使得自认成了传闻规则和意见规则的例外。通常情况下，在民事案件中使用"自认"（admission）一词，在刑事案件中使用"自白"（confession）一词。《1995年证据法》仅使用了自认一词，既适用于民事程序，也适用于刑事程序。

【23】尽管《1995年证据法》81(1)规定自认是传闻规则的例外，第82条又对该自认进行了进一步限制，即仅限于第一手的口头或者书面自认证据。

【24】《1995年证据法》第83条将根据第81条采纳的自认限定用于作出自认的当事人的案件以及提出该证据的当事人的案件。该证据不能用于第三方案件，除非该第三方同意。

【25】《1995年证据法》第84条规定了民事程序和刑事程序中自认可采性的基本要求。该条取代了普通法上的自愿性要求，规定自认或者自认过程应当没有受到暴力、胁迫、不人道或者有损人的尊严的行为或者采取这些行为之威胁的影响。该规定没有提及这些影响的来源，因此从事这些行为的人并不限于调查人员。根据84(2)，受到提出的自认证据所反对的当事人必须先就是否存在这种影响提出异议，然后要求提出该证据的当事人应当提出证据使法院确信该自认以及自认的过程没有受到这些因素的影响。

【26】《1995 年证据法》85(2) 规定："关于自认的证据不可采，除非自认是在其真实性不可能受到不利影响的情况下所作出的。"这一规定关注的是作出自认的环境。如果作出自认的环境可能导致自认不可靠，则该自认不可采，而不论作出的自认本身是否真实。根据 189(3)，在关于被告的自认是否应当在刑事程序中被采纳为证据（无论是否是行使自由裁量权）的预备性问题听审中，对该自认真实与否的问题不予审理，除非该问题是被告提出的。这是因为在这些情况下作出的自认本身真实与否的问题，不是由审判法官确定的问题，而是要由陪审团确定的问题。"作为预备性问题，审判法官应当确定自认的可靠性是否遭到了取得该自认的方式的贬损。"[25] 法官在作出该决定时应当考虑 85(3) 规定的所有因素。

【27】在实践中，《1995 年证据法》第 86 条仅适用于要求就讯问强制性录音录像的案件之外的案件，或者本应当强制性录音录像但是有合理理由未进行强制性录音录像的案件。

【28】依据《1995 年证据法》第 88 条之规定，寻求提出自认的当事人首先应当承担说服负担，然后由法院按照比较低的"合理"标准判定具体某人作出了自认，最后要由事实审判者确定有关人员是否作出了自认。

【29】*Petty & Maiden v R*[26] 案件曾确立了这样的普通法原则，即不能从被告未能或者拒绝在审判前提出辩护或者解释而作出不利推论。《1995 年证据法》第 89 条之规定仅涉及被告针对调查人员的询问或者表述未能回答或者回应的情况，因此，比该普通法原则的适用范围更窄。所以，对于该条没有涵盖的情况，继续由普通法来加以调整。

---

25 Australia Law Reform Commission, ALRC 26, vol 1, para 765.

26 (1991) 173 CLR 95.

【30】《1995 年证据法》第 90 条吸收了普通法的公平裁量权原则。公平性本身是一个界限不是很清晰的概念，无法进行准确地界定，但是保证被告获得公平的审判是其应有之义。不公平性主要关注的是自认的可靠性，以及在审判时使用该自认反对被告的不公平性。

【31】《1995 年证据法》第 91 条规定，关于在澳大利亚或者海外程序中作出的裁决或者事实认定的证据，不得采纳来证明在该程序中的争议事实的存在。这体现了澳大利亚普通法的思想，即这样的证据仅仅是证明另一法院的意见的证据。[27]91(2) 规定，"根据本节不能采纳来证明某事实之存在的证据，即使因其他目的具有相关性，也不得用于证明该事实。"换言之，这些证据可以用于证明这些证据的存在、作出时间、法律效力等事项，但是即便如此也不得用于证明其包含的事实。第 92 条针对本条规定了若干例外。

【32】《1995 年证据法》92(2) 规定，在民事程序中，定罪判决证据具有可采性，但是仅可以反对被定罪之当时人或者该当事人通过其提出主张的人。这是因为第三方很难就该定罪判决提出反对，而被定罪之人则有机会来就争议问题进行抗辩、提出证据、进行交叉询问、上诉。赋予定罪判决的证明力将取决于具体情况。如果其证明力很低，可能会适用第 135 条或者第 136 条。这一规定并没有确立该定罪判决应当被视为正确的推定。这一规定也没有就定罪判决的种类进行区分。此外，民事判决不能采纳用来证明其所依据的事实，这是因为与刑事定罪判决相比，其证明力显然要低。"它是在当事人选择的证据基础上判定的，他们不像公诉人那样义务提供所有已知的相关证据。此外，其证明标准仅仅是依据的概论权衡，因此在原告提起的成功诉讼与不成功诉讼之间，没有什么太大区

27　See *National Mutual Life Association of Australia Itd v Grosvenor Hill (Qld)* [2001] FCA 237, BC200100855.

别。" [28]

【33】保留是在一般规则之后就特别立法的规定予以的特别考虑。《1995 年证据法》92(1) 规定，"与因诽谤提起的程序（包括刑事程序）中提交的定罪证据的可采性和效力有关的法律"不受影响。换言之，如果在诽谤罪程序中，某人是否犯罪是争议问题，则该人的定罪判决则可能是该人犯有该罪行的结论性证据。

【34】《1995 年证据法》第 3.6 节规定，倾向与巧合证据不可采，除非进行了预先通知，并且证据具有重大证明价值。但是第 101 条对检控方提出的倾向证据和巧合证据进行了进一步限定，即检控方提出的关于被告的倾向证据或者关于被告的巧合证据，不能用于反对被告，除非上述证据的证明价值严重超过了（substantially outweigh）其可能给被告造成的任何损害后果。因此，这一规定给检控方设定了很重的证明负担。

【35】《1995 年证据法》第 101A 条注释 2 指出，插入第 101A 条，是为了回应澳大利亚最高法院在 *Adam v The Queen* (2001) 207 CLR 96 案件中的判决。在 2008 年修正之前，第 102 条规定，仅仅与证人可信性相关的证据不具有可采性。在 Adam 案中，澳大利亚最高法院判定，应当对第 102 条进行字面解释，因此在证据不仅仅因与证人可信性相关的情况下，则不受第 102 条调整，即使该证据不能采纳用作其他用途。如果证据不受第 102 条调整，则与证人的可信性有关而具有可采性。第 101A 条反对这种立场，澳大利亚法律改革委员会认为，"证据既与可信性有关，也与争议事实有关，但是不能为后者目的采纳，则应当与其他可信性证据一样遵守同样的规则。" [29]因此，如果证据与可信性有关，但是就其他目的也具有相关性和可

28 Australia Law Reform Commission, ALRC 26, vol 1, para 781.

29 Australia Law Reform Commission, ALRC 102, para 12.14.

采性，则该证据就不是可信性证据。

【36】在 2008 年修正之前，《1995 年证据法》103(1) 规定，"在对证人进行交叉询问中提出的证据，如果该证据具有重大证明价值，则可信性规则不适用于该证据。"澳大利亚法律改革委员会认为，许多事项都可以说与证人的可信性有关，但是对于评估证人证言的真实性和准确性没有什么影响。如果证人在评估证人证言的可信性方面没有什么重大证明价值，则可能会不必要地延长审判时间，损害事实审判者对证人可信性的适当评估，干扰事实争点。[30] 因此，修正后的《1995 年证据法》103(1) 规定，"在对证人进行交叉询问中提出的证据，如果该证据会严重影响对证人可信性的评估，则可信性规则不适用于该证据。"

【37】《1995 年证据法》108A 之规定，旨在允许为传闻证据所反对的当事人，在作出传闻者不出庭情况下，就该作出传闻者提出可信性证据。

【38】《1995 年证据法》110 (1) 规定："传闻规则、意见规则、倾向规则和可信性规则并不适用于被告提出的用于证明（直接或者暗示）被告在总体上或者具体方面是一个具有良好品性之人的证据。"采纳被告提出的良好品性证据，是因为赋予刑事被告这样的绝对权利，有利于最小化错误定罪的危险。此外，在特定情况下，这种证据对于被告而言是至关重要的，"在错误辨认情况下，被告没有自己的不在犯罪现场证据，良好品性可能是将其从辨认证人的错误中挽救出来的唯一方法。经过权衡，保留这种保护是明智的，尽管这样的证据的证明力很低。"[31]

【39】《1995 年证据法》第 111 条之规定允许刑事程序中的被

30　See Australia Law Reform Commission, ALRC 102, para 12.28.

31　Australia Law Reform Commission, ALRC 26, vol 1, para 802.

告就其他共同被告的品性提出专家意见证据。在普通法上，*Lowery v The Queen*[32] 案件就是一个典型案件。这一案件涉及两个被告：Lowery 和 King。他们因对一名 15 岁的女孩施虐和毫无动机的谋杀被判有罪。在审判时他们提出了"害人"辩护，每个人都说对方对犯罪承担全部责任。King 在自己的辩护中，传唤了一名心理学家，其证言支持 King 作出的不利于 Lowery 的证言。最后，两个被告都被定罪。Lowery 提出上诉，称心理学家的证言不应当被采纳。枢密院维持了审判法官采纳该证言的裁决，驳回了 Lowery 的上诉。

【40】《1995 年证据法》对排队辨认没有进行界定。但是《1914年犯罪法》第 3ZM 条、第 3ZN 条和第 3ZP 条就联邦犯罪有关的排队辨认要求和程序进行了规定。

【41】《1995 年证据法》第 114 条规定，检控方提出的视像辨认证据不可采，除非符合该条规定的其他条件。这是考虑到目击证人的辨认通常更不可靠，与其他证据类型相比更难以评估，以交叉询问来进行检验并不能为被告提供足够的保护。排队辨认则比其他辨认方法更为可靠。因此，本条实际确立了排队辨认在证据法上的优先地位。换言之，排队辨认是采纳辨认证据的一个前提条件。

【42】《1995 年证据法》第 118 条就主要目的是获得律师提供的法律建议情况下进行的秘密交流和制作的秘密文件，规定了法律建议特免权。

【43】《1995 年证据法》第 119 条就主要目的是针对诉讼而获得律师提供的法律建议情况下进行的秘密交流和制作的秘密文件，规定了法律建议特免权。这一规定与第 118 条在很大程度上是平行的，但是二者在主要目的的内容、特免权对第三方交流的适用、针对文

---

32 [1974] AC 85.

件的一般方法上是不同的。在本条中，秘密文件不需要是委托人或者律师制作的。

【44】《1995 年证据法》第 127 条规定了神职人员特免权。根据该条规定，身为或者曾为任何教堂或者教派之神职人员的人员，有权拒绝披露在其是神职人员之时，有人曾向其作出宗教自白，或者该宗教自白的内容。因此，该特免权属于神职人员或者曾是神职人员之人。进行宗教自白的人是否有泄露该自白的意愿不具有相关性。

【45】《1995 年证据法》第 128 条规定了证人反对被迫自我归罪的特免权问题。Griswold 曾说"反对被迫自我归罪的特免权是人类在自身文明化的斗争过程中最伟大的里程碑之一"，[33] 曾被称为"自由的基本堡垒"。[34] 赋予证人反对被迫自我归罪的特免权，有利于维护证人尊严，有利于鼓励证人作证，从证人这里获得证言，有利于避免伪证。证人反对被迫自我归罪的特免权一度被认为仅仅适用于司法程序，即允许证人或者当事人在审判或者具有中间性质的审前程序中拒绝回答问题或者披露文件。但是澳大利亚最高法院在 *Pyneboard Pty Ltd v TPC*, (1983) 152 CLR 328 案件中明确反对这一限制，使得这一特免权适用于任何强制取得信息的情形。在司法程序中，这一特免权被判定适用于可能披露"任何惩罚、刑罚、没收或者开除教籍"的情况。[35]《1995 年证据法》第 128 条则将其限定在司法程序中。128(1) 和（3）规定，在证人反对作出具体证言或者关于具体事项的证言，是因为该证言可能倾向于证明该证人存在实施了违反或者起因于

33 E Griswold, *The Fifth Amendment Today*, Harvard Uni Press, Cambridge, 1955, 7.

34 *Pyneboard v Trade Practices Commission* (1983) 45 ALJR 609, 621 (Murphy J); *Baker v Campbell* (1983) 49 ALR 385.

35 *Redfern v Readfern* [1891] P139.

澳大利亚法律或者外国法律的犯罪；或者应当对民事处罚承担责任，则法院应当确定该异议是否存在合理根据，以决定是否使用该特免权。128(4) 规定，如果法院确信有关证据并不倾向于证明该证人实施了违反或者起因于外国法律的犯罪，或者根据外国法律应当对民事处罚承担责任，并且正义利益要求证人作证，则法院可以要求证人作证。在法院据此要求证人作证的情况下，要为证人提供证人豁免。因此，该规定改变了普通法的规定，使得该特免权仅仅适用于审判，且不适用于证言可能使证人牵涉没收或者开除教籍的情形。

【46】《1914 年犯罪法》第三章规定的犯罪，是与司法有关的犯罪（OFFENCES RELATING TO THE ADMINISTRATION OF JUSTICE），包括提供虚假证言、欺骗证人、贿赂证人、毁灭证据、共谋提出虚假指控等罪行。

【47】《1995 年证据法》第 135 条规定，如果证据的证明价值将会为下列危险所严重超过，则法院可以拒绝采纳该证据：(a) 该证据可能给一方当事人造成不公平的损害；或者 (b) 该证据可能具有误导性或者迷惑性；或者 (c) 该证据可能导致或者造成不合理的时间耗费。这一规定既适用于刑事程序，也适用于民事程序，与普通法主要存在以下不同：（1）135(a) 既适用于民事案件也适用于刑事案件，而在普通法上则不适用于民事案件。换言之，在普通法上，在民事案件中，在证据的损害效果超过其证明价值时，不存在拒绝采纳该证据的自由裁量权。（2）135(b) 和 (c) 对应的是普通法上的法律相关性概念。根据普通法的法律相关性概念，在存在损害、混淆、时间耗费等情况时，要由提出证据的当事人使法官确信证据具有足够的证明价值。第 135 条则改变了普通法的做法，由反对该证据的当事人说明证据应当被排除。

【48】《1995 年证据法》第 138 条规定，不当或者非法取得的

证据不得被采纳，除非采纳这些证据的可取性大于其不可取性。这一规定既适用于民事程序也适用于刑事程序。在普通法上，自由裁量权也要求进行政策权衡。然而进行权衡的天平一侧是证据表明被告有罪的程度，另一侧则没有得到清晰的界定。[36] 澳大利亚法律改革委员会认为，"在处理非法和不当取得的证据问题上，自由裁量方法似乎是最适当的方法。……这个领域相互冲突的关切，以及情况的复杂多变，使得这样的方法成为必需。"[37] 为了减少法官行使自由裁量权的困难，避免判决的过大差异，138(3) 规定了法院在进行这种权衡时所要考虑的因素，包括但是不限于该证据的证明价值；该证据在程序中的重要性；相关犯罪、诉因或者抗辩的性质以及程序标的的性质；不当行为或者违法的严重性；该不当行为或者违法行为是故意的还是过失造成的；该不当行为或者违法行为是否违反了《公民和政治权利国际公约》所认可的人的权利或者与此不一致；是否就不当行为或者违法行为已经提起或者可能提起任何其他程序（无论是否为法院程序）；在不从事不当行为或者违反澳大利亚法律行为的情况下获得证据的难度（如果有的话）。这一规定大大提高了就非法证据排除进行抗辩的可操作性和可预测性。

第 4 章—证明

【1】 "Justice of the Peace" 译为"太平绅士"。澳大利亚太平绅士的主要职能是进行公证和主持宣誓陈述书之宣誓。《2002 年太平绅士法》（Justices of the Peace Act 2002）第 8 条规定，太平绅士

---

36 See Australia Law Reform Commission, ALRC 26, vol 1, para 468.

37 Australia Law Reform Commission, ALRC 26, vol 1, para 964.

的职能是行使《1900 年宣誓法》（the Oaths Act 1900）或者其他法律所赋予或者规定的职能。该法第 5 条规定，符合下列所有条件的人，才能被任命为太平绅士：(a) 该人至少 18 岁；(b) 该人得到了立法会（the Legislative Assembly or the Legislative Council）成员的任命提名；(c) 该人达到了规章规定的被任命为太平绅士的标准。该法第 4 条规定，州长可以根据部长的推荐，任命太平绅士。太平绅士任期 5 年，可再次获得任命。

【2】在邮品问题上，《1995 年证据法》第 160 条设立了推定，即预付邮资寄给澳大利亚或者外部领地指定地址的某人的邮品，推定于邮件寄发后第四个工作日寄达指定地址，提出足够证据对该推定提出疑问者除外。根据该规定，对方当事人只要"提出足够证据对该推定提出疑问"，而不需要证明相反，就会消灭该推定。

【3】澳大利亚法律改革委员会认为，普通法上的补强要求应当废除，但是与伪证罪有关的补强要求应当保留。在普通法上，在检控方依据直接口头证言来反驳被告的陈述时，为了证明证言的虚假性，必须要有两个证人，或者一个得到了补强的证人。

【4】因迟延引起的"法证上的不利"，通常是指因迟延使得被告失去了对证人等进行足够检验的机会，或者不能足够地组织辩护等情况。新南威尔士法律改革委员会曾指出，"取决于具体情况，它们可能很容易察觉，也可能不易察觉。一方面，它们包括从关键证人的死亡到具体证据的灭失……另一方面，它们可能更集中于因拖延导致的对'正义的整体质量'的一般性损害，例如失去了调查所称犯罪情况的机会，现在对报案人的证言进行足够检验的难度。"[38]

---

38 Australia Law Reform Commission, ALRC 102, para 18.134.

【5】根据《1979 年澳大利亚联邦警察法》，联邦警察机构由下列人员构成：(a) 澳大利亚联邦警察机构行政长官；(b) 澳大利亚联邦警察机构副职行政长官；(c) 澳大利亚联邦警察机构雇员；(d) 澳大利亚联邦警察机构特别成员；以及 (e) 特别保护服务人员。澳大利亚联邦警察机构雇员是指根据该法第 24 条聘用的人员。该法第 24 条规定，澳大利亚联邦警察机构行政长官代表联邦，可以以书面形式聘用人员作为雇员。该聘用可以设定条件。这些条件可以涉及试用期、公民身份、基本素质要求、安全与品性审查、健康审查、保密要求等。根据该法第 40E 条，行政长官可以依照其确定的条件，任命某人为澳大利亚联邦警察机构特别成员，以帮助履行该机构之职能。该特别成员在任命期间，拥有法律明确规定的权力和职责，以及在其任命文件中列明的权力和职责。

【6】《1995 年证据法》第 177 条规定，当事人可以通过书面的专家证明书来证明专家意见，而不需要传唤专家证人出庭。这种做法，必须遵循该法规定的通知要求，即一般至迟在听审前 21 日送达对方当事人。对方当事人可以要求该专家出庭作证。在这种情况下，专家证明书不可采。

第 5 章—其他规定

【1】《1995 年证据法》第 187 条之规定反映了普通法的立场，即法人不能主张反对被迫自我归罪的特免权。

【2】《1995 年证据法》第 188 条之规定源于《1971 年证据法》第 88 条。《1971 年证据法》已废止。

重要译名对照表

act 法 法律

adduce 提出

admissibility 可采性

admission 自认

affirmation 郑重声明

Australian legal practitioner 澳大利亚法律执业者

beyond reasonable doubt 排除合理怀疑

certain 某些

certificate 证明书

coincidence evidence 巧合证据

commence 施行

competence 作证能力

conduct of proceeding 程序运行

corroboration 补强

credibility 可信性

cross examination 交叉询问

defendant 被告

duplicate 复本

evidence in chief 主问证据 / 主答证据

evidential presumption 证据推定

evidentiary effect 证据效力

examination in chief 主询问

examine 检视

faith and credit 信赖

forensic disadvantage 法证不利 法证上的不利

gazette 公报

give evidence 作证

governor of a state 州长

governorgeneral 总督

hearsay rule 传闻规则

impound 扣管

inspect 查阅 查验

interlocutory proceeding 中间程序

interpreter 传译人员

justice of the peace 太平绅士

law 法律

leading question 诱导性问题

leave 许可

legal presumption 法律推定

litigation 诉讼

magistrate 治安法官

oath 宣誓

ordinance 法令

overseas proceeding 海外程序

particular 具体的

personal knowledge 亲身知识

preliminary question 预备性问题

previous representation　先前表述

prior inconsistent statement　先前不一致陈述

proceeding　程序

Proclamation　《公告》

provision　规定

reexamination　再询问

religious text　宗教经卷

royal assent　御准

rule of practice　法院程序规则

sovereign　元首

specified　特定的　列明的

stamp duty　印花税

subpoena　传证令　传票

subsection　款

tendency evidence　倾向证据

unfair prejudice　不公平的损害

图书在版编目(CIP)数据

澳大利亚联邦证据法:中英对照/澳大利亚司法部编;
王进喜译. —北京:中国法制出版社,2013.8
ISBN 978 - 7 - 5093 - 4618 - 1

Ⅰ.①澳… Ⅱ.①澳… ②王… Ⅲ.①证据 - 法学 -
研究 - 澳大利亚 Ⅳ.①D961.15

中国版本图书馆 CIP 数据核字(2013)第 116900 号

策划编辑:袁笋冰   责任编辑:袁笋冰   封面设计:李　宁

澳大利亚联邦证据法:中英对照
AODALIYA LIANBANG ZHENGJUFA:ZHONGYING DUIZHAO

经销/新华书店
印刷/涿州市新华印刷有限公司
开本/880×1230 毫米 32   印张/ 14.75 字数/ 400 千
版次/2013 年 8 月第 1 版   2013 年 8 月第 1 次印刷

中国法制出版社出版
书号 ISBN 978 - 7 - 5093 - 4618 - 1   定价:48.00 元

北京西单横二条 2 号 邮政编码 100031   传真:66031119
网址:http://www.zgfzs.com   编辑部电话:66066627
市场营销部电话:66033296   邮购部电话:66033288